THE CLOSING DRAMA AT THE END OF THE AGE

THE CLOSING DRAMA AT THE END OF THE AGE

Is Christ's Coming One Coming or in Two Phases?

A Study In The Book Of Revelation

M DEAN KOONTZ

iUniverse, Inc.
Bloomington

The Closing Drama at The End of The Age
Is Christ's Coming One Coming or in Two Phases?

iUniverse books may be ordered through booksellers or by contacting:

iUniverse
1663 Liberty Drive
Bloomington, IN 47403
www.iuniverse.com
1-800-Authors (1-800-288-4677)

ISBN: 978-1-4502-5307-9 (sc)
ISBN: 978-1-4502-5308-6 (ebk)

Printed in the United States of America

iUniverse rev. date: 10/31/2011

CONTENTS

AUTHOR'S PREFACE

When I was younger, I used to love to do picture puzzles. They were great to do in the evening when the more active outdoor activities of the day could no longer be pursued. Some puzzles were harder than others, and your puzzle of choice had to do with how much expendable time you had. Some puzzles took several evenings to complete, and during the course of the day, a piece here and a piece there would be fitted in. Each puzzle took quite a bit of concentration, time and patience. I usually began by trying to put all the related pieces together in one group (color and content). The border went in first, so that the picture was framed. Then I worked from the outside in. There was always a great feeling of accomplishment when the picture lay completely finished before me.

I thought of my puzzle days when someone recently commented to me that the book of *Revelation* was a puzzle to them. I took the comment to mean that they were pretty sure it was beyond comprehension—at least, their comprehension. *Revelation* is puzzling in many respects. It gives a broad view of end time events climaxing with the coming of Christ in the clouds with power and great glory. But to really understand the book, it is necessary to gather the pieces of the puzzle from many places in the Scripture, and then fit them into the framework of *Revelation*. This requires some time and patience, but the end result is satisfying, and a more complete picture is seen.

As I began a study in the book of *Revelation* a few years ago, I found myself experiencing a healthy tension between two admonitions of our Lord regarding this book and its message. At the beginning, a **blessing** is pronounced on those who read it, hear it, and heed its words. So I approached the study with great eagerness to receive those promised blessings. Those blessings abound! But at the conclusion of the book there are solemn words of **warning** for those who add to or subtract from it. They are extremely sobering. Listen to them again.

> *"I warn everyone who hears the words of the prophecy of this book: If anyone **adds anything** to them, God will add to him the plagues described in this book. And if anyone **takes words away** from this book of prophecy, God will take away from him his share in the tree of life and in the holy city, which are described in this book" (22:18-19).*

I'm not at all sure that I fully understand the import of our Lord's warning here, but his words did convey to me in no uncertain terms that I needed to take special care as I began this study. And the reason should be obvious. **There is no other book in the Scriptures that has been more added to and subtracted from than this book!** So, to ask oneself the questions what does it say? What does it mean? What does it mean for me today? is crucial, because of our Lord's warning for would-be interpreters.

I began by earnestly asking the Lord to enable me to render a true appraisal of its contents and meaning. With all of my study of Scripture, in over 50 years of active ministry, I still wondered if it would be possible for me to actually let the Scriptures speak for themselves? I suspected it wouldn't be easy. We tend to become fixated in what we have been taught, and do not often ask the question, Is what I have been taught that which corresponds to the truth of Scripture?

The book of *Revelation* is all about the Second Coming of Christ. It seems to me that Scripture teaches His coming will be singular—one climactic coming at the end of the age. In its pages history moves to a climax. All the pathways of prophecy converge there, and reach their final fulfillment in that great and glorious event, the Second Coming of our Lord Jesus Christ. All that began in *Genesis* finds its consummation in *Revelation* at the glorious appearing in the clouds of our great God and Savior, Jesus Christ.

My approach to this study was as thorough and as systematic as I could make it. These steps were followed:

Step 1. After the first few chapters that introduce my theme, that Christ's coming is one climactic coming at the end of age, the consummation of Daniel's Seventieth Week of Years, I have given some attention to the *schemata* of the book. By the schemata I mean how the book is put together. An attempt to understand this at the outset is crucial, because so many mistakes in interpretation have been made simply because the structure of the book has been largely ignored or misunderstood. These, admittedly, are my own deductions from a careful reading of the text of *Revelation*. Many see it differently, I know. I offer my conclusions for the reader's consideration.

Step 2. I went through the entire Old Testament extracting all the passages I could find that dealt in any way with the end of the age and God's prophetic consummation of all things as they relate to *Revelation*. It is important to review this evidence, because the book of *Revelation* is impossible to understand without knowledge of the prophetic word. Actually, there are well over 300 allusions, quotations, and citations from the Old Testament in the book of *Revelation*. By *allusion*, we mean that one or more words can be traced to a known body of text. A *quotation* consists of a general reproduction of the original so that there isn't any doubt of its source, and *a citation* is a fairly exact reproduction of the words of the original text. There are no direct citations in *Revelation* from the Old Testament; the phraseology is often fragmentary or inexact, but they do indicate what a profound influence the Hebrew canon had on the thinking of John, the Seer.

Step 3. Next, I copied out every passage in the New Testament that referred in any way to the Second Coming. I did not comment on these references, but gave each section a caption beginning with the words "at the coming of Christ" such and such will happen.

Step 4. Then I used the text of *Revelation* itself, in bold type for easy reading, with appropriate, and, hopefully, clarifying notes. The passages from the Old and New Testament that directly relate to the text of *Revelation* were fitted in where they most likely occur, not just the reference, but also the actual text. As you read the book of *Revelation,* it will be possible to see how Old and New Testament passages help clarify meanings and find their fulfillment. Within the framework of this last and climactic week of history (particularly the last half week of Daniel's 70th week of years), all Scripture reaches its consummation and fulfillment. No wonder a blessing is pronounced on the one who reads, hears, and heeds its words!

Step 5. I did not ignore the commentaries. The insights of others are important and of interest to me. I saved them for last, because I wanted to draw my own conclusions from a personal examination of Scripture. Only after doing the above did I go back to read and review them to see if I had overlooked anything that should be included in a clarifying way. I have purposely refrained from giving variant opinions from the different commentators, but have tried to select the meaning that, in my opinion, is most consistent with the content and context of *Revelation.*

After all this, the one thing of which I am still absolutely sure is that Jesus is coming again! That is the ultimate blessed hope of every believer. Although the general timing of that wonderful event is earnestly debated and is important to consider, it is not the most important focus. I believe, as our Lord emphatically expressed, that we as believers can know *generally* when He will return, but *not specifically* i.e. the hour, the day.

Is it possible that some of us living now will still be alive when we hear the trumpet call and the voice of the archangel beckoning us upward? Yes, I believe so. However, we must be cautious. Former generations have thought the same, so we must refrain from speaking dogmatically. As we have now entered the twenty-first century, the growing conviction among evangelical believers is that something is going to happen soon. Once again the focus of the world is on the Middle East, and a search is on for a peace agreement that will allow the Palestinians and Israelis to live side by side with minimal conflict. The debate continues to rage over who will control Jerusalem, and have jurisdiction over the site of the Temple Mount. Someone has recently suggested that God should decide. We're certain that He will be the deciding factor. Although He doesn't seem to be consulted much in all of this, His sovereign purpose cannot be thwarted (Rev. 17:17). Certain events are occurring in our world such as wars, internecine strife within nations, famines, plagues, earthquake, and hurricanes, which seem of apocalyptic proportions. Thousands are left homeless

There is the great need for God's holiness to be vindicated, His redemption to be consummated, His righteousness to fill the earth, His glory and honor to be lifted up in the eyes of all mankind. Only the coming of our Lord can accomplish all that.

Finally, I'm aware of the difficulty of being solely bound by Scripture, but certain principles in approaching this study of prophecy seem important to underscore if we are to avoid adding to or subtracting from our Lord's words.

Principle 1 *We need to avoid, as much as possible, anything that rests upon surmise or mere probability;* but include only what is supported either by direct proof from Scripture, or by reasonable deductions from Scripture. Comparing Scripture with Scripture is the only way to arrive at a consistent rendering of the truth.

Principle 2 *The proof offered in support of any interpretation should be taken from the Scripture itself.* I believe that whatever information is essential for the interpretation of Scripture is to be found somewhere in the Bible itself. The Bible is its own best commentary. History, of course, must be appealed to for prophetic fulfillment, but interpretation of Scripture depends on what Scripture says about itself. The Word of God needs no defense. A few references in Revelation are not clear by appealing to Scripture such as the seven thunders mentioned in chapter 10. Their meaning is lost to us, but they are not crucial to an overall understanding of the message of the book.

An understanding of the original languages, both Hebrew and Greek, is helpful, of course, but not essential. A number of our modern translations do a good job of translating the original into English. The translators rendered the meaning as accurately as they could, and their accuracy enables us to interpret what the original authors meant. It is important that we take the normal, natural, and customary sense when studying the text. A literal, face value reading is usually the correct one. If the plain sense makes good sense, it is probably the right sense. Context, too, is important. Someone has put it well, "A text taken out of context is no more than a pretext."

Principle 3 *Whenever a statement or opinion is offered to the reader for his or her acceptance, we should feel bound to give along with it the proofs by which we believe it to be established.* There is always the temptation to render an opinion without proof. We should be sure to clarify that it is only an opinion if proof is not readily available.

Our method of approach in this book, as we have indicated, is to gather all the passages from the Old and New Testament that speak about end-time events and the second coming of our Lord, and then attempt to show how they complement and clarify the text of *Revelation*. I consider

Revelation to be the unifying guide to the understanding of last things in the Bible. Old Testament passages appear to be both interpretive and illustrative in the *Revelation*. By far the largest part of the material comes from the apocalyptic prophets, Isaiah, Daniel, Ezekiel, and Zechariah. The Revelation employs the Old Testament terminology quite freely, but organizes the thought in its own way. After reviewing both the Old Testament and New Testament passages, I was impressed with the fact that all the materials needed for our understanding of Christ's second coming at the end of the age are contained in the Bible itself. That is as it should be, for what other book has been given by God to illuminate our thinking and confirm our belief.

Principle 4 *The very nature of things revealed in the Revelation emphasizes the truth that its message was intended to be understood by the ordinary believer.* So many believers assume that a study of the *Revelation* is far beyond their comprehension, and thus they defer to study it on the grounds that to do so is futile and confusing. But consider, it is the *only* New Testament book that promises blessing on the one who reads it, hears it and takes its message to heart (1:3). Why should we miss out on that blessing? Its message was directed by our Lord to the individual members of the various churches scattered throughout Asia-Minor, not to the intellectual elite of that day. It is a book of symbols, to be sure, but all its symbols are either obvious natural ones, or else have their roots planted in the Old Testament prophets and the figurative language of Jesus and His apostles.

Finally, let me affirm that I am well aware of human fallibility, my fallibility, in understanding, and if my readers should disagree with my conclusions, then I ask of them a measure of kindly toleration. I believe that they, with equal sincerity, seek to know the mind of God as I do. But along with toleration, I beg for openness, a willingness to interact with what is presented before dismissing it out-of-hand.

DEDICATION

To my two sons, Philip and Mark, of whom I am justifiably proud. You are good husbands, wonderful fathers, and faithful followers of our Lord Jesus Christ. This book Is a challenge to you is to build strong foundations for yourselves and your families as you eagerly long for and anticipate the coming of our Lord Jesus Christ in power and great glory. May the blessings this book of Revelation promise be your.

PART 1

Christ's Coming: The Climax of the Ages

1

THE THEME OF THIS STUDY: THE CLIMAX OF THE AGES

Among those whose faith rests securely in God's revealed truth in the Scriptures, the second coming of our Lord Jesus Christ at the end of the age is a given. It will be the climax of history, the end of this age, as we know it, and the beginning of a new and glorious age of righteousness in the millennial kingdom. Every generation of believers has lived with the knowledge that they could be the generation living on earth when this climactic event occurs.

The theme of this study is that the Lord's coming is consistently seen as *a singular event*. Not one coming in two phases, but one climactic event. The revelation of the Lord is seen by most expositors as a climactic event at the end of the age. The question is, are there two aspects or phases of His coming either before the seven years, in the middle of the seven years, or during the last half of the week of years? It seems to me that if a period of time intervenes, there are really two comings. I have searched in vain for a clear statement in Scripture that there will be two aspects to Christ's Second Coming, one *for* the Church in a rapture in the clouds, and then a second coming sometime later, *with* the Church, back to earth. I must confess that I taught this view for many years, always with some nagging reservations.

However, the singular coming of our Lord is easily demonstrated. The burden of proof for a two-phased coming rests with those who teach it. In this study, I have no desire to refute those views, but only to declare what I believe the Scriptures clearly state. That the Bible consistently emphasizes a singular event can be seen from a simple reading of the text

*"Tell us, what will be the sign of **your coming** (singular) and of the end of age" (Matthew 24:3).*

*"For as the lightning comes from the east and flashes to the west, so will **the coming** (singular) of the Son of Man" (Matthew 24:27).*

*"But as it was in the days of Noah, so it will be at **the coming** (singular) of the Son of Man" (Matthew 24:37).*

*"That is how it will be at **the coming** (singular) of the Son of Man" (Matthew 24:39).*

*"But each in his own turn: Christ, the first fruits; then, **when he comes,** those who belong to him. Then the end will come."(1 Corinthians 15:21-24).*

*"But what is our hope, our joy, or the crown in which we will glory **in the presence of** (or at the coming of) our Lord Jesus Christ **when he comes**? (1 Thessalonians 2:19).*

*"May he give you inner strength that you may be blameless and holy before God, even our Father, **in the presence of** (or at the coming of) our Lord Jesus with all his holy ones of our Lord Jesus Christ with all his saints) (1 Thessalonians 3:13).*

*"According to the Lord's own word, we tell you that we who are still alive, who are left till **the coming** (singular) of the Lord."(1 Thessalonians 4:15).*

*"May God himself, the God of peace, sanctify you through and through. May your whole spirit, soul and body be kept blameless at **the coming** (singular) of our Lord Jesus Christ" (I Thessalonians 5:23).*

*"Concerning **the coming** (singular) of our Lord Jesus Christ and our being gathered to him." (2 Thessalonians 3:1).*

"And then the lawless one will be revealed, whom the Lord Jesus will overthrow with the breath of his mouth and destroy by the splendor (epiphany) *of **his coming*** (singular)*" (2 Thessalonians 2:8).*

*"Be patient, then, brothers, until the Lord's **coming** (singular)" (James 5:7).*

*". . . we told you about the power and **coming** (singular) of our Lord Jesus Christ . . ." (2 Pet. 1:16)*

"Where is this 'coming' (singular) he promised?" (2 Pet. 3:4).

*". . . as you look forward to the day of God and speed its **coming** (singular)" (2 Pet. 3:12).*

*"And now, little children, continue in him, so that when he appears we may be confident and unashamed before him at **his coming** (singular)" (I John 2:28).*

In every case, without exception, Christ's second coming is spoken of as a singular event at the climax of the age. There is not even the slightest hint of two comings or a two-phased coming. If such is to happen, the Bible is silent about it, and this is truly remarkable since this event is so important. The coming (singular) of our Lord has been and continues to be the blessed hope of the church. In the next chapter, I want to comment briefly on the three words that are used in Scripture to describe Christ's climactic coming.

2

HIS CLIMACTIC COMING:
THE KEY WORDS USED

Though we do not know the *exact* time of Christ's return, we can know the *approximate* time. And the words that are frequently used to describe His return give us a clue *generally* as to when His return will occur. These three words are *parousia, apocalypse, and epiphany*, or as they are variously translated, coming, revelation, and appearing. We want to examine them briefly. Do they indicate a one or two phased coming of our Lord? There isn't a uniform rendering of these words, that is, the Greek words are not always translated by the same English words, but that should not deter us.

1. Parousia: The Coming of the Lord in Real Presence

The word *parousia* is the most frequently used word in the New Testament in reference to the coming of Christ. It is from *para* meaning with, and *ousia*, meaning being, and it denotes both an arrival and a consequent presence with. It occurs twenty-four times in the New Testament in a variety of ways. Pre-tribulationists suggest that this word is used in a general way and not in any specific sense. They assign certain references, quite arbitrarily, to the rapture that they assert occurs prior to the tribulation when Christ comes *for* his church, and others to the revelation, when He comes *with* His church. Such a distinction seems unwarranted, since all the references seem to refer to one coming, and not two phases of one coming.

The first mention of it is in the Olivet Discourse when the disciples questioned the Lord, *"Tell us,"* they said, *"when will this happen, and what will be the sign of your coming (parousia) and of the end of the age" (Matthew 24:3)?* The reply the Lord gives them mentions a number of things that will constitute the beginning of "birth pangs" or "sorrows". The things that immediately precede His coming are mentioned in all the Synoptic Gospels . . . Jerusalem surrounded by armies, the abomination of desolation, a period of great tribulation, celestial disturbances, then His climactic coming on the clouds of heaven and the angelic harvesting or gathering of the elect from the far flung corners of the earth. In verse 15, Jesus specifically alludes to the *abomination that causes desolation* spoken of by the prophet Daniel. Then he adds, *". . . let the reader understand."* It should be noted that Jesus' reference to Daniel 9 and 12 indicates that the reference pointed to a distant future event in the middle of a week of years. Thus, they do not refer to the events that happened a few years later in the destruction of Jerusalem and the temple in 70 A.D. The seals, trumpets, and bowls describe that week of seven years in the Revelation, and the sequence is noticeably similar.

In all the synoptic gospel accounts of the Olivet Discourse we need to begin with the climactic coming of Christ in glory, and work backward. This backward tracing of events details the signs that will immediately precede His coming in the clouds, and they constitute the 70th week of Daniel's prophecy with the emphasis on the last half week of years (3 1/2 years).

At The End of the Age

Our Lord used the same word in his teaching about the end of the age. *"For as the lightning comes from the east and shines as far as the west, so will be the coming (parousia) of the Son of Man" (Matt. 24:27).* It will be like a bolt of lightning, glorious, visible, and evident to all.

His Coming Will Be Like It Was In The Days Of The Flood

"As it was in the days of Noah, so it will be at the coming (parousia) of the Son of Man; they knew nothing about what would happen until the flood

came and took them all away. That is how it will be at the coming (parousia) of the son of Man" (Matthew 24:37, 39). Jesus seems to be saying that those in the world better be ready, because when He comes, it is too late to get ready. It will be sudden, as it was in Noah's day, (although ample warning had been given), and it will be marked by finality. Everything was going on as usual, and then the rains came, and Noah took his family inside the ark, shut the door, and all opportunity for those on the outside to repent and believe was over. Many books that are being written today seem to reflect the view that the coming of Christ will constitute a wakeup call to the world, and many will then believe. That doesn't seem to be what Jesus is saying here.

His Coming With All His Holy Ones

"May he strengthen your hearts so that you will be blameless and holy in the presence of (before) our God and Father when our Lord Jesus comes (parousia) with all his holy ones"(1 Thessalonians 3:13).

Paul tells us in I Thessalonians 2:19 who will be with the Lord at His coming, *"For what is our hope, our joy, or the crown in which we will glory in the presence of (before) our Lord Jesus when he comes (parousia)? Is it not you?"*

It is argued by some that our Lord must have come "for" his saints in order for him to come "with" all his saints, and that suggests a two-phased coming. Not necessarily. First, there is strong evidence that *"all his saints"* here may refer to his angelic armies. The original reference is probably from Zechariah 14:5, *"Then the Lord my God will come, and all the holy ones with him."* However, it could be both the angelic hosts and the saints. We have to include in our thinking Revelation 17:14 where the conquering Christ has with him when he comes to wage war *"the called, chosen and faithful."*

> *"They will make war against the Lamb, but the Lamb will overcome them because he is Lord of lords and King of king, and **with him will be his called, chosen and faithful followers"** (Rev. 17:14).*

Their "rapture and resurrection" occurred at the end of the tribulation period in chapter 14 with the harvest at the end of the age. In chapter 15, just before the bowls of wrath are poured out, they are seen in heaven, and the time frame in chapter 19 suggests that this is the same event as the Marriage Supper of the Lamb where the Bridegroom comes to take his Bride. Then the battle occurs, and all the holy ones (angels and believers) are with him in the final conquest. *"When the Son of Man comes in his glory, and **all the angels with him** . . . " (Matthew 25:31).* A parallel passage in the Revelation is chapter 19 and verse 13, *"The armies of heaven **were following him,** riding on white horses and dressed in fine linen, white and clean . . . "* The marriage supper had just preceded this, indicating that rapture and revelation are closely related events.

The Resurrection and The Rapture

This is the word used in reference to the resurrection and the rapture of the saints. *". . . we tell you that we who are still alive, who are left till the coming (parousia) of the Lord, will certainly not precede those who have fallen asleep . . . we will be caught up together with them in the clouds to meet the Lord in the air" (1 Thessalonians 4:15, 16).* His coming will be attended by a shout of command, the voice of the archangel, the trumpet of God. This is certainly not a secret coming!

The reference to His coming (parousia) is repeated in chapter 5 and verse 23, *"May God himself, the God of peace, sanctify you through and through. May your whole spirit, soul and body be kept blameless at the coming (parousia) of our Lord Jesus Christ."*

The Destruction of the Antichrist

It is also used with reference to the destruction of the Antichrist in 2 Thessalonians 2:1-3. *"Concerning the coming (parousia) of our Lord Jesus Christ and our being gathered to him . . . "* Here his coming is associated with the Day of the Lord. Paul must be talking about the same "coming" (parousia) that he was referring to in his first letter to the Thessalonian believers. Here he adds that it will not come until the rebellion occurs and the man of lawlessness is revealed. *"And **then** the lawless one will be revealed, whom the Lord Jesus will overthrow with the breath of his mouth and destroy by the splendor of his coming (the epiphany of His parousia)".* This most certainly occurs after the great tribulation.

We conclude, naturally, on the basis of this word, that the rapture of the living saints, the resurrection of believers, and the judgment of the Antichrist will all take place at the same time, namely, at the *parousia* of Jesus Christ at the end of the tribulation. It will be a glorious event, for when Christ destroys the Antichrist it will be by the brightness (epiphany) of his coming (2 Thessalonians 2:8). The parousia will bring salvation and judgment, salvation of the saints and judgment upon the world.

2. Apocalypse: The Revelation

The second word is the word "revelation," meaning the "apocalypse," "taking the wraps off," the "unveiling." It occurs eighteen times in the noun form, and twenty-six times in the verb form. It is derived from *kalupto*, to cover, and with the prefix, to uncover, and thus to reveal.

Does the Bible say we are waiting for the rapture, or does it say we are waiting for the revelation? Actually, the Bible says we are waiting for the revelation, not the rapture! Paul states that Christians are *"waiting for the revelation of our Lord Jesus Christ" (I Corinthians 1:7).* Here is where the King James Version confuses us, for it uses the word "coming" whereas the word is actually "revelation." Now, if we are waiting for the revelation, then we are not waiting for the rapture **unless the rapture occurs at the same time,** and if we are waiting for the revelation, then we are waiting for an event that will occur at the end of the tribulation period! This word "revelation" is the word Paul uses in Second Thessalonians 1:7-8 when he writes that God will recompense tribulation to those who now afflict the church and will also give rest to those who are now afflicted. If the affliction is to be rendered to the ungodly at the revelation of Christ, then the rest given to the saints will also be at the same time.

The Apostle Peter (I Peter 1:6-7) has a similar exhortation and instruction:

> *"In this greatly rejoice, though now for a little while you may have had to suffer grief in all kinds of trials. These have come so that your faith—of greater worth than gold, which perishes even though refined by fire—may be proved genuine and may result in praise, glory and honor **when Jesus Christ is revealed.**"*

How long is faith to hold out? Until the end of the tribulation period when the Lord shall be revealed! Look at verse 13:

> *"Therefore, prepare your minds for action; be self-controlled; set your hope fully on the grace to be given you* **when Jesus Christ is revealed.***"*

What is Peter saying? He is speaking to a group of suffering Christians, and he promises that God's grace will be given to them abundantly at the revelation of Jesus Christ. Evidently the church will be on earth at the revelation, which comes at the end of tribulation period. Again Peter writes, *"But rejoice that you participate in the sufferings of Christ, so that you may be overjoyed* **when his glory is revealed***" (I Pet. 4:13).* There is that same word again, "revelation," or the verb form, "be revealed."

These verses are rather puzzling if Christians are not to be on earth at the time of the revelation, but they make sense if Christians are to undergo suffering right up until the end of the tribulation period when the revelation admittedly occurs! This word, it appears to me, has a definite reference to believers and expresses the believers' hope. Certainly we believe in the rapture, but it is the revelation that is presented as the hope of the believers, not the rapture. We wait for the revelation of the Lord Jesus Christ! The rapture, of course, occurs at the same time, but it is significant that the Bible does not say we are to wait for it or that it is our blessed hope!

Luke 17:30 reveals that the revelation will be sudden, like in the days of Noah and in the days of Lot. When He comes, there will be no second chance for earth-dwellers to believe. You are either ready or it will be too late.

3. Epiphany: The Appearing

The third word is "epiphany," often translated "appearing" or "brightness," because it has to do with a "shining upon." The noun form, *epiphaneia is* from *phaino* that, in the Active Voice, means to shine, and in the Passive Voice, to be brought forth into light, to appear, to become evident. It speaks of a shining forth, a glorious event.

All the glory and light of God will be seen in the person of Jesus Christ! This is an excellent word to use with reference to our Lord's return.

The epiphany comes at the end of the tribulation period, the revelation of Christ that brings judgment upon the world. Paul writes that Christ will slay the Antichrist with the "epiphany of his parousia"—the brightness of his coming (2 Thessalonians 2:8). It is clear that the epiphany does occur at the end of the tribulation when the Antichrist is destroyed. However, the epiphany is also the object of the believer's hope. It is the "blessed hope." What does the Bible say about this?

Turn to Paul's first letter to Timothy chapter 6, verse 14. *"I charge you to keep this command without spot or blame until **the appearing of our Lord Jesus Christ,** which God will bring about in his own time . . . "* Paul tells Timothy to keep this commandment until what event? The rapture? No, the epiphany! And the epiphany comes at the end of the tribulation period! What point would there have been for Paul to tell Timothy to keep the commandment until the epiphany if Timothy, or any other Christian, were not to be present when the epiphany occurred?

Let us look at another passage, this one very familiar, one we often quote about our own prospects of reward. Paul writes to Timothy in the second epistle,

> *"Now there is in store for me the crown of righteousness, which the Lord, the righteous Judge, will award me on that day, and not only to me, but also to all who have longed for **his appearing"** (2 Tim. 4:8).*

When do we receive our rewards? Paul says we receive our rewards at the epiphany of the Lord that comes at the end of the tribulation period. The Bible says all who have loved his appearing—not the rapture—will receive the crown of righteousness when He comes in glory, the revelation of the Lord Jesus Christ.

Now, let's turn to one more important passage. What is the blessed hope of the Christian? Is it the rapture, or is it the epiphany? The Bible says it is the epiphany of our Lord Jesus Christ! In Titus, chapter 2 and verse 13. Paul writes, *". . . while we wait for the blessed hope—**the glorious appearing** of our great God and Savior, Jesus Christ. "* The blessed hope is definitely and clearly declared to be the epiphany, the glorious appearing of our Lord. Since the epiphany does come at the end of the tribulation period, at the revelation of our Lord in glory, then the believers' hope centers upon a wonderful event of deliverance that will occur at the end of the tribulation period, not prior to it. We do have a blessed hope, thank God, and it is the rapture, but also the appearing in glory of our most wonderful Savior and Lord, Jesus Christ! They are one and the same.

So Christ will destroy the Antichrist by the brightness of his coming, the epiphany of his parousia. The two words are synonymous as to time. When will the rapture occur? At this same parousia. When will the resurrection take place? At the parousia and the revelation and the epiphany of our Lord Jesus Christ! All refer to one grand and glorious and climactic event! Yes, the revelation has to do with judgment (II Thessalonians 1:7), but it also is the great event for which the believer is waiting and upon which he sets his hope. The blessed hope centers our attention not on ourselves, not on our escape, but upon the Lord Jesus himself, His coming at the climax of the age!

Christ's coming is also seen as the climax of a "week" of seven years that we sometimes refer to as Daniel's Seventieth Week. The Sixty-Ninth week of Daniel's vision prophesied the first advent of our Lord, and His being cut off by crucifixion. This 70th week ushers in a sequence of events culminating in the second coming of our Lord. We will look at this more carefully in the next chapter.

Before going on, please read carefully the charts that pinpoint the various places in the New Testament where the above words occur. Is there any indication in these references that there are two phases of His coming in view rather than one climactic coming?

The Parousia

A presence, *para* meaning with, and *ousia*, meaning being, denotes both an arrival and a consequent presence with.

The Coming	Text
1 **The Question About His Coming And Signs Attending It** **(Matthew 24:3, 27)**	"Tell us," they said, "when will this happen, and what will be the sign of your coming (parousia) and of the end of the age?" "For as the lightning comes from the east and flashes to the west, so will be the coming (parousia) of the Son of Man."
2 **His Coming Will Be Like The Day When The Flood Came on The Earth** **(Matthew 24:37, 39)**	"As it was in the days of Noah, so it will be at the coming (parousia) of the Son of Man...they knew nothing about what would happen until the flood came and took them all away. That is how it will be at the coming (parousia) of the Son of Man."
3 **His Coming In Relation To The End Of The Age** **(I Cor. 15:23)**	"But each in his own turn: Christ the firstfruits; then, when he comes (parousia), those who belong to him. Then the end will come..."
4 **The Hope And Joy Of His Coming** **(I Thes. 2:19)**	"For what is our hope and joy, or the crown in which we will glory in the presence (parousia) of our Lord Jesus Christ when he comes? Is it not you? Indeed, you are our glory and joy."
5 **His Coming With All His Holy Ones** **(I Thes. 3:13)**	"May he strengthen your hearts so that you will be blameless and holy in the presence of our God and Father when our Lord Jesus comes (parousia) with all his holy ones." (Probably angels here, rather than saints)
6 **The Living And Dead Will Rise To Meet The Lord in the Air At His Coming** **(I Thes. 4:15-16)**	"...we tell you that we who are still alive, who are left till the coming (parousia) of the Lord, will certainly not precede those who have fallen asleep...we will be caught up together with them in the clouds to meet the Lord in the air."
7 **Kept Blameless Until His Coming** **(I Thes. 5:23)**	"May God himself, the God of peace, sanctify you through and through. May your whole spirit, soul and body be kept blameless at the coming (parousia) of our Lord Jesus Christ."

The Parousia - continued

The Coming	Text
8 Things Attending His Coming (2 Thes. 2:1-3)	"Concerning **the coming** (parousia) of our Lord Jesus Christ and our being gathered to him..." (This must be referring to I Thes. 4:16-17) Here as in I Thes. 5, it is associated with The Day of the Lord "...saying that the day of the Lord has already come...that day will not come **until**...the rebellion occurs and the man of lawlessness is revealed..."
9 His Coming Marks The Overthrow of the Lawless One (2 Thessalonians 2:8)	"And then the lawless one will be revealed, whom the Lord Jesus will overthrow with the breath of his mouth and destroy by **the splendor of his coming** (the epiphany of His parousia)."
10 Waiting For His Coming Requires Patience (James 5:7, 8)	"Be patient, then, brothers, until **the Lord's coming** (parousia)...you too, be patient and stand firm, because **the Lord's coming** (parousia) **is near**."
11 His Coming Brings Judgment On The Whole World Like In The Judgment of The Great Flood (2 Peter 3:4f, 12)	They will say, "Where is this '**coming**' (parousia) he promised? (Note: Peter uses the two great judgments to illustrate his point: the universal judgment by water and the universal judgment by fire. In other words, the universal judgment came when the flood came, and the universal judgment at the end of age comes when Jesus returns. This he calls 'the day of God" in verse 12= the day of the Lord. "...as you look forward to the day of God and speed **its coming** (parousia)."
12 His Appearing Is The Same As His Coming (I John 2:28)	"And now, dear children, continue in him, so that when he **appears** (phaino--root of epiphany) we may be confident and unashamed before him **at his coming** (parousia).

The Apocalypse

Derived from apo and kalupto meaning to cover, or to veil and with prefix to uncover

The Revelation	Text
1 **The Revelation of Jesus Christ** **(Rev. 1:1)**	"The **revelation** of Jesus Christ, which God gave him to show his servants what must soon take place."
2 **The Revelation Eagerly Awaited** **(I Cor. 1:7)**	"Therefore you do not lack any spiritual gift as you eagerly wait for our Lord Jesus Christ **to be revealed**."
3 **At The Revelation,** **Judgment On Unbelievers, While** **Believers Marvel And Are Glorified** **(2 Thes. 1:7-8)**	"God is just: He will pay back trouble to those who trouble you and give relief to you who are troubled, and to us as well. This will happen when the Lord Jesus **is revealed** from heaven in blazing fire with his powerful angels. He will punish those who do not know God and do not obey the gospel of our Lord Jesus Christ. They will be punished with everlasting destruction and shut out from the presence of the Lord and from the majesty of his power on the day he comes to be glorified in his holy people and to be marveled at among all those who have believed."
4 **Salvation Is Revealed When Christ Is** **Revealed** **(I Peter 1:6, 7)**	"..shielded by God's power until the coming of the salvation that is ready **to be revealed** in the last time...when Jesus Christ is **revealed**."
5 **Grace Given When Christ Is Revealed** **(I Pet 1:13)**	"..set your hope fully on the grace to be given you when Jesus Christ is **revealed**."
6 **Believers Rejoice When Christ Is** **Revealed** **(I Pet. 4:13)**	"But rejoice that you participate in the sufferings of Christ, so that you may be overjoyed when **his glory is revealed**.
7 **The Revelation Will Be Sudden** **(Luke 17:30)**	"It will be just like this on the day the Son of Man is **revealed**." (Like in the days of Noah and in the days of Lot) Sudden, with no second chance!

The Epiphany

The noun form, epiphaneia, from phaino, in Active Voice, to shine; in Passive Voice, to be brought forth into light, to appear, to become evident, a shining forth

The Appearing	Text
1 His Glorious Appearing In God's Own Time (I Timothy 6:14, 15)	"I charge you to keep this command without spot or blame until the appearing of our Lord Jesus Christ, which God will bring about in his own time..."
2 His Glorious Appearing Will Bring In The Kingdom Age (2 Timothy 4:1)	"In the presence of God and of Christ Jesus, who will judge the living and the dead, and in view of his appearing and his kingdom, I give you this charge..."
3 His Glorious Appearing—A Time of Rewards (2 Timothy 4:8)	"Now there is in store for me the crown of righteousness, which the Lord, the righteous Judge, will award me on that day—and not only to me, but also to all who have longed for his appearing."
4 His Glorious Appearing Is The Blessed Hope For Which We Wait (Titus 2:13)	"...while we wait for the blessed hope—the glorious appearing of our great God and Savior, Jesus Christ..."
5 His Glorious Appearing Marks The Defeat Of The Lawless One (2 Thessalonians 2:8)	"And then the lawless one will be revealed, whom the Lord Jesus will overthrow with the breath of his mouth and destroy by the splendor (epiphany) of his coming (parousia)." (Note: The epiphany (appearing) and the parousia (coming) are the same event.)
6 His Glorious Appearing Will Be Like Lightning That Lights Up The Sky From East to West (Matthew 24:27)	"For as lightning that comes from the east is visible (phainetai) even in the west, so will be the coming (parousia) of the Son of Man."
7 His Glorious Appearing Is His Coming (I John 2:28)	"And now, dear children, continue in him, so that when he appears (phaino–root of epiphany) we may be confident and unashamed before him at his coming (parousia)."

3

THE CLIMACTIC WEEK
AT THE END OF THE AGE

Each succeeding generation of believers is to live with the earnest expectation that our Lord could return in their lifetime. There will be one generation, however, that will witness certain events that will climax with His glorious return in the clouds of the sky. This generation will enter the Seventieth Week of Daniel's prophecy, and will know the general time of His coming although not the "day and hour" of His return (Matthew 24:36).

The Jews had a "seven" of years as well as a "seven" of days. This Biblical "week" of years was very familiar to any Jew. (See Leviticus 25:3-4). The Jewish year was a year of 360 days, 12 months of 30 days (See Genesis 7:11, 24; 8:3,4). (See chart that follows showing the fulfillment in the first coming of Christ.)

Although many do not acknowledge it, there is a definite gap between the 69th and 70th week of Daniel's prophecy. The "ruler" who has come and the "ruler" that will come are different. The powerful, charismatic leader of the "end time" will arise out of a 10 nation confederacy, conquer three kings, and take control of the other seven who give their power and authority to "the beast" (Rev. 17:13). Then Christ will return in the clouds, defeat the beast, and inaugurate His kingdom that will never pass away (Daniel 7:11-14).

Daniel indicates that the event that initiates the seventieth week will be a covenant that will be confirmed "with many" (presumably the nation Israel) by the "the ruler."(Daniel 9:27; 7:24-25). This may not be easily recognizable since it will involve a confederation of nations with their leaders that will confirm it. Israel has entered into agreements with many nations, some public, while others are secret. Having consolidated his power, Antichrist will later manifest his true intent in the middle of the week when he erects his "abomination" in the rebuilt temple. Daniel 12:11 moves this event to the "time of the end" (12:4). *"From the time that the daily sacrifice is abolished and the abomination that causes desolation is set up, there will be 1,290 days (1,260 days plus 30 days)."*

The first three and one-half years of that future seven-year period are called "the beginning of birth pangs or sorrows" (Matthew 24:8). False Christs, wars, famine, and pestilence will characterize it. The four horses of the apocalypse ride forth, and one-quarter of the world's population will be affected. Although we are probably not there yet, these conditions described under the first four seals have already taken a vast toll in many nations.

The Great Tribulation begins at the mid-point of the seventieth week. The covenant will be suddenly broken, and Antichrist will reveal his true character and intent, demanding compliance from the Jews. His image will be erected in the temple, worship directed to him will be required, and all will be compelled to receive a mark to demonstrate fidelity. Many who refuse will be put to death or taken into captivity. Those in Jerusalem are warned to "flee when they see" the abomination set up. To remain in the city means almost certain death. The persecution spreads to include Christians, and will evidently be worldwide in its scope. The fifth seal with the martyred dead probably pictures the outbreak of persecution, as The Great Tribulation gets under way. The martyrs under the altar cry, *"How long!"* and they are told to wait a little longer until the rest of their brethren would be gathered in through martyrdom. This seems to indicate that persecution of believers will gradually increase until it reaches a climax, and the Lord cuts it short by His dramatic intervention from heaven. The great multitude of chapter 7 will include many of those brethren soon to be killed. Empowered by Satan, the Antichrist will seek to establish a counterfeit new world order in direct opposition to our Lord and His kingdom. He will invade the Holy Land, and set up his headquarters there. This Gentile occupation force marks the beginning of the end for the Times of the Gentiles, as Daniel's great image depicting the succession of empires crashes to the ground at the coming of our Lord, the *"rock cut out of a mountain, but not made by human hands."*

Two witnesses will arise at this time, sent on their mission by God Himself, and empowered to do the miraculous. They will strongly oppose this counterfeit regime, showing powerfully and convincingly that the coming Christ is the focal point of prophetic history. The witnesses, probably Moses (representing the Law) and Elijah (representing the Prophets), will encourage true believers, and warn the world of impending judgment. Their mission lasts for the entire period of 42 months or 3 1/2 years. The "beast out of the Abyss" attacks the witnesses, overpowers them, and puts them to death. The world rejoices and celebrates, but suddenly the witnesses come to life again after 3 1/2 days, and are caught up to heaven. A great earthquake then occurs, and seven thousand people are killed. When their mission concludes, the second woe or sixth trumpet is finished, and the third woe or last trumpet is about to sound. This must mean that most of the trumpet judgments occur during The Great Tribulation period. We do not believe that they constitute the beginnings of the Day of the Lord, but are partial and preparatory, and give the world one more chance to repent. From what is said at the conclusion of chapter 9, their intent seems to be remedial in nature even though they failed to accomplish that desired result.

Since this week of years is a week of consummations, chapter 12 ushers on to the final stage of history seven persons depicting the characters which have in some way figured in the spiritual drama of redemption from the very beginning of time, but are now to be seen in their final manifestation on this last stage. They will run their course and reach their climax at the end of the 3 1/2 year period of great tribulation. The age-old conflict between the "seed" of the Woman and Satan is shown (Genesis 3:15). John's chief purpose seems to be the showing of this enmity between the serpent and the woman, and thus depiction of the Christ Child moves from incarnation to ascension for the sake of brevity. Michael and his angelic cohorts are successful in casting Satan out of heaven to earth. Michael ceases to restrain Satan's evil intentions, and Satan is permitted to engineer his last diabolical scheme. Knowing that his time is short, he tries to destroy the Israel of God, as he has sought to do down through the ages. God provides His protection for Israel. In anger, Satan turns to persecuting "the rest of her offspring." By their description, they are the faithful followers of Christ who unashamedly testify to their faith in Him, and thus infuriate the Evil One. Satan energizes the Beast out of the Sea giving him his power, his throne, and great authority. His authority extends for the full 42 months. Mankind worships both the dragon and the beast. He makes war against the saints, as Daniel had prophesied, and conquers them. They endure great hardship, many taken captive and many others slain. They suffer much for their faithfulness to the Lord. The Beast out of the Sea is assisted by The Beast out of the Earth, a false prophet that performs signs and miracles, erects an image of the first beast, and introduces a mark on the right hand and forehead of his subjects that determines their ability to buy and sell. It also makes them a target for execution if they refuse the mark. Daniel prophesies that all this will come to a close at the coming of the "son of man" in the clouds (Daniel 7:11-13). In connection with His return, the Antichrist and false prophet will be thrown into the pit of Hell (Rev. 19:20, Satan will be bound (Rev. 20:3), the goat and sheep nations will be judged (Matt. 25:31-34), and the marriage supper of the Lamb will take place.

"SEVENTY WEEKS ARE DETERMINED UPON THY PEOPLE AND UPON THY HOLY CITY"

Note: The first 69 weeks of years is literal; the 70th week must be also

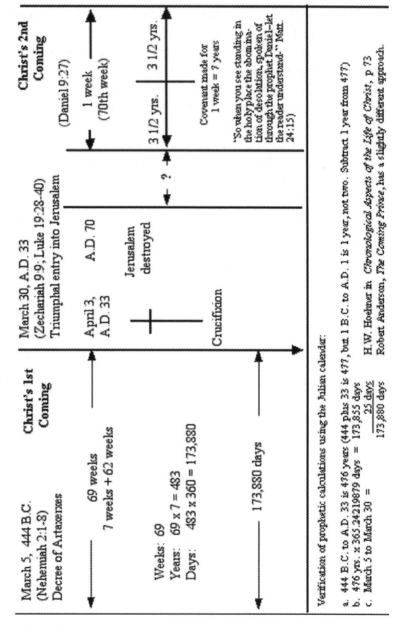

March 5, 444 B.C.
(Nehemiah 2:1-8)
Decree of Artaxerxes

Christ's 1st Coming

March 30, A.D. 33
(Zechariah 9:9; Luke 19:28-40)
Triumphal entry into Jerusalem

Christ's 2nd Coming

(Daniel 9:27)
1 week
(70th week)

69 weeks
7 weeks + 62 weeks

April 3, A.D. 33

A.D. 70
Jerusalem destroyed

Crucifixion

Weeks: 69
Years: 69 x 7 = 483
Days: 483 x 360 = 173,880

173,880 days

3 1/2 yrs.   3 1/2 yrs.

Covenant made for
1 week = 7 years

"So when you see standing in
the holy place the abomination of desolation, spoken of
through the prophet Daniel--let
the reader understand." Matt.
24:15)

?

Verification of prophetic calculations using the Julian calendar:

a. 444 B.C. to A.D. 33 is 476 years (444 plus 33 is 477, but 1 B.C. to A.D. 1 is 1 year, not two. Subtract 1 year from 477)

b. 476 yrs. x 365.24219879 days = 173,855 days

c. March 5 to March 30 = 25 days
                          173,880 days

H.W. Hoehner in *Chronological Aspects of the Life of Christ*, p 73
Robert Anderson, *The Coming Prince*, has a slightly different approach.

Daniel's Time Lines For The End Of The Age

"War will continue until the end, and desolations have been decreed. He will confirm a covenant with many 'for one seven.' In the middle of the 'seven' he will put an end to sacrifice and offering. And on a wing of the temple he will set up an abomination that causes desolation, until the end that is decreed is poured out on him." (Daniel 9:27). 'From the time that the daily sacrifice is abolished and the abomination that causes desolation is set up, there will be 1290 days. Blessed is the one who waits for and reaches the end of the 1335 days" (12:11).

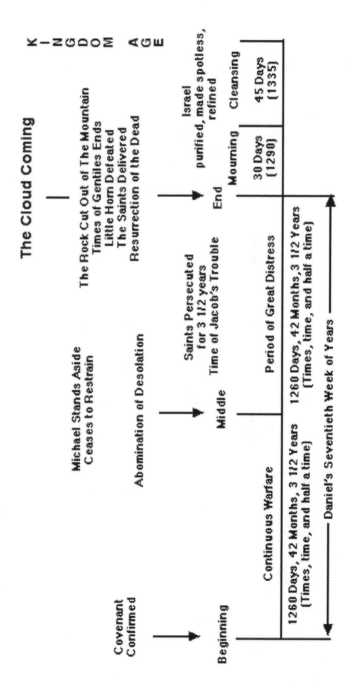

The Cloud Coming

KINGDOM OF AGE

The Rock Cut Out of The Mountain
Times of Gentiles Ends
Little Horn Defeated
The Saints Delivered
Resurrection of the Dead

Israel purified, made spotless, refined

Mourning — 30 Days (1290)
Cleansing — 45 Days (1335)

End

Saints Persecuted for 3 1/2 years
Time of Jacob's Trouble

Michael Stands Aside
Ceases to Restrain

Abomination of Desolation

Middle

Period of Great Distress

1260 Days, 42 Months, 3 1/2 Years
(Times, time, and half a time)

Continuous Warfare

1260 Days, 42 Months, 3 1/2 Years
(Times, time, and half a time)

Covenant Confirmed

Beginning

—— Daniel's Seventieth Week of Years ——

4

THE CLIMACTIC DAY
AT THE END OF THE WEEK

In pursuing our theme that the Lord's coming will be one climactic coming at the end of the age, it should prove instructive to review the places in the New Testament where that final or last "Day" is found. To aid us in this, I have prepared a chart that brings all of these references immediately before us for our careful study and comparison.

The references in their entirety seem to militate against the view that the "last days" refer to the period of time from the advent of Christ until the destruction of Jerusalem in A.D. 70. The claim is that this period of some 40 years marks the transition from the Old Covenant to the New, Israel replaced by the Church.

The first observation is that we are not told whether this is a single day of 24 hours, or an extended day. What is important is that it is a climactic day, and once it arrives, the curtain falls on this age as we know it, and rises again at the dawning of a new day, a new age, the kingdom age.

These references, almost without exception, refer to the day of Christ's return when this present age will be brought to its conclusion and his everlasting kingdom over the new heaven and the new earth universally established. The various designations seem to point to one specific terminal day—"the end of the age", "the end", "the day", "that day", "the day of the Lord", "the day of God", "the great day", "the day of wrath", "the day of judgment", "the day of redemption", and "the last day"—and these are not meant to denote different days, but the one last climactic day when Christ returns.

Surely, our Lord did not intend that we see this "day" as a long period of time. Seeing this as the consummating day of the age-the end, the last day-accords well with all the scenarios describing our Lord's return in virtually every New Testament reference to his coming.

It will be a day on which many climactic events occur:

+ A day when the harvest of the good and bad seed takes place
+ The day when Christ will be revealed
+ A day that will surprise unbelievers
+ A day of anticipation and expectancy for believers
+ A day of rewards for God's people
+ A day of terror and judgment for unbelievers
+ A day of wrath on an ungodly world
+ A day of resurrection
+ A day of redemption

Our Lord Jesus Christ will appear in glorious manifestation in the clouds of the sky. He will be the focal point for "every eye shall see him." We know from other references that the last great battle will take place, and the nations will be judged, a remnant of Israel will be saved, the satanic triumvirate will be defeated and consigned to Hell and the Abyss. And Christ will begin the new age of righteousness. What a glorious day that will be!

This climactic day at the end of the age is designated the Day of the Lord, Day of Christ, and Day of God. In the Old Testament, it is pictured as a "day of visitation" (Isaiah 10:3), a day "of the wrath of the Lord" (Ezek. 7:19), a "great day of the Lord" (Zephaniah 1:14). The entire conception in the Old Testament is one of deep darkness and fearful foreboding.

In the New Testament, there are elements of hope and joy and victory associated with this day. That is because it is the day when Christ comes in the glory of His Father. But there is a dark background to the bright picture, for it still remains a "day of wrath" (Rom. 2:5), a "great day" (Rev. 6:17, Jude 9), a "day of God" (2 Pet. 3:12), a "day of judgment" (Mt. 10:15; 2 Pet. 3:7; Rom. 12:16).

Sometimes it is called "that day" (Mt. 7:22; I Thessalonians 5:4; 2 Tim. 4:8), and again it is called "the day" without any qualification whatever, as if it were the only day worth counting in all the history of the world and of the race. To the unbeliever, it is a day of terror for it brings awful judgment; to the believer, a day of great joy for on this day the rapture, resurrection, and reward will occur. The entire New Testament, but especially Paul's letters, is suffused with this longing for the Parousia, the day of Christ's glorious manifestation, his very real presence, and his everlasting establishment of the kingdom age of righteousness. It points in every instance to one coming at the climax of the age, and not to two phases or aspects of one coming separated by a period of time.

"That Day" in Zechariah

I was struck by Zechariah's use of "that day" in the last three chapters of his oracle concerning the restoration of Israel. He uses the phrase 19 times in all, and the information that is given is intriguing, affording us details concerning the Lord's return that are found no where else. He outlines several events that occur on "that day." The following are a few of particular interest:

1. The gathering of the nations against Jerusalem
2. The Lord intervening in Israel's behalf
3. A spirit of grace and supplication poured out on the inhabitants of Jerusalem
4. Looking on Him whom they have pierced and mourning
5. A fountain opened for the cleansing of Jerusalem's inhabitants
6. A period of great suffering for God's people
7. A remnant spared and refined by testing
8. The feet of the Lord standing on the Mount of Olives, and it splitting in two from east to west forming a great valley
9. The remnant flees through this mountain valley
10. **The Lord coming with all His holy ones with him**
11. The uniqueness of that day
12. The survivors from the nations worship the King, the Almighty, and celebrate the Feast of Tabernacles in the kingdom age.

The Climactic Day of All Days

The End of the Age This climactic end marks the return of Christ, the harvest of both the good and bad seed, a time of judgment and reward.	Matt. 13:39 Matt. 13:40 Matt. 13:49 Matt. 24:3 Matt. 28:20	The harvest is the end of the age. So it will be at the end of the age. This is how it will be at the end of the age. What will be the sign of Your coming, and of the end of the age? I am with you always, to the very end of the age.
The End This is the "end" and thus marks a terminal point, a climax to this age as we know it. Then the new age of the kingdom will begin as Christ comes and begins to reign.	Matt. 10:22 Matt. 24:6 Matt. 24:13 Matt. 24:14 I Cor. 1:8 I Cor. 15:24 Heb. 3:6 Heb. 3:14 Heb. 6:11 I Pet. 4:7 Rev. 2:26	He who stands firm to the end will be saved. But the end is still to come. He who stands firm to the end will be saved. Then the end will come. He will keep you strong to the end. Then the end will come. Hold on to the end. Hold firmly till the end the confidence we had at first. Show the same diligence...to the very end. The end of all things is near. He who...does my will to the end.
The Day It is singular and climactic, because it marks the final day when Christ returns.	Matt. 25:13 Luke 17:30 Rom. 2:16 I Cor. 3:13 Heb. 10:25	You do not know the day or the hour. The day the Son of Man is revealed. The day when God will judge men's secrets. The Day will bring it to light. As you see the Day approaching.

That Day
 	
The same as "the day." It is so designated without any qualification, as if it were the only day worth counting in all the history of the world and of the race. Again, it refers to that climactic day of the Lord's coming.
	Matt. 7:22
	Matt. 24:36
	Luke 10:12
	Luke 21:34
	I Thess. 5:4
	2 Thess. 2:3
	
	2 Tim. 1:12
	
	2 Tim. 1:18
	2 Tim. 4:8
		Many will say to me on that day, 'Lord, Lord."
		No one knows about that day or hour.
		It will be more bearable on that day for Sodom.
		That day will close on you unexpectedly like a trap.
		So that this Day should surprise you like a thief.
		That Day will not come until the rebellion (the
		    apostasy, the falling away) occurs.
		He is able to guard what I have entrusted to him for
		    (until) that day.
		That he will find mercy from the Lord on that day!"
		The crown...which the Lord...will award to me
		    on that day.

The Climax of The Last Day
(continued)

The Day of the Lord The Day of Christ's return and the outpouring of God's wrath on an unbelieving world.	I Cor. 1:8 I Cor. 5:5 2 Cor. 1:14 Phil. 2:16 I Thess. 5:2 2 Thess. 2:2	So that you will be blameless on the day of our Lord Jesus Christ. That his spirit be saved on the day of the Lord. We will boast of you in the day of the Lord Jesus. That I may boast on the day of Christ. The day of the Lord will come like a thief in the night Saying that the day of the Lord has already come.
The Day of God Same as the Day of the Lord.	2 Pet. 3:12	As you look forward to the day of God.
The Great Day Same as the Day of the Lord. A time of judgment and wrath.	Acts 2:20 Jude 6 Rev. 6:17 Rev. 16:14	The great and glorious day of the Lord. The judgment on the great Day. The great day of their wrath has come. The battle on the great day of God Almighty.
The Day of Wrath Same as the Day of the Lord.	Rom. 2:5 Rev. 6:17	Storing up wrath against yourself for the day of God's wrath. The great day of their wrath has come.
The Day of Judgment Same as the Day of the Lord.	Matt. 10:15;11:22;11:24 Matt. 12:36 2 Pet. 2:9 2 Peter 3:7 I John 4:17	It will be more bearable...on the day of judgment Men will have to give account on the day of judgment. To hold the unrighteous for the day of judgment Being kept for the day of judgment. Confidence on the day of judgment.
The Day of Redemption	Eph. 4:30	You were sealed for the day of redemption.
The Last Day His coming marks the translation and the resurrection of believer.	John 6:39 John 6:40 John 6:44 John 6:54 John 11:24	I will raise them up at the last day. I will raise them up at the last day. I will raise them up at the last day. I will raise them up at the last day. He will rise again in the resurrection at the last day.

"That Day" In The Vision Of Zechariah

Order of Events	Text
The Nations Gather Against Jerusalem	"**On that day**, when all the nations of the earth are gathered against her, I will I make Jerusalem an immovable rock for all the nations. All who try to move it will injure themselves" (12:3).
The Lord Almighty Fights For Them	"**On that day** I will strike every horse with panic and its rider with madness," declares the Lord. I will keep a watchful eye over the house of Judah, but I will blind all the horses of the nations. Then the leaders of Judah will say in their hearts, 'The people of Jerusalem are strong, because the Lord Almighty is their God" (13:4-5).
Jerusalem Will Not Be Overthrown The Lord Shields And Fights For Them	"**On that day** I will make the leaders of Judah like a firepot in a woodpile, like a flaming torch among sheaves. They will consume right and left all the surrounding peoples, but Jerusalem will remain intact in her place"(12:6). "**On that day** the Lord will shield those who live in Jerusalem, so that the feeblest among them will be like David, and the house of David will be like God, like the Angel of the Lord going before them" (12:8).
Spirit Of Grace And Supplication The Lord Appears To Them The Clans Mourn	"**On that day** I will set out to destroy all the nations that attack Jerusalem. And I will pour out on the house of David and the inhabitants of Jerusalem a spirit of grace and supplication. They will look on me, the one they have pierced, and they will mourn for him as one mourns for an only child, and grieve bitterly for him as one grieves for a firstborn son" (12:9-10). (Quoted in Revelation 1:7)
A Fountain For Cleansing Opened	"**On that day** a fountain will be opened to the house of David and the inhabitants of Jerusalem, to cleanse them from sin and impurity." (13:1)
Idolatry And False Prophets Banished	"**On that day**, I will banish the names of idols from the land, and they will be remembered no more," declares the Lord Almighty....also the false prophets. (13: 2). "**On that day** every prophet will be ashamed of his prophetic vision." (13:4)
A Remnant Spared 1/3 Refined And Tested	"...Strike the shepherd, and the sheep will be scattered, and I will turn my hand against the little ones. In the whole land," declares the Lord, 'two-thirds will be struck down and perish; yet one-third I will bring into the fire; I will refine them like silver and test them like gold. They will call on my name and I will answer them; I will say, 'They are my people,' and they will say, 'The Lord is our God.'"(13:7-9). See Daniel 12:10.

"That Day" In The Vision Of Zechariah

Order Of Events	Text
The Great Battle At The End Of The Age	"The day of the Lord is coming...I will gather all the nations to Jerusalem to fight against it; the city will be captured, the houses ransacked, and the women raped. Half of the city will go into exile, but the rest of the people will not be taken from the city. Then the Lord will go out and fight against those nations, as he fights in the day of battle. (14:1-3).
Touchdown On The Mount Of Olives	"On that day his feet will stand on the Mount of Olives, east of Jerusalem, and the Mount of Olives will be split in two from east to west, forming a great valley, with half moving north and half moving south. You will flee by my mountain valley, for it will extend to Azel. You will flee as you fled from the earthquake in the days of Uzziah king of Judah. (14:4-5)
The Lord Comes In Glory With His "Holy Ones"	"Then the Lord will come, and all the holy ones with him" (14:5).
Celestial Changes	"On that day there will be no light, no cold or frost. It will be a unique day, without daytime or nighttime—a day known to the Lord. When evening comes, there will be light." (14:6-7).
King Over The Whole Earth	"On that day living water will flow out from Jerusalem, half to the eastern sea and half to the western sea, in summer and in winter. The Lord will be king over the whole earth. On that day there will be one Lord, and his name the only name" (14:8-9).
Panic!	"On that day men will be stricken by the Lord with great panic..." (14:13).
Feast Of Tabernacles Observed By Survivors	"Then the survivors from all the nations that have attacked Jerusalem will go up year after year to worship the King, the Lord Almighty, and to celebrate the Feast of Tabernacles..." (14:16).
All Set Apart Unto The Lord	"On that day HOLY TO THE LORD will be inscribed—on bells, pots, bowls..." (14:20-21).

5

THE CLIMACTIC NATURE
OF THE OLIVET DISCOURSE

The Olivet Discourse, as found in the parallel passages of Matthew 24, Mark 13, and Luke 21, constitutes the main body of our Lord's teaching regarding His return to earth. It is really the definitive passage, and all other passages in Scripture relating to the Lord's Second Coming should be interpreted in the light of what He says here.

In keeping with our theme that the second coming of Christ is depicted in Scripture as one climactic appearing at the end of the age, we wish to show from a careful reading of The Olivet Discourse in all three synoptic gospels that everything moves to a determined end reaching a climax in the glorious appearing of our Lord in the clouds of heaven.

That end time events move toward a climax is seen in a series of phrases that our Lord uses taken in the order of their occurrence.

*"the sign of your coming and of **the end of the age**"*

*"but **the end** is still to come (or will not come right away)"*

*"All these are **the beginning** of birth pains . . . "*

*"he who stands firm **to the end** will be saved"*

"then the end will come"

*"I have told you **ahead of time**"*

>*"**Immediately after** the distress of those days"*

>*"**At that time** the sign of the Son of Man will appear in the sky"*

>*"So, when you see **all these things** (signs), you know that it is near, right at the door"*

>*"**When these things begin to take place,** stand up and lift up your heads, because your redemption is drawing near"*

>*"**When you see these things happening,** you know that the kingdom of God is near"*

The only place the Second Coming is mentioned is at the climax of a whole series of events.

>*"**At that time** (the time when the celestial disturbances appear) the sign of the Son of Man will appear in the sky, and all the nations of the earth will mourn. They will see the Son of Man coming on theclouds of the sky, with power and great glory. And he will send his angels with a loud trumpet call, and they will gather his elect from the four winds, from one end of the heavens to the other" (Matt. 24:30-31).*

Furthermore, this sequence almost exactly parallels the opening of the seals in Revelation 6 which span the entire Seventieth Week of years, and climax with Armageddon, the Wrath of the Lamb and the Day of the Lord, all aspects of His coming at the end of the age.

So our Lord answers the question of his disciples, *"When will be the sign of your coming and of the end of the age?"* It cannot be demonstrated that Jesus is talking about the end of the Jewish age, and the destruction of Jerusalem. If we approach the passage without previous bias, His answer is quite clear and unambiguous. He will come in one climactic appearing at the end of the age, ushering in a series of events that will bring the curtain down on this age as we know it, and usher in a new age of righteousness.

What does the phrase "this generation" mean in the Olivet Discourse?

Matthew 14:29
Mark 13:24
Luke 21:25, 26

After mentioning the fig tree parable, Luke repeats the idea: *"Even so, when you see **these things** happening, you know that **the kingdom of God is near"** (21:31).* It is clear that "these things" do not include the parousia itself. It is obviously pointless to say, "When you see the Son of Man coming in glory, you know that He is near." Matthew's version also points out that all cosmic events must be realized, before we can say that the parousia is near and the last generation has arrived: *"Even so, when you see all these things, you **know that it is near, right at the door.** I tell you the truth, **this generation** will certainly not pass away until **all these things** have happened"* (Matt. 24:33, 34).

Matthew mentions the "shaking" of heavenly bodies or cosmic upheavals as the last sign before the coming of Christ (Matt 24:29). Only when all these cosmic signs have occurred, can we know that the last generation has come.

. Of His parousia He said: *"No one knows that day or hour, not even the angels in heaven, nor the Son, but only the Father. Be on guard! Be alert! You do not know when that time will come!"* *(Mark 13:32, 33).* This answers the second question of Jesus' disciples concerning the timing of His second coming (Matt. 24:3).

Jesus looked forward to the generation that will live at "the end" of time. The phrase "the end" is similar to the one in Daniel and is used repeatedly for the end of the age (not the end of the Jewish age) (Matt. 10:22; 13:39; 24:3, 13, 14; 28:20).

Likewise, the sixth seal (Rev. 6:12-17) portrays the last generation on earth and its experience of the shaking of heaven and earth. That generation alone will see the "all things" that Christ predicted. It will be the generation that lives when the seven last plagues fall on the Babylonian world, at the moment when it decides to destroy the followers of Christ.

Luke's Gospel presents the cosmic signs as an unbreakable unit and process that introduces the return of Christ for the last generation: *"There will be signs in the sun, moon and stars. On the earth, nations will be in* *anguish and perplexity at the roaring and tossing of the sea. Men will faint from terror, apprehensive of what is coming on the world, for **the heavenly bodies will be shaken.** At that time they will see the Son of Man coming in a cloud with power and great glory. When these things begin to take place, stand up and lift up your heads, because **your redemption is drawing near"** (Luke 21:25-28).*

The generation that witnesses all these things is the one that will live during the seven last plagues or as they are poured out on the earth, and will certainly not pass away before it sees the advent of Christ.

The Olivet Discourse In Matthew, Mark, And Luke
Compared With Revelation

Event	Matthew	Mark	Luke	Revelation
	24:1-44	13:1-37	21:5-36	Herod's temple was destroyed in 70 A.D.
Discussion about the Temple	1 Jesus left the temple and was walking away when his disciples came up to Him to call his attention to its buildings.	1 As He was leaving the temple, one of His disciples said to Him, 'Look, Teacher! What massive stones! What magnificent buildings!"	5 Some of His disciples were remarking about how the temple was adorned with beautiful stones and with gifts dedicated to God.	The temple in heaven is mentioned several times. This is the heavenly temple after which the earthly tabernacle was designed.
Its magnificence	2 'Do you see all these things?' He asked. 'I tell you the truth, not one stone here will be left on another; every one will be thrown down."	2 'Do you see all these great buildings?' replied Jesus. 'Not one stone here will be left on another; every one will be thrown down."	6 But Jesus said, "As for what you see here, the time will come when not one stone will be left on another; every one of them will be thrown down."	When John is instructed to measure 'the temple of God" in Rev. 11:1, this may refer to a rebuilt temple in the last days. Its location seems to be in Jerusalem.
Its destruction predicted	3 As Jesus was sitting on the Mount of Olives, the disciples came to Him privately.	3 As Jesus was sitting on the Mount of Olives opposite the temple, Peter James, John and Andrew asked him privately.		
The inquiry as to the sign of his coming and the end of the age	"Tell us," they said, "when will be the sign of your coming and of the end of the age?"	4 "Tell us, when will these things happen? And what will be the sign that they are all about to be fulfilled?"	7 "Teacher," they asked, "when will these things happen? And what will be the sign that they are about to take place?"	

The Olivet Discourse In Matthew, Mark, And Luke
Compared With Revelation

Event	Matthew	Mark	Luke	Revelation
Many deceivers	4 Jesus answered: "Watch out that no one deceives you. 5 For many will come in my name, claiming, 'I am the Christ,'	5 Jesus said to them: "Watch out that no one deceives you. 6 Many will come in my name, claiming, 'I am he,'	8 He replied: "Watch out that you are not deceived. For many will come in my name, claiming, 'I am he,'' and, 'The time is near.'	
Many deceived	and will deceive many.	and will deceive many.	Do not follow them.	
Wars and rumors of wars	6 You will hear of wars and rumors of wars, but see to it that you are not alarmed. Such things must happen, **but the end is still to come.**	7 When you hear of wars and rumors of wars, do not be alarmed. Such things must happen, **but the end is still to come.**	9 When you hear of wars and revolutions, do not be frightened. **These things must happen first, but the end will not come right away."**	**First Seal: White horse** Conquest, war "...a conqueror bent on conquest" (6:2)
Internecine strife within and between nations	7 Nation will rise against nation, and kingdom against kingdom.	8 Nation will rise against nation, and kingdom against kingdom.	10 Then he said to them: 'Nations will rise against nation, and kingdom against kingdom.	**Second Seal: Red horse:** Internecine strife "...to take peace from the earth and to make men slay each other" (6:4)
Famines Earthquakes Pestilences Fearful events Great signs from heaven	There will be famines and earthquakes in various places. 8 **All these are the beginning of birth pains.**	There will be earthquakes in various places, and famines. **These are the beginning of birth pains.**	11 There will be great earthquakes, famines and pestilences in various places, and fearful events and great signs from heaven.	**Third Seal: Black horse:** Famine "A quart of wheat for a day's wages, and three quarts of barley for a day's wages, and do not damage the oil and the wine!" (6:6)

The Olivet Discourse In Matthew, Mark, And Luke
Compared With The Revelation

Event	Matthew	Mark	Luke	Revelation
Persecution Prison Death	9 **Then** you will be handed over to be persecuted and put to death,	9 You must be on your guard.	12 But **before all this,**	**Fourth Seal: Pale horse:**
	and you will be hated by all nations because of me.	You will be handed over to the local councils and flogged in the synagogues.	they will lay hands on you and persecute you. They will deliver you to synagogues and prisons, and	Death by sword, famine and plague, and by wild beasts
	10 **At that time** many will turn	On account of me you will stand before governors	you will be brought before kings and	**Fifth Seal** Persecution
Apostasy	away from the faith and will	and kings as witnesses to	governors, and all on account of my	People slain because of the
Betrayal	betray and hate each other,	them.	name.	Word of God and the testimony
Deception	11 and many false prophets will appear and deceive many people.			they had maintained (6:9)
Increase of wickedness	12 Because of the increase of wickedness, the			
Love grows cold	love of most will grow cold,			
	13 but **he who stands firm to the end will be saved.**			
The gospel of the kingdom first preached to all nations— then the end will come	14 And this gospel of the kingdom will be preached in the whole world as a testimony to all nations, and **then the end will come.**	10 And the **gospel must first be preached** to all nations.		"The gospel preached as a testimony to all nations" is a theme that runs through Revelation. This must refer to a latter day world wide witness.

The Olivet Discourse In Matthew, Mark, And Luke
Compared With The Revelation

Event	Matthew	Mark	Luke	Revelation
The Holy Spirit will speak through the witnesses, and grant wisdom to them	Note: Warnings by our Lord in Matthew 10:17-22 to His disciples as they go forth to witness are similar to what He says here about the future persecution of His witnesses in the last day. He seems to transcend the moment and project the future. Which explains the reference to His coming before they complete their mission.	11 Whenever you are arrested and brought to trial, do not worry beforehand about what to say. Just say whatever is given you at the time, for it is not you speaking, but the Holy Spirit.	14 But make up your mind not to worry beforehand how you will defend yourselves. 15 For I will give you words and wisdom that none of your adversaries will be able to resist or contradict.	
Family loyalties are replaced by expediency		12 Brother will betray brother to death, and a father his child. Children will rebel against their parents and have them put to death. 13 All men will hate you because of me,	16 You will be betrayed even by parents, brothers, relatives and friends, and they will put some of you to death. 17 All men will hate you because of me. But not a hair of your head will perish.	"This calls for patient endurance on the part of the saints who obey God's commandments and remain faithful to Jesus" (Rev. 14:12)
	(v 13 above here repeated for 13 He who stands firm to the end will be saved.	but he who stands firm to the end will be saved.	By standing firm you will gain life.	

36

The Olivet Discourse In Matthew, Mark, And Luke
Compared With The Revelation

Event	Matthew	Mark	Luke	Revelation
The abomination of desolation	15 So when you see standing in the holy place	14 When you see	20 When you see Jerusalem being surrounded by armies, you will know that	"But exclude the outer court; do not measure it, because it has been given to the Gentiles. They will trample on the holy city for 42 months." (Rev. 11:1)
The mid-point of the Seventieth Week	the abomination that causes desolation, spoken of through the prophet Daniel–let the reader understand–	the abomination that causes desolation standing where it does not belong–let the reader understand–	its desolation is near.	Daniel places this at the mid-point of the 70th week.
Flee for your lives! A warning to Israel.	16 then let those who are in Judea flee to the mountains. 17 Let no one on the roof of his house go down to take anything out of the house.	then let those who are in Judea flee to the mountains. 15 Let no one on the roof of his house go down or enter the house to take anything out.	21 Then let those who are in Judea flee to the mountains, let those in the city get out, and let those in the country not enter the city.	"Because of the signs he was given power to do on behalf of the first beast, he deceived the inhabitants of the earth. He ordered them to set up an image in honor of the beast who was wounded by the sword and yet lived. He was given power to give breath to the image of the first beast, so that it could speak and cause all who refused to worship the image to be killed." (Rev. 13:14-15).
	18 Let no one in the field go back to get his cloak.	16 Let no one in the field go back to get his cloak.	22 For this is the time of punishment in fulfillment of all that has been written.	
Dreadful for pregnant and nursing mothers.	19 How dreadful it will be in those days for pregnant women and nursing mothers!	17 How dreadful it will be in those days for pregnant women and nursing mothers!	23 How dreadful it will be in those days for pregnant women and nursing mothers!	

The Olivet Discourse In Matthew, Mark, And Luke
Compared With The Revelation

Event	Matthew	Mark	Luke	Revelation
Unequaled great distress **The Great Tribulation**	20 Pray that your flight will not take place in winter or on the Sabbath. 21 For **then there will be great distress, unequaled from the beginning of the world until now—and never to be equaled again.**	18 Pray that this will not take place in winter, 19 because those will be days of **distress unequaled from the beginning, when God created the world, until no—and never to be equaled again.**	23 There will be great distress in the land and wrath against this people.	Daniel says this will last for 3 1/2 years. Since the Israeli remnant will go on to 1290 days and 1335 days, this period of trial is cut short. It is a time of purification and mourning for Israel.
The days shortened by the Lord	22 If those days had not been cut short, no one would survive, but for the sake of the elect those days will be shortened.	20 If the Lord had not cut short those days, no one would survive. But for the sake of the elect, whom he has chosen, he has shortened them.	24 They will fall by the sword and will be taken prisoners to all the nations.	The church will be raptured right after the Tribulation of 42 months. If anyone is to go into captivity, into captivity he will go. If anyone is to be killed with the sword, with the sword he will be killed. This calls for patient endurance and faithfulness on the part of the saints." (Rev. 13:10).
Jerusalem occupied by Gentiles			Jerusalem will be trampled on by the Gentiles until the times of the Gentiles is fulfilled.	They (the Gentiles) will trample on the holy city for 42 months (Rev. 11:2).

The Olivet Discourse In Matthew, Mark, And Luke
Compared With The Revelation

Event	Matthew	Mark	Luke	Revelation
Great deception False Christs False Prophets	23 At that time if anyone says to you, 'Look, here is the Christ!' or, 'There he is!' do not believe it. 24 For false Christs and false prophets will appear and perform great signs and miracles to deceive **even the elect-if that were possible.**	21 At that time if anyone says to you, 'Look, here is the Christ!' or, 'Look, there he is!' do not believe it. 22 For false Christs and false prophets will appear and perform great signs and miracles to deceive **the elect-if that were possible.** 23 So be on your guard;		And he (the false prophet) performed great and miraculous signs, even causing fire to come down from heaven to earth in full view of men (Rev. 13:13).
No one can mistake Christ's coming	25 See, I have **told you ahead of time.** 26 So if anyone tells you, 'There he is, out in the desert,' do not go out; or, 'here he is, in the inner rooms,' do not believe it. 27 For as lightning that comes from the east is visible even in the west, **so will be the coming of the Son of Man.** 28 Wherever there is a carcass, there the vultures will gather.	**I have told you everything ahead of time.**		

The Olivet Discourse In Matthew, Mark, And Luke
Compared With The Revelation

Event	Matthew	Mark	Luke	Revelation
Celestial disturbances following the tribulation	**29 Immediately after** the distress (tribulation) of those days the sun will be darkened, and the moon will not give its light; the stars will fall from the sky,	**24 But in those days, following that distress,** the sun will be darkened, and the moon will not give its light; **25** the stars will fall from the sky,	**25** There will be signs in the sun, moon and stars. On the earth, nations will be in anguish and perplexity at the roaring and tossing of the sea. **26** Men will faint from terror, apprehensive of what is coming on the world,	**Sixth Seal: Celestial Disturbances** "The sun turned black like sackcloth made of goat hair, the whole moon turned blood red, and the stars in the sky fell to earth, as late figs drop from a fig tree when shaken by a strong wind. The sky receded like a scroll, rolling up, and every mountain and island was removed from its place. (Rev. 6:12-14).
	and the heavenly bodies will be shaken.	and the heavenly bodies will be shaken.	for the heavenly bodies will be shaken.	For the great day of their wrath has come, and who can stand ? (6:17)
Christ comes on the clouds with power and great glory!	**30 At that time** the sign of the Son of Man will appear in the sky, and all the nations of the earth will mourn. They will see the son of Man coming on the clouds of the sky, with power and great glory.	**26 At that time** men will see the Son of Man coming in clouds with great glory.	**27 At that time** they will see the Son of man coming in a cloud with power and great glory.	**Look, he is coming with the clouds,** and every eye will see him, even those who pierced him; and all the peoples of the earth will mourn because of him. So shall it be. Amen. (Rev. 1:7).

The Olivet Discourse In Matthew, Mark, And Luke
Compared With The Revelation

Event	Matthew	Mark	Luke	Revelation
			28 When these things begin to take place, stand up and lift up your heads, because your redemption is drawing near.	
The trumpet blast and the gathering of the elect by the angels	31 And he will send his angels with a loud trumpet call, and they will gather his elect from the four winds, from one end of the heavens to the other.	27 And he will send his angels and gather his elect from the four winds, from the ends of the earth to the ends of the heavens.		"Another angel came out of the temple and called in a loud voice to him who was sitting on the cloud, 'Take your sickle and reap, because the time to reap has come, for the harvest of the earth is ripe." (Rev. 15:15).
The lesson of the fig tree	32 Now learn this lesson from the fig tree: As soon as its twigs get tender and its leaves come out, you know that summer is near. 33 Even so, when you see all these things, you know that it is near, right at the door.	28 Now learn this lesson from the fig tree: As soon as its twigs get tender and its leaves come out, you know that summer is near. 29 Even so, when you see these things happening, you know that it is near, right at the door.	29 He told them this parable: "Look at the fig tree and all the trees. 30 When they sprout leaves, you can see for yourselves and know that summer is near. 31 Even so, when you see these things happening, you know that the kingdom of God is near.	
These things				
This generation	34 I tell you the truth, this generation will certainly not pass away until all these things have happened.	30 I tell you the truth, this generation will certainly not pass away until all these things have happened.	32 I tell you the truth, this generation will certainly not pass away until all these things have happened.	

The Olivet Discourse In Matthew, Mark, And Luke
Compared With The Revelation

Event	Matthew	Mark	Luke	Revelation
	35 Heaven and earth will pass away, but my words will never pass away.	31 Heaven and earth will pass away, but my words will never pass away.	33 Heaven and earth will pass away, but my words will never pass away.	The trustworthiness of God's Word is emphasized throughout the Revelation
No one knows the day or hour	36 No one knows about that day or hour, not even the angels in heaven, nor the Son, but only the Father.	32 No one knows about that day or hour, not even the angels in heaven, nor the Son, but only the Father.		Revelation indicates that Christ's coming is sometime after the Great Tribulation concludes and the unusual celestial disturbances begin. Thus no hour or day for His return is indicated.
As in the days of Noah when the flood came	37 As it was in the days of Noah, so it will be at the coming of the Son of Man. 38 For in the days before the flood, people were eating and drinking, marrying and giving in marriage, up to the day Noah entered the ark; 39 and they knew nothing about what would happen until the flood came and took them all away. That is how it will be at the coming of the Son of Man			

The Olivet Discourse In Matthew, Mark, And Luke
Compared With The Revelation

Event	Matthew	Mark	Luke	Revelation
Two men Two women	40 Two men will be in the field; one will be taken and the other left.. 41 Two women will be grinding with a hand mill; one will be taken and the other left.			This surely speaks of the **rapture** of true believers. And it locates it at the coming of Christ after the tribulation and the celestial disturbances appear.
Be on your guard!		33 Be on guard! Be alert! You do not know when that time will come.	34 Be careful, or your hearts will be weighed down with dissipation, drunkenness and the anxieties of life, and that day will close on you unexpectedly like a trap.	
It may come and trap you Keep watch!	42 Therefore keep watch, because you do not know on what day your Lord will come. 43 But understand this: If the owner of the house had known at what time of night the thief was coming, he would have kept watch and would not have let his house be broken into. 44 So you also must be ready, because the Son of Man will come at an hour when you do not expect him.		35 For it will come upon all those who live on the face of the whole earth. 36 Be always on the watch,	Notice that the commands to watch and to be ready are found within the context of "these things"—the signs that immediately precede the coming of the Lord.

43

The Olivet Discourse In Matthew, Mark, And Luke
Compared With The Revelation

Event	Matthew	Mark	Luke	Revelation
Pray that you may escape!	45 Who then is the faithful and wise servant, whom the master has put in charge of the servants in his household to give them their food at the proper time? 46 It will be good for that servant whose master finds him doing so **when he returns**. 47 I tell you truth, he will put him in charge of all his possessions. 48 But suppose that servant is wicked and says to himself, 'My master is staying **away a long time**,' 49 and he then begins to beat his fellow servants and to eat and drink with drunkards. 50 The master of that servant will come **on a day when he does not expect him and at an hour he is not aware of.** 51 He will cut him to pieces and assign him a place with the hypocrites, where there will be weeping and gnashing of teeth.	34 Its like a man going away: He leaves his house and puts his servants in charge, each with his assigned task, and tells the one at the door to keep watch. 35 Therefore keep watch because **you do not know when** the owner of the house will come back--whether in the evening, or at midnight, or when the rooster crows, or at dawn. 36 If he comes suddenly, do not let him find you sleeping. 37 What I say to you, I say to everyone: "Watch!"	and pray that you may be able to escape all that is about to happen, and that you may be able to stand before the Son of Man.	

<small>A thief in the night!</small>

44

6

TIME-LINE REFERENCES WHICH SHOW THAT THE COMING OF CHRIST WILL BE AT THE CLIMAX OF THE AGE

Most time-line references are to the second half of the 70th Week of Daniel known as The Great Tribulation or The Great Distress.

Time-Line No. 1
Daniel's Seventieth Week, Daniel 9:24-27

Failure to see that Revelation must be interpreted in the light of prophetic predictions lends itself to much error in interpretation. Revelation is seen as the climax to a 3 1/2 year period of time. Why 3 1/2 years? Because it corresponds to the second half of a "week" of seven years mentioned in Daniel 9. This period of time, according to Daniel, occurs at *"the time of the end"* (9:27; 12:40; 12:4; 12:9; 12:13)

> *"Seventy 'sevens' are decreed for your people and your holy city to finish transgression, to put an end to sin, to atone for wickedness, to bring in everlasting righteousness, to seal up vision and prophecy and to anoint the most holy. Know and understand this: From the issuing of the decree to restore and rebuild Jerusalem until the Anointed One, the ruler, comes, there will be seven 'seven,' and*

*sixty-two 'sevens.' It will be rebuilt with streets and a trench, but in times of trouble. After the sixty-two 'sevens,' the Anointed One will be cut off and will have nothing. The people of the ruler who will come will destroy the city and the sanctuary; **the end** will come like a flood: War will continue **until the end** and desolations have been decreed. He will confirm a covenant with many for **one 'seven.' In the middle of the 'seven'** he will put and end to sacrifice and offering. And on a wing of the temple, he will set up an abomination that causes desolation, **until the end** that is decreed is poured out on him."*

These verses describe for us a week of years still in the future at "the end" of the age. In the Olivet Discourse, Jesus specifically makes reference to The Abomination of Desolation spoken of by Daniel. Daniel fixes this occurrence at the mid point of the week of years. In referring to the time of our Lord's Second Coming, we must begin with His coming and work our way backward. In the Olivet Discourse Jesus pinpoints His coming sometime after the second half of Daniel's 70th week is completed, after the Great Tribulation and the celestial disturbances occur.

Counting backward we have:
Christ's Coming in the clouds of glory.
Celestial disturbances
Period of great distress
Abomination that causes desolation
Gospel of kingdom preached in the whole world
Severe persecution
Famines, earthquakes
Nation rising against nation, kingdom against kingdom, wars and rumors of war
False Christs deceiving many

There are those who insist that *Revelation* is a prophecy of the approaching destruction of Jerusalem in A.D. 70, showing that Jesus Christ had brought the New Covenant and the New Creation. At that time, the last vestiges of the Old Covenant were destroyed, and Israel is terminated in God's future planning. This makes the "last trumpet" blast the destruction of Jerusalem. Thus, according to them, *Revelation* should not be interpreted futuristically. *Revelation*, according to them, is history. It has already been fulfilled.

There seems to be something missing from this scenario, namely, the rapture and resurrection of the elect and Christ coming in power and great glory. Can it actually be demonstrated that Christ came back then, and will not be revealed in any future time?

Time Line No. 2
The Times of the Gentiles, Daniel 2:44, Revelation 11:2, Revelation 17:12

". . . *the Gentiles will trample on the holy city* ***for 42 months***" *(Rev. 11:2).*

Note Luke's version of this in the Olivet Discourse,

> *"There will be great distress in the land and wrath against this people. They will fall by the sword and will be taken as prisoners to all the nations. Jerusalem will be trampled on by the Gentiles **until the times of the Gentiles are fulfilled**" (Luke 21:12-14).*

The Times of the Gentiles began with the captivity of Judah to Babylon under Nebuchadnezzar, which marked the final demise of the Israeli monarchy. The point of Nebuchadnezzar's dream in Daniel 2, and Daniel's vision in chapter 7 is the course of Gentile domination. In regard to the colossus, Daniel has revealed to him that

> ***"In the time of those kings*** *(the 10 toed or ten horned confederated kingdom of the last day), the God of heaven will set up a kingdom that will never be destroyed. It will crush all those kingdoms and bring them to an end, but it will endure forever" (Dan. 2:44).*

This will be the time when the *"rock cut out of the mountain, not by human hands, will strike the statue on its feet of iron and clay and smash them" (2:34).*

The whole colossus comes crashing down! When will this occur? Will it be, as claimed by some, when Jerusalem is destroyed by Titus? Revelation 11 seems to indicate that it will occur sometime after the end of the 42 month period or The Great Tribulation, when Antichrist, who heads these 10 kingdoms in the last day will be overthrown by the coming of our Lord and those with Him—*"his called, chosen and faithful followers."* I believe this will occur in connection with the *revelation* of His coming at Armageddon (Rev. 17:12-14; 19:11ff). Again this coming is a climactic coming at the end of the age.

Time Line No. 3

The Cloud Coming of our Lord and the Overthrow of the Little Horn, Daniel 7:11-14

> *"Then I continued to watch because of the boastful words the horn was speaking. I kept looking until **the beast was slain** and its body destroyed and thrown into the blazing fire.*
>
> *In my vision at night I looked, and there before me was **one like a son of man, coming with the clouds of heaven.** He approached the Ancient of Days and was led into his presence. He was given authority, glory and sovereign power; all peoples, nations and men of every language worshiped him. His dominion is an everlasting dominion that will not pass away, and his kingdom is one that will never be destroyed."*

The phrase "son of man" occurs in Revelation 14:14 *with obvious intent. "I looked, and there before me was **a white cloud, and seated on the cloud was one "like a son of man"** with a crown of gold on his head and a sharp sickle in his hand."* This corresponds with the first resurrection at the end of the age according to our Lord in Matthew 13.

This obviously occurs at the Great Unveiling of our Lord in Revelation 19:20, *"But the beast was captured and with him the false prophet who had performed the miraculous signs on his behalf . . . the two of them were thrown alive into the fiery lake of burning sulfur."*

Then shortly after this, the judgment takes place, **the dead are raised,** and they *"reigned with Christ a thousand years" (Rev. 20:4).*

Time Line No. 4

The Timing of the Restrainer Being Removed or Taken out of the Way, Daniel 12:1, 2 Thessalonians 2:7-8, Revelation 12:7-9

> *"**At that time** Michael, the great prince who protects your people, will arise (stand aside). There will be a time of distress such as has not happened from the beginning of nations until then.*

The timing of this, according to Daniel 11:40 is *"at the end of the age."*

> *"For the secret power of lawlessness is already at work; but the one who now holds it back will continue to do so **till he is taken out of the way.** And then the lawless one will be revealed, whom the Lord Jesus will overthrow with the breath of his mouth and destroy by the splendor of his coming."*

> *"And there was war in heaven. Michael and his angels fought against the dragon, and the dragon and his angels fought back. But he was not strong enough, and they lost their place in heaven. The great dragon was hurled down—that ancient serpent called the devil, or Satan, who leads the whole world astray. He was hurled to earth, and his angels with him."*

Revelation places this event at the mid-point of the 70th Week, because Satan goes on in his anger, and pursues and persecutes the people of God for 1,260 days or 3 1/2 years (Rev. 12:6).

Please note that I Thessalonians 4 gives no time-frame reference for the coming of Christ except to connect it with the Day of the Lord in chapter 5. However, 2 Thessalonians chapter 2, connecting it to the same event, does give us some guidelines as to when it will occur. *"Concerning the coming of our Lord Jesus Christ, and **our being gathered to him . . . "** (2:1).* He again connects His coming with the Day of the Lord in verse 2, and says it will be preceded by a time of apostasy or rebellion, and the appearing of *"the man of lawlessness, the man doomed to destruction."* The Restrainer is removed or stands aside. Christ will come and *"overthrow (him) with the breath of his mouth and destroy (him) by the splendor of his coming." (v. 8).* It seems much more natural to connect the "restrainer" with Michael rather than the Holy Spirit, as many do.

Time Line No. 5
The Order of Daniel's Seventieth Week in the
Olivet Discourse & Revelation 6

Matthew 24 closely parallels The Seals in Revelation 6. The mid-point reference is found in 24:15

> *"So when you see standing in the holy place the abomination that causes desolation, spoken of through the prophet Daniel—let the reader understand—then let those who are in Judea flee to the mountains . . . . "*

That this occurs at the mid-point of the seven years is shown by Daniel's prophecy in 9:26-27,

> *"The end will come like a flood: War will continue until the end, and desolations have been decreed. He will confirm a covenant with many for one 'seven.'* **In the middle of the 'seven' he will put an end to sacrifice and offering. And on a wing of the temple he will set up an abomination that causes desolation, until the end that is decreed is poured out on him."*

The order, then, using the parallel references in Matthew 24 and Revelation 6 would be as follows:

The Olivet Discourse. Order of Signs leading up to the End of the Age

1. Counterfeit Christs
2. Wars & rumor of wars
3. Famine & earthquakes
   (These are the beginning of birth pangs or sorrows)

4. Persecution & death, increase of wickedness
5. Gospel preached to the whole world
6. **Abomination of Desolation**-Mid-point 3 1/2 years to this point
7. The Great Tribulation . . . 3 1/2 years in duration
8. Celestial disturbances *"Immediately after the distress of those days*
9. **The Son of Man coming on the clouds with power and great glory**
10. The nations mourn. The gathering by the angels of the elect from one end of heaven to the other

Revelation 6 Order of the Seals

1. A Conqueror bent on conquest.
2. Internecine Strife—War
3. Famine
4. Death by sword, famine, plague, and wild beasts
5. Persecution and death (martyrs under the altar)
6. Celestial disturbances
7. **The Day of the Lord** *"the face of him who sits on the throne and from **the wrath of the Lamb.** The great day of their wrath has come, and who can stand?"*

Time-Line No. 6
The Angel and the Little Scroll

The next time-frame reference is found in Revelation 10 where John saw the mighty angel coming down from heaven with the Little Scroll that was sealed. A careful comparison of Revelation 10 and Daniel 12 shows that the imagery is the same. In Daniel 12 one angel says to the *'man clothed in linen, who was above the waters'*, *"How long will it be before these astonishing things are fulfilled?"* The "astonishing things" are the things just mentioned in the opening verses of chapter 12:

1. Michael, who has been a protector of Israel, arises (or stands aside), the effect of which is to make Israel vulnerable to The Lawless One who desires their ruin. Michael, the Restrainer, ceases to hold back the Evil One at **the mid-point** of Daniel's Seventh Week. At this point in the Revelation (Ch 12), Michael and his angelic

army succeed in casting Satan out of the heavenly realm to earth. Satan, in rage, relentlessly pursues the Israeli remnant.

2. A time of unparalleled **"great distress"** occurs called the Great Tribulation.

3. The **deliverance** of the redeemed then occurs . . . *'those whose name is found written in the book of life.'* The inference is that this occurs following the time of "great distress." These who are delivered correspond to the "saints" of both Daniel and Revelation—the believing Church. According to Paul in I Thessalonians 4, the rapture of the living and the resurrection of the dead occur simultaneously at the Lord's Return.

4. The **resurrection** of the dead also occurs at this time . . . *"multitudes who sleep in the dust of the earth will awake: some to everlasting life, others to shame and everlasting contempt."* The New Testament parallel to this is Paul's word to the church in Thessalonica:

    > *"God is just: He will pay back trouble to those who trouble you and give relief to you who are troubled, and to us as well. This will happen when the Lord Jesus is revealed from heaven in blazing fire with His powerful angels. He will punish those who do not know God and do not obey the gospel of our Lord Jesus.* ***They will be punished with everlasting destruction and shut out from the presence of the Lord and from the majesty of his power on the day he comes to be glorified in his holy people and to be marveled at among all those who have believed."*** *(2 Thessalonians 1: 6-10)*

5. In Verse 7, the angel seems to be referring to Israel who will be preserved by God to enter the kingdom alive as the believing Remnant. The angel says that after 3 1/2 years, *"the power of the holy people has been finally broken."* They will be humbled and declare their need for the True God, and *"many will be purified, made spotless and refined . . . " (v. 10).* This corresponds with what Zechariah predicted in Zechariah 13:7-9 concerning Israel:

    > *"Awake, O sword, against my shepherd, against the man who is close to me!" declares the Lord Almighty. "Strike the shepherd, and the sheep will be scattered, and I will turn my hand against the little*

ones. In the whole land, declares the Lord, two-thirds will be struck down and perish; yet one-third will be left in it. **This third I will bring into the fire; I will refine them like silver and test them like gold.** *They will call on my name and I will answer them; I will say, 'They are my people,' and they will say, 'The Lord is our God.'"*

The angel in Daniel 12 *"lifted his right hand and his left hand toward heaven, and I heard him swear by him who lives forever, saying, 'It will be for a time, times and a half time (v 7).* Now that Daniel's sealed scroll is opened, and the time frame is revealed for the end times, the angel in Revelation 10 says, *"There will be no more delay! But in the days when the seventh angel is about to sound his trumpet,* **the mystery of God** *will be accomplished, just as he announced to his servants the prophets" (v 6-7).* The "mystery of God" must refer to the restoration of Israel. This is pictured in Revelation 14 with the 144,000 Jewish Remnant standing with the Lamb on Mt. Zion.

The reference in Daniel 12 extends the 1260 days, 42 months, and 3 1/2 years time-frame for Israel to 1290 days. Sometime during this 30 day period of Israel's mourning, the Little Horn will be overthrown by Christ at His coming, and an additional 45 days is added, which in the Jewish calendar takes us to 1335 days or Hanukkah, when the temple was originally cleansed from the desecration that occurred there in the days of Antiochus Epiphanes.

All of this coincides perfectly with what our Lord said in the Olivet Discourse,

> *"For* **then there will be great distress,** *unequaled from the beginning of the world until now . . . and never to be equaled again" (Matt. 24:21* note the similarity of language to Daniel 12:1).

> **"Immediately after the distress of those days** *the sun will be darkened, and the moon will not give its light; the stars will fall from the sky, and the heavenly bodies will be shaken. At that time the sign of the Son of Man will appear in the sky, and all the nations of the earth will mourn. They will see the Son of Man coming on the clouds of the sky, with power and great glory. And he will send his angels with a loud trumpet call, and they will gather*

his elect from the four winds, from one end of the heavens to the others" (Matt. 24:29-31).

It is at this point that Jesus says, *"If those days had not been cut short, no one would survive, but for the sake of the elect those days will be shortened" (Matt. 24:22).*

"Immediately after the distress of those days . . . " is a time-line reference. We know that the distress of those days lasts for 3 1/2 years. The saints will be persecuted for 3 1/2 years, so that the celestial disturbances associated with the sixth seal do not occur **until the tribulation period is over.** But doesn't our Lord say those days will be shortened? Please note that there is no reference in Matthew 24 to the actual length of the great distress. That is confirmed for us in Daniel. And a possible explanation for the shortened days is to be found there also in Daniel 12. By "cut short" and "shortened" are we to understand Jesus as saying that Daniel's time-frame reference of 1260 days for the saints to be "oppressed" and "handed over" to the Lawless One will be shortened, say to 1200 days. That would seem to be a contradiction. What He probably is saying is that this time of distress will be so severe that God will not permit it to go farther than His will has allowed, that is, no longer than 1260 days. Christ's coming, sometime following this period of distress, will cut short the Beast's rampage against the people of God, and he will come to his "appointed end." Remember, Daniel has told us that the course to the end will last for another 75 days beyond the 1260. Thus 1260 days does cut the whole process short.

Time Frame No. 7
The Two Witnesses, Revelation 11:3

*And I will give power to my two witnesses and they will prophesy for **1,260 days . . .** " (Rev. 11:3).* Malachi tells us that God will send his witnesses *"**before** that great and dreadful day of the Lord comes" (Mal.4:5). Remember the law of my servant **Moses**, the decrees and laws I gave him at Horeb for all Israel. See, I will send you the prophet **Elijah** before that great and dreadful day of the Lord comes." (Mal. 4:4-5)*

54

"Now when they have ***finished*** *their testimony . . .* "They are killed. "*After the three and a half days . . .* " they are brought back to life by God and caught up to heaven.

Note Hosea's word concerning unrepentant Israel in Hosea 6:1-2,

> "*Come, let us return to the Lord. He has torn us to pieces but he will heal us; he has injured us but he will bind up our wounds.* ***After two days he will revive us; on the third day he will restore us,*** *that we may live in his presence.*"

"***At that very hour*** *there was a severe earthquake . . .* "The city collapses, and 7, 000 are killed.

"***The second woe has passed;*** *the third woe is coming soon*" (v 14). This is the sixth trumpet or second woe, which immediately precedes the seventh trumpet (v. 15), the third woe. This means that the sixth trumpet finishes as the two witnesses complete their task at the end of 42 months, and are killed and subsequently caught up to heaven. **So the seventh trumpet must follow The Great Tribulation.** The seventh trumpet sounds the arrival of our Lord. This would make it parallel to the Seventh Seal of which it is a part. The loud voices from heaven in connection with the sounding of the seventh trumpet announce:

1. The kingdom of the world has become the kingdom of our Lord
2. Christ has taken his great power and has begun to reign.
3. His wrath has come upon the angry nations.
4. The time for the dead to be judged has come.
5. The time for the saints to be rewarded has come.
6. The time for destroying those who destroy the earth has come.

In 11:19 we have **the terminal statement,** "*And there came flashes of lightning, rumblings, peals of thunder, an earthquake and a great hailstorm.*" This seems to show that the event is parallel to the Seventh Seal, because we have the same **terminal statement** there, "*Then the angel took the censor, filled it with fire from the altar, and hurled it on the earth; and there came peals of thunder, rumblings, flashes of lightning and an earthquake.*" (Rev. 8:5). A similar terminal statement occurs at the end of the Bowl Judgments indicating that the seventh bowl is also parallel to the seventh Seal and the seventh Trumpet. *"Then there came flashes of lightning, rumblings, peals of thunder and a severe earthquake" (16:18).*

Time Line No. 8
The Persecution of Israel by The Dragon

*"The woman was given the two wings of a great eagle, so that she might fly to the place prepared for her in the desert, where she would be taken care of for **a time, times and half a time,** out of the serpent's reach" (Rev. 12:14)*

The time-line again is 3 1/2 years. This will be a time of great distress for Israel as a nation. It is probably just a remnant of Israel that are sealed and protected by God. These will consist of those who refuse to worship the Beast and receive his mark. There will occur in Israel at this time a great apostasy or falling away, such as occurred during the time of Antiochus. Paul writes that God will give them a *"strong delusion so that they will believe the lie" (2 Thessalonians 2:11).* Again, we have the time frame of the Great Tribulation given.

Time Line No. 9
The Authority of Antichrist, Revelation 13:5-7

*"The beast was given a mouth to utter proud words and blasphemies and to exercise his authority **for forty-two months** . . . He was given power to make war against the saints and to conquer them" (Rev. 13:5).*

This is the same time-frame as given in Daniel 7:25, *"The saints will be handed over to him for **a time, times and half a time."** Again, it seems clear, that Christ will not return for His own until sometime after the Great Tribulation concludes.

Time-line No. 10
The Celestial Disturbances, Joel 2:28-32

*"And afterward, I will pour out my Spirit on all people. Your sons and daughters will prophesy, your old men will dream dreams, your young men will see visions. Even on my servants, both men and women, I will pour out my Spirit in those days. I will show wonders in the heavens and on the earth, blood and fire and billows of smoke. The sun will be turned to darkness and the moon to blood **before the coming of the great and dreadful day of the Lord.** And everyone who calls on the name of the Lord will be saved."*

Peter says the outpouring of the Spirit fulfills Joel's prophecy. He seems to be saying that the whole Messianic era between the two comings of Christ is looked upon as the age of the Spirit, poured out—not just in a drizzle, but in a downpour on His people. Although there are spiritual conditions for receiving the Spirit, there are no social conditions, whether sex, or age, or rank. *"Everyone who calls on the name of the Lord will be saved."*

The age of the Spirit finds its consummation at the end of the age, when celestial wonders will occur just before the day of the Lord which is the second coming of the Lord.

The prophesy of Isaiah confirms this:

"See the day of the Lord is coming—a cruel day, with wrath and fierce anger—to make the land desolate and destroy the sinners within it. The stars of heaven and their constellations will not show their light. The rising sun will be darkened and the moon will give its light. I will punish the world for its evil, the wicked for their sins" (Isaiah 13:9-11)

Zephaniah says the same thing:

*"**The great day of the Lord is near**—near and coming quickly. The day will be a day of wrath, a day of distress and anguish, a day of trouble and ruin, a day of darkness and gloom, a day*

of clouds and blackness, a day of trumpet and battle cry . . . "
(Zephaniah 1:14-16).

John says the same thing in Revelation 6:12-17:

"There was a great earthquake. The sun turned black like sackcloth
made of goat hair, the whole moon turned blood red, and the stars
*in the sky fell top earth . . . **for the great day of their wrath has***
***come,** and who can stand?"*

And our Lord, quoting the above passage from Isaiah 13, tells us
that these celestial disturbances will occur ***"after the tribulation of those***
days," and just before his coming,

"At that time *they will see the Son of Man coming on the clouds of*
the sky with power and great glory . . . " (Matthew 24:29, 30)

Time-Line No. 11
Christ Will Remain In Heaven Until The Time When God Restores All Things, Acts 3:19-21

"Repent, then, and turn to God, so that your sins may be wiped out,
that times of refreshing may come from the Lord, and that he may
*send the Christ, who has been appointed for you—even Jesus. **He***
***must remain in heaven until** the time comes for God to restore*
everything, as he promised long ago through his holy prophets"

When does God restore everything? It must be at the end of the
age after the renovation of heaven and earth by fire, and just before the
millennial age is inaugurated. Thus, again, it shows Christ coming at the
climax of the age, one climactic coming.

Peter speaks graphically of this time.

*"But **the day of the Lord will come like a thief.** The heavens will*
disappear with a roar; the elements will be destroyed by fire, and
the earth and everything in it will be laid bare. Since everything
will be destroyed in this way, what kind of people ought you to be?

*You ought to live holy and godly lives **as you look forward to the
day of God** and speed its coming. **That day** will bring about the
destruction of the heavens by fire, and the elements will melt in
the heat. But in keeping with his promise we are looking forward
to a new heaven and a new earth, the home of righteousness (the
restoration)"* (2 Pet. 10-13).

Time Line No. 12
The Redemption of the Old Creation and the New,
Romans 8:18-25

*"I consider that our present sufferings are not worth comparing
with **the glory that will be revealed in us.** The creation waits
in eager expectation **for the sons of God to be revealed.** For the
creation was subjected to frustration, not by its own choice, but by
the will of the one who subjected it, in hope that the creation itself
will be liberated from its bondage to decay and brought in to **the
glorious freedom of the children of God.** We know that the
whole creation has been groaning as in the pains of childbirth right
up to the present time. Not only so, but we ourselves, who have the
first fruits of the Spirit, groan inwardly as we wait eagerly for **our
adoption as sons, the redemption of our bodies.** For in this
hope we were saved. But hope that is seen is no hope at all. Who
hopes for what he already has? But if we hope for what we do not
yet have, we wait for it patiently.*

Paul tells us that some kind of glory will later be revealed in us. The
creation awaits this revelation (v 19). The creation has been subjected
temporarily to emptiness, but it will be freed from corruption and share in
the freedom of the glory of God's children. Verse 21 seems to be a reprise of
verse 19. The creation groans in anticipation of its deliverance. We likewise
eagerly await our full adoption as sons of God and the redemption of our
bodies (which obviously occurs at the Rapture and the Resurrection. We
conclude from this that the reason the creation is awaiting our bodily
redemption is that it will be redeemed from corruption at the same time. If
the creation has been freed from corruption and emptiness at the Rapture

how can it be subjected to plagues thereafter? So the coming of our Lord must occur as the bowl judgments are poured out and the renovation of the earth that Peter mentions takes place. Again this speaks of a climactic coming at the end of the age.

7

THE TIMING OF HIS COMING: SHOULD IT MATTER?

The theme of a series of popular, best-selling books, the so-called *Left Behind* series-is that the Church will be raptured prior to Daniel's Seventieth Week, and those left behind whose loved ones have been removed, will now be faced with the decision to reject or accept Christ, and if they do accept him, they must expect to undergo persecution at the hands of the Man of Lawlessness. These "late-comers" become overcomers. They are sort of a hybrid-Church, a second part of "Christ's Body" who will be martyred or raptured (a second rapture for these?) when Christ comes back in the second of a two-phased return at the end of the tribulation. This kind of scenario is simply **not** found in our Lord's teaching!

I have a real concern about this *second-chance* opportunity for all earth dwellers following the rapture. What we are being told is that the rapture of the Church will witness more dramatically than any words to the necessity to trust Christ—thus holding out a second chance to repent to all those who were not believers when the rapture occurred?

If, as many teach, the Church will not be here during the terrible period described in the Revelation equivalent to Daniel's Seventieth Week, why, as believers, should we worry ourselves about it other than indulging a morbid curiosity as to Israel's final destiny? Why should we be concerned about something that will take place primarily for Israel? Why should we who compose His church even bother studying the book of Revelation since we will be raptured at the beginning of chapter 4? We could skip chapters 5-18, and begin our study again in chapter 19 with the

Hallelujah Chorus, the marriage supper, and the revelation of our Lord when He rides forth on His white charger to engage the rebellious nations since these intervening chapters have little relevance for the Church. John is careful to tell us at the very beginning of Revelation that the message it contains is "for the churches."

The paradox of the Lord's promised return creates a unique challenge for the church. The *what* is certain, the *when* obscure. The truth of the promise for the believer fosters hope; the uncertainty of the time of its fulfillment is a summons to watchfulness, endurance, and faith.

But, the same truth is a two-edged sword. For the unbeliever, this message of certainty and uncertainty presents a warning and a challenge. Jesus seems to be saying, "How foolish to go on with daily living as though there were plenty of time for spiritual and eternal things sometime in the future." Scripture never promises us a future. James's warning is to the point *"Be patient, then, brothers, until the Lord's coming" (James 5:7).* He has already reminded his readers of the uncertainty about tomorrow, *"Why, you do not even know what will happen tomorrow. What is your life? You are a mist that appears for a little while and then vanishes" (4:14).* He goes on to warn that those who know what they should be doing and don't do it are sinning their life away. The Lord's coming in every generation has always been seen as near!

Where did the idea come from that there would be a second chance for earth dwellers at the Coming of our Lord? In that climactic moment when He returns, all opportunity is over.

Two thousand years have gone by since that note of urgency and immediacy was sounded. Jesus underlines in various ways that no one knows the day or the hour when He will return except the Father. And we better be ready, because when He comes, it is too late to get ready. It will be sudden and it will be marked by finality.

He illustrates it by a reference to the first judgment. In Noah's day, everything was going on as usual in the world, and then the rains came, and Noah took his family inside the ark, **shut the door,** and **all opportunity for those on the outside to repent and believe was over.**

He illustrates it again by referring to two men going about their normal tasks of working in their fields, and two women, pursuing what they ordinarily do, grinding grain to make bread, and the Lord comes, and one will be taken, the other left. Again there is finality, no chance for decision making at that point. **No time to get ready if not ready!**

Then Jesus inserts his thesis—that which he is emphasizing, underlining, stressing—*"Keep watch, because you do not know on what day your Lord will come (24:42).* Please note that this warning is given in the context of the final countdown to His coming when the signs in the heavens begin to appear.

Then He goes right on to illustrate it by a reference to His thief-like coming. *"If the owner of the house had known at what time of night the thief was coming, he would have kept watch and would not have let his house be broken into" (24:43).* And once again He repeats His warning. *"So you also must be ready, because the Son of Man will come at an hour when you do not expect him" (24:44).*

But our Lord is not finished pressing home His point—that of the necessity of watchful expectancy, and therefore readiness. He mentions the contrast between the faithful and foolish servant. The former goes about his appointed tasks all the while mindful that his master could return and expect an accounting. The foolish servant reasons, "Well, my master has been gone a long time, and I suspect he isn't coming any time soon." So he misuses his authority, and blends into the worldly scene, and generally lives as if there is no future accountability, and then His master comes **"when he does not expect him and at an hour he is not aware of."** There is no opportunity to repent his foolish ways. He is summarily and severely judged. The faithful servant is commended for his consistent attention to and obedience of His master's wishes. He is rewarded by given even greater responsibility.

Again, He underscores what He has been saying by the story of the bridegroom's coming in relation to the wedding banquet that parallels the marriage supper in Revelation 19. Without detailing the typical Hebrew wedding, the main point is obvious. Five virgins were ready, five were not when the bridegroom suddenly comes. Those who were ready went into the wedding banquet, **and the door was shut** (25:10). Again that note of awful finality! And those who weren't ready cry out in distress, *"Open the door for us!"* And the reply of the Bridegroom is, *"I tell you the truth, I don't know you."*

And yet again, Jesus doesn't leave it there, but presses on with still another illustration. We call it the Parable of the Talents (25:14). It stresses again the truth that we who know Him as Lord must be faithfully "occupying until He comes." Those who did faithfully work while they watched, who were good stewards of what they had received, were rewarded with more. The one, who did nothing with his entrustment, was summarily and severely judged. *"Throw that worthless servant outside . . . "* The wicked servant tried to excuse his inaction, but the master called him "you lazy servant!"

Actually, although it is often given separate treatment, the judgment of the nations teaches the same thing. The Son of Man comes in his glory, and gathered before him are two groups "the sheep and the goats". They are rewarded or judged according to their reception or rejection of "the brethren", the witnesses of the last day who announce, *"Repent, for the kingdom of heaven is at hand."* (See context in Matthew) But at that point, **there is no second chance for repentance.** The unrighteous are summarily and severely judged, and the righteous inherit the everlasting kingdom, *"they will go away to eternal punishment, but the righteous to eternal life"* (25:46).

The Second Coming prophecy, then, as found in Matthew 24 presents a paradox for the believer. There is a paradox of certainty and uncertainty. Jesus promises a sure return, but its time is undisclosed. The believer knows **what,** not **when.** *"The Son of Man **will come** (certainty) at an hour when you do not expect him"* (uncertainty). And it is clear that this element of uncertainty is the design of God, intended to create a particular response or tension in the servant of God: *"Therefore keep watch, because you do not know on what day your Lord will come . . . **So you also must be ready,** because the Son of Man will come at an hour when you do not expect him"* (Matt. 24:42, 44).

All of the Gospel writers seem to point to one climactic coming of Christ at the end of the age. And at His appearing He will reward the faithful, and judge the wicked.

Thus, I do not see, as many are suggesting, a second chance for unbelievers after His coming in the clouds of glory. Peter insists that there was no second chance for those who had rejected the warnings of Noah. The flood came and they were all outside the ark of safety except the eight souls within. And then he says that when the Lord comes and the fire falls, there will be no opportunity to repent then. There will be no period of time when repentance can take place. God's long suffering and the day of opportunity will be over. The lost will be lost forever; the saved will be secure forever. And the Lord waits as long as He can for everyone who will repent to repent. He delays—He waits—He hopes. And that should speak to us today! Do we really believe that there is a day just ahead that God's patience finally runs out, and His wrath overflows on an unbelieving world, and some of those who are unbelievers are our neighbors, our friends, even our nearest and dearest loved ones?

I do not mean to be morbid, but have you thought lately what it might mean to be finally lost forever. The whole world is lost in the darkness of sin. That's why Jesus came—to seek and to save those who are lost. He talked about the one lost sheep, the one lost coin, the one lost son, and how the Father and Son are on a search and rescue mission to save the lost.

I remember when I was very young, we used to listen enraptured to a Singing Lady who lived down the street from us. There was one song she sang that made a deep impression on my childish heart. It was about two little babes that were lost one day in dark woods, and after wandering all day, and night settled in, they lay down and finally died from exposure. The only part I still recall was the conclusion, and you can imagine what havoc such a song played on my childish emotions. It went something like this:

> And when they were dead, a robin so red
> Carried strawberry leaves, and over them spread.
> And all the daylong he sang them a song,
> And the poor little babes were left all alone.

Lost and left all alone! That thought was retained through all of these years. We read in the papers of those who are lost in some mountain wilderness, and literally thousands join in the search at a prodigious cost of time and money, but no one seems to mind if, after all this, the lost one is found at last.

In the Bible, the word for man, make no mistake about it, is lost! We talk about finding God. I wish we would quit using that phraseology. Never is it true that we cannot manage to find God. Always it is true that we cannot manage to lose Him. That was Adam's problem, back there among the trees in the garden. It was Jacob's problem, and David's problem. Not how to find Him, but how to lose Him. There are times when we talk about finding God in Christ. It is truer to say in Him God finds us.

The great truth embodied in the uncertainty regarding the timing of His coming is that God is waiting, patiently waiting for men to everywhere repent and turn to Him before it is too late. Do we understand that we are somehow involved in the process? Jesus said, "Go, make disciples . . . baptize them . . . teach them." **His last command should be our first concern.**

Do we really see people around as lost? We face today a twofold problem in winning the lost. There is the appalling unconcern of God's children for the lostness of the lost, and there is the awful unawareness of the lost to their true condition. There isn't anyone more pathetic than one who is lost and knows not that he is lost, or one who is sick and knows not that he is sick.

In the parable of the prodigal son it says, He came to himself . . . then he came to the father. But the truth is His father came to him. Once we turn our face homeward, while we are a great way off, our Father will outstrip the wind, and come to meet us. Our Father waits and hopes and longs for the prodigal's return, and when He sees him, runs and kisses him when he comes.

> Yet a great way off He saw me,
> Ran to meet me as I came;
> As I was my Father loved me,
> Loved me in my sin and shame.

All of us live with the certainty of Jesus Return—His Coming again in the clouds of glory. That is our blessed hope! But it is not a hope for the unbeliever! Is the Rapture only a wake-up call for unbelievers, or does it signal the end of opportunity to believe?

I believe C.S. Lewis underscores my concern here. Listen to his pointed words.

> God is going to invade this earth in force. But what's the good of saying you're on his side then, when you see the whole natural universe melting away like a dream and something else, something it never entered your head to conceive comes crashing in. Something so beautiful to us and so terrible to others that none of us will have any choice left. This time it will be God without disguise; something so overwhelming that it will strike either irresistible love, or irresistible horror into every creature. It will be too late then to choose your side. There is no use saying you choose to lie down, when it's become impossible

to stand up. That will not be the time for choosing; it will be the time when we discover which side we really have chosen, whether we realize it or not. Now, today, in this moment, is our chance to choose the right side. God is holding back to give us that chance. It will not last forever; we must take it or leave it.

Before leaving this, I must mention a second concern that I have about the view that says the Church will be raptured before Daniel's Seventieth Week. Who in his right mind wouldn't want to be exempt from that terrible time of trial? But if, as Scripture seems to say, Christ's coming is at the end of the age, and following the Great Tribulation (last 3 1/2 years of the 7 year period), then the saints, *"those who obey God's commandments and hold to the testimony of Jesus"* mentioned in chapter 12, will suffer persecution at the hand of Antichrist and his False Prophet. A *"great multitude"* of redeemed ones will *"come out of The Great Tribulation"* probably through martyrdom. Should this indeed be so, there is a great need for God's people to be in the Word, and to build into their lives strong spiritual backbones that will not collapse when the storm comes. The Church down through the ages has never been exempt from trials, and even today in godless countries they are suffering greatly, imprisoned and killed for their faith in Christ. For a persecuted church, the key responses are not self-defense or escape, but a bold witness, standing firm to the end, perseverance, patient endurance, wisdom, faithfulness, and a willingness to die if necessary. Jesus warned that we must build our lives continually on Him and His Word as the only foundation with sufficient strength to withstand whatever comes. One cannot build his house on rock after the storm breaks; that must be done before. When to any one of us an important crisis comes, the solemn fact is that either we are ready or not ready—it is too late to get ready. A man must have resources of a strong spiritual life, grounded in faith, exercised in moral habit, in touch with adequate reserves of power, **before** the emergency. He cannot extemporize spiritual life when, in a crisis, he suddenly needs it. After all, as someone has well said, "Religion is worth while when you need it; but you can't have it then, if you haven't had it before!"

PART 2

The Schemata

1

EXPLANATION OF THE SCHEMATA: HOW THE BOOK OF REVELATION IS PUT TOGETHER

The chief question concerning how *Revelation* is put together is whether we should take the structure of the book in a straightforward chronological sense or allow for some form of recapitulation to take place. My personal opinion is that it should not be taken sequentially. It seems to follow some form of progressive parallelism.

An understanding of how the book is set up is vitally important to knowing when the various recorded events occur. A failure to look at the structure closely has led to many errors in interpretation. Various scenarios have been put forth. I offer this view for your careful consideration.

Anyone familiar with the Bible knows that the number seven is the most significant symbolic number in Scripture, appearing in some manner in almost six hundred passages. Seven is also important because it is the sum of two other numbers with sacred and symbolic importance, three and four. It seems to be God's number for completion and perfection.

Because of the frequent use of the number seven in *Revelation*, it should be carefully studied because it is important in an understanding of how the book is structured.

Sevenfold Prologue
Sevenfold Vision of the Sovereign Christ
Seven Beatitudes

Seven Stars
Seven Angels
Seven Branched Candelabra
Seven Spirits
Seven Churches
Sevenfold Message to the Churches
Seven Positions Around the Throne
Seven Horns and Seven Eyes
Seven Seals
Seven Trumpets
Seven Persons
Seven Administrative Angels
Seven Bowls
Seven Heads
Sevenfold Epilogue

The Seven Seals encompass the entire period of the seventieth week of years (predicted by Daniel). The seventh seal brings to an end Daniel's Seventieth Week. The Seven Trumpets judgments occur during the last 3 1/2 years of this week of years, and are not sequential to the Seventh Seal but included in it. The Bowls are not sequential to the Trumpets, but are included in the Seventh Seal and the Seventh Trumpet. All the Sevens terminate at the same point—the Day of the Lord and the coming of Christ.

For purposes of this discussion, we will concentrate on the primary series of seven:

The Seven Churches
The Seven Seals
The Seven Trumpets
The Seven Bowls

The Seven Churches

The opening chapter tells us clearly that the entire letter was written to and for the churches, *"Write, on a scroll what you see and send it to the seven churches . . . "* It warns them of what is to come. This strongly indicates that the church that exists in the end time will have to face the terrors of Satan's energized man, the Man of Lawlessness.

The message was timely for these churches, but timeless for the church of all ages, just as Paul's seven letters to the churches to which he wrote then are for the church of every age. Christ's message to each church was His message to all churches, then and now. Our Lord tells each church what they are doing right, and what they are doing wrong, and then He tells them what they should do as they anticipate His coming. Even the messages that announce His coming seem to move to a climax.

The theme of "overcomers" is prominent in each letter, and runs throughout the book of Revelation. What are they to overcome? They are to overcome the beast and his mark, refusing to worship him or his image. This will bring suffering, even death, but their faithfulness will be rewarded in the New Jerusalem by their reigning with Him. How do they overcome? *"They over came him by the blood of the Lamb and by the word of their testimony; they did not love their lives so much as to shrink from death" (12:11).* (See the chart "The Overcomers" which follows this section).

Another indication that the Church will be present during the time of Great Distress is the mention of the persecuted "saints" under the altar after the 5th seal is opened (occurring somewhere near the mid-point of the Daniel's Seventieth Week or shortly thereafter), and The Great Multitude of saints that will suffer from the hand of The Two Beasts mentioned in chapter 13. This multitude corresponds to those *"fellow servants and brothers who were to be killed as they had been (6:11)."*

The closing chapter of Revelation confirms that the message of the entire book was written to the churches, *"I, Jesus, have sent my angel to give you this testimony for the churches" (22:16).* The nation Israel is certainly in view in the book, but the book is not written primarily to Israel, but for the Church.

The Seven Seals

The Seven Seals give us a preview of the entire week of seven years. Jesus describes the first four seals as *"the beginning of sorrows or birth pangs"* They picture conditions in general, conditions that are even now widespread on the earth, but will intensify as the end approaches. The martyrs seen under the altar are probably the first wave of those killed as

Antichrist shows himself for who he really is at the mid-point of the week. More will be put to death as the persecution intensifies.

The six seals opened by the Lamb take us to the climax of the ages. Some insist that all seven seals must be broken before the contents of the scroll are revealed. This does not seem to be the case, because we are given a view of what will unfold as each seal is opened. John continues to watch as the sixth seal is opened and the terrestrial and celestial disturbances unfold. It is obviously an announcement of the impending Day of the Lord. The imagery is taken from the prophecy of Isaiah concerning that awful day. I believe it also parallels Revelation 19, with the description of the Lord appearing in glory leading his heavenly hosts into battle. The recipients of judgment are the same *"kings of the earth, the princes, the generals, the rich, the mighty and every slave and every free man."* There the Great Supper of God is described in graphic detail as the carrion birds are summoned to *"eat the flesh of kings, generals, and mighty men, of horses and their riders, and the flesh of all people, free and slave, small and great" (Rev. 19:18).*

Still further, John sees that the time of wrath has come *"from the face of him who sits on the throne and from the wrath of the Lamb! For the great day (Day of the Lord) has come, and who can stand?" (6:16).*

This demonstrates that the seals include the entire period leading up to the Day of the Lord and the Coming of Christ in glory. The Trumpets and the Bowls are included in the Seventh Seal. But are we justified in saying that they occur sequentially, that is, that the Trumpets follow the sixth seal in sequence. I don't think so, and for the following reason.

Chapters 7 and 14 constitute the bookends of The Great Tribulation. Chapter 7 is an explanatory passage that begins the period of great distress. When John says, *"After this I saw four angels standing at the four corners of the earth, holding back the four winds of the earth to prevent any wind from blowing on the land or on the sea or on any tree,"* he is not necessarily speaking sequentially, but describing the next thing that he saw. What he saw was two people groups who will be present on the earth during this stressful period of time leading up to the Day of the Lord.

The 144,000

Do the 144,000, who are obviously Jewish, go through the Tribulation? Yes, but only the elect remnant will be under special protection. In Chapter

12, the Israeli Remnant is seen again under the symbol of the Woman who births the Man Child. And she is pursued and persecuted for 1260 days, but is protected by God for that period of time in the place prepared for them in the desert. Chapter 7 indicates that she is doubly protected . . . sealed as God's own for protection against the Trumpet judgments soon to come upon the earth. The wind was prevented from blowing on the land or on the sea or on any tree—precisely the same areas upon which the Trumpet judgments fall. To reinforce this, the fifth trumpet angel unleashes a horde of demonic locust-like creatures that torment those on the earth *"who did not have the seal of God on their foreheads."* Obviously those who did have the seal of God are present, but in some way protected.

My conclusion is that the Remnant is protected from these partial judgments that begin soon after they are sealed much as God in Goshen protected Israel when the plagues came on Egypt. And she is also protected from the wrath of the Dragon who has just been cast out of heaven by Michael. This occurred at the mid-point of the week. Another picture of the Lord's protection of Israel is Zechariah's vision of the Lord coming down and his feet touching the Mount of Olives, and a great earthquake occurring forming a great valley through which they can flee to safety eastward.

The Trumpets

When the Trumpets sound, they progress to the same point as the sixth seal. The sixth trumpet takes us to the Euphrates, where the mounted troops are summoned, 200,000,000 strong, to kill 1/3 of mankind. This is certainly either Armageddon or preparation for Armageddon, because the same thing happens with the pouring out of sixth bowl of wrath. A warning is given in 16:15, which is the typical warning of the Day of the Lord, *"Behold, I come like a thief!"* *"Then they gathered the kings together to the place that in Hebrew is called Armageddon" (16:16).*

We are not sure when the trumpets begin, but we do know from chapter 11 that the two witnesses prophesy for 42 months (the time frame of the Great Tribulation), are killed by Antichrist, and then brought back to life and caught up into heaven. This occurs, according to Revelation 11:14 as a part of the sixth trumpet (2nd woe), or right at the end of the Tribulation, just before the last trumpet sounds. The sixth trumpet, then, must be blown at the end of the tribulation, making the first five trumpets occur during the Great Tribulation. It, therefore, parallels the sixth seal. And Jesus, in the Olivet Discourse, says that the celestial disturbances that constitute the sixth seal occur immediately after the period of great distress or at the end of the Tribulation or last 3 1/2 years of the week. That the Trumpet Judgments take some time is indicated by the demonic cavalry who torment unbelievers for a space of 5 months—*"those who did not have the seal of God on their foreheads."*

The Great Multitude

But there is a second group of people mentioned in chapter 7 that will go through the Tribulation, and somewhere during the Tribulation will be taken out of it, probably not by rapture, but by martyrdom. I believe it is a logical conclusion that this great multitude of blood-washed followers of Christ is the group referred to when the martyred souls under the altar (fifth seal) are told to *"wait a little longer, until the number of their fellow servants and brothers who were to be killed as they had been was completed" (6:11)*. It is true that they are spoken of as being *"before the throne"* and the recipients of their well deserved reward, but they *"come out of the Great Tribulation"* so they must have gone through it or at least part of it. John seems to be speaking of them proleptically, that is, as if the event described occurred before it actually did take place. Their great suffering at the hands of the Dragon, the Antichrist and the False Prophet, is described for us in 12:17; 13:7, 10, 16; 14:12-13. They are sustained and strengthened by God, but not necessarily protected in the same sense as the Israeli Remnant are. The remnant is specifically protected that they may be preserved alive, believing in Christ, and entering the kingdom when He returns.

The Little Scroll. The Time-Frame for The Last Half of Daniel's Seventieth Week or The Great Tribulation (Chapter 10)

We have a similar explanatory section following the sixth trumpet. Chapter 10 pictures the opening of Daniel's sealed scroll, and that scroll specifically answered the question *"How long will it be before these astonishing things are fulfilled?"* The answer given was *"It will be for a time, times and half a time."* The time frame is expanded 75 more days making a total of 1335 when Antichrist is overthrown, and the temple is cleansed.

The indication from Daniel 12 seems to be that the Lord will return after 1260 days when the first resurrection takes place (same time as the rapture). The remnant believes, Antichrist will be defeated around 1290 days at Armageddon, and the temple will be cleansed at the end of another 45 days (Hanukkah).

Once the time frame is established the mighty angel of Revelation 10 says, *"There will be no more delay!"* Then he announces the soon sounding of the seventh or last trumpet, and tells John that he has more work to do, before the sounding of that trumpet which signals the Coming of our Lord.

Chapter 11 describes a Gentile occupation force that will move into Jerusalem, which corresponds to the breaking of the covenant with Israel, and the setting up of the abomination in the rebuilt temple (perhaps a hastily rebuilt temple on Mount Moriah). This, according to Daniel occurs at the mid-point of the Tribulation. The occupation will be for the duration of 42 months . . . the time indicated in Daniel's sealed scroll. And at the end of those 42 months The Times of the Gentiles will come to a close with the rock hewn out of the mountain striking the 10 toes of the colossus. This, of course, signals the setting up of the kingdom and the overthrow of the "little horn." All of this takes place at the conclusion of The Great Tribulation of 3 1/2 years.

The Two Witnesses (Chapter 11)

Second, two witnesses, forerunners of the Coming King, will hold forth for the same period of time given as 1,260 days. They complete their witness and are killed, miraculously brought back to life, and taken up. This completes the second woe or the sixth trumpet and the seventh trumpet sounds indicating the Coming of our Lord. It announces that the time has come for His reign to begin, His wrath to be executed, rewards to be given, and judgment on earth-dwellers to take place. Again, this is the Day of the Lord. So we are back to the sixth and seventh seal that also indicate the Day of the Lord and the Lord's Coming.

Chapters 12 and 13 continue this explanatory section, and go back again to tell us what will happen to the two people groups mentioned in chapter 7. It fills in the blanks for John's readers of events transpiring *before* the seventh trumpet blows and our Lord comes in glory. Chapter 14, then, is the other bookend of The Great Tribulation, and describes Christ's Appearing, first to the believing remnant of Israel on Mt. Zion, and then in the air for the harvest of the earth—both the righteous and unrighteous. The latter brings us again to the Day of the Lord and Armageddon. Chapter 14 introduces us to seven administrative angels that give a preview of what is soon to come.

Chapter 12 tells us that Michael casts Satan out of heaven (mid-point of the 70th week), The Dragon pursues and persecutes the Israeli Remnant for "times, time, and half a time", but God protects them for that same period from Satan's destroying wrath. The Antichrist is energized by Satan, and wreaks havoc on the people of God . . . "the saints." He is given such power for 42 months. A mark is set up so that anyone who does not receive it and worship the Beast will be subject to deprivation and death. This tells us what will happen to the second people group mentioned in Chapter 7. Will all of this "great multitude" be martyred? Probably not, but the residue, still living, will be soon raptured at His coming, and will join their brothers and sisters in the first resurrection which also occurs at the same time (I Thessalonians 4).

Daniel seems to indicate that Israel, that is, the believing remnant, will still be on the earth vulnerable to the Satanic Triumvirate past the 1260 days until 1290 days. During this time, they will experience Satan's final attempts to destroy them. They are called "blessed" in Daniel because they patiently wait for and reach, not just the 1290 days when Antichrist is overthrown, but 1335 days when the temple is cleansed even as it was in the days of Antiochus Epiphanes. This is also a possible explanation for Jesus' words in Matthew 24:21-22, *"For then there will be great distress, unequaled from the beginning of the world until now—and never to be equaled again. If those days had not been cut short, no one would survive, but for the sake of the elect those days will be shortened."* Daniel says that the people whose names are written in the book (of Life) will be delivered. And this at the first resurrection when Christ comes. But there will be those who will *"be purified, made spotless and refined"* while the wicked continue to be wicked. These are those who will need to wait and reach 1290 days and 1335 days. These are the saved and protected remnant of Israel.

The Seven Bowls of Wrath

Now soon after His coming or in connection with it, the Bowls of Wrath are poured out. In the Bowls, God's ultimate purpose in wrath will have been realized. It is contended by some that the Trumpet judgments are the "beginning" of God's wrath, and the Bowls are therefore the "completing" of God's wrath. I personally do not believe that the Trumpets constitute a part of the Day of the Lord. As indicated above, I believe they span the last half of Daniel's week, and are partial and intended to be remedial. It is the nature of God to give the world every chance to repent and turn from their wicked ways. There is much witness that goes on during the Tribulation. The trumpets are a further witness. That they did not accomplish their purpose of bringing people to repent is the conclusion drawn at the end of chapter 9, *". . . they still did not repent . . . Nor did they repent . . . " (9:20-21).*

I would offer one final argument that the seals, trumpets, and bowls are not sequential, but progressively parallel. By sequential, I mean the trumpets follow the seals, and the bowls follow the trumpets. What seems to be true is that they work like three hour glasses set to go off at given intervals, but all running out at the same time, thus climaxing with the great Battle of Armageddon and the Coming of Christ, both of which constitute the Day of the Lord. The bowls are evidently poured out in quick succession, and the sixth and seventh bowl bring us to Armageddon and The Coming of Christ. Chapter 15 opens with God's people in heaven worshipping before the throne, so the Church will be raptured just before Armageddon begins and the bowls are poured out. This agrees with Revelation 19 with the Marriage Supper of the Lamb occurring first, then the Great Supper of God and the Coming of the King of kings and Lord of lords.

This seems to be borne out also by the terminal statements that occur at the end of the Seals, Trumpets and Bowls. (See chart at the end of this chapter) As the Seventh Seal is opened (8:5) *"Then the angel took the censor, filled it with fire from the altar, and hurled it on the earth; and there came peals of thunder, rumblings, flashes of lightning and an earthquake."* As the Seventh Trumpet sounds (11:19) *"Then God's temple in heaven was opened, and within his temple was seen the Ark of the Covenant. And there came flashes of lightning, rumblings, peals of thunder, an earthquake and a great hailstorm."* As the Seventh Bowl is poured (16:17) *"Out of the temple came a loud voice from the throne saying, "It is done!" Then there came flashes of lightning, rumblings, peals of thunder and a severe earthquake."* This can hardly be considered a random use of language. What it signals is climax. That Christ's Coming is *climactic* at the end of the age. (See chart at the end of this chapter)

In chapter 14 we have a preview of what will come. We have there what we might expect to happen. Christ appears on Mt. Zion, and with him 144,000, who have been protected, who believe on Him when they see Him appear, and who enter the kingdom prepared for them. The Great Multitude now in heaven, sing the song of redemption, a welcoming song for the 144,000.

Then we have a final declaration of the "eternal gospel." We next have a declaration of Babylon's fall. Then comes a severe warning to all who bear the mark of the beast, and finally, we have Christ coming on the cloud, and the harvest of the earth, which according to Matthew 13 is of both the righteous and unrighteous corresponding to the rapture and the first resurrection. The second harvest is the great wine press of the wicked who are judged at Armageddon. In Chapter 15, just before the Bowls of Wrath are poured out, the redeemed are seen in heaven rejoicing that they have been victorious over the Beast. Chapters 16, 17, and 18 are explanatory giving more detail about the Day of the Lord, and the victory of the King of kings and Lord of lords. Chapter 19 is the grand finale, the great Hallelujah Chorus of the redeemed sung for their Lord at the Marriage Supper (equivalent to the rapture and resurrection) and followed immediately by the grand unveiling of Christ coming in triumph with the armies of heaven following.

So the coming of Christ is seen to occur in several places, each depicted as climactic:

> As the last seal is opened.
> As the last trumpet sounds.
> As the harvest of the earth occurs.
> As the bowls are poured out.
> As Mystery Babylon falls
> As the marriage supper takes place.
> As the battle of Armageddon begins.

A Few Reflections on the Final Judgments

In chapter 20 and verse 4, John sees *"thrones on which were seated those who had been given authority to judge."* This judgment could include the Bema judgment seat as well as the judgment of the nations, since Christ refs in the context of Matthew 25 to several who are judged, because they were not ready when Christ came.

Actually, in that context, our Lord speaks of the judgment of those who were found unprepared at his coming and thus became the objects of His judgment. Paul reminded his Corinthian readers that *"we must all appear before the judgment seat of Christ, that each one may receive what is due him for the things done while in the body, whether good or bad" (2 Corinthians 5:10, 11, 14).* Then he says that since we know what it is to live in the fear of the Lord, we try to persuade men to be reconciled to Christ while there is still time, and not to receive God's grace "in vain." The fear of the Lord and our love for the Lord (the two are not mutually exclusive) become the great motivating force for effective witness.

Our Lord in Matthew 24 and 25 alludes to several judgment scenes. At the end of chapter 24 he talks about the faithful and wise servant who the master puts in charge of his household, and he comes back and finds him faithfully fulfilling his trust. He is rewarded by given greater responsibilities. But if that servant had been wicked and lived life as if the master would never return, doing what he pleased and living sensually, when the master returned unexpectedly, he would be condemned to hell. *"He will cut him to pieces and assign him a place with the hypocrites, where there will be weeping and gnashing of teeth" (24:51).*

Then he talks about the ten virgins—five wise and five foolish. This furnishes light on The Marriage Supper. The five were ready and waiting with their lamps trimmed and full of oil. The other five were not prepared, because they didn't really believe the bridegroom was coming soon. Unexpectedly, he came, and they were shut out. He said to them, *"I tell you the truth, I don't know you."* Next, he gives the parable of the talents with a similar application. To those who had been faithful with their entrustments He said, *"Come and share your master's happiness!"* To the one talent man who did nothing, He said, *"Throw that worthless servant outside, into the darkness, where there will be weeping and gnashing of teeth."* Now he speaks of His coming in relation to the nations. This has been misunderstood by many, who feel the Lord introduces a new basis for salvation and the kingdom—that of works. Jesus is talking about the witness that went out during the Tribulation period—those who had been faithful in their testimony to Christ, and faithful to the truth of God's Word. The people in those nations that stand before the Lord were recipients of the witness as it went out. They were separated, sheep on the right, goats on the left. The righteous enter the kingdom, because they ministered to the messenger who came in Christ's name. As they witnessed, Christ's messengers suffered, experiencing deprivation, disease, and imprisonment because of their testimony. Those who rejected His messengers, and did nothing to alleviate their suffering, but only added to it, were sent away *"to eternal punishment."* It is significant, therefore, that in Revelation 20, when the thrones were set up, and those given authority to judge sat on them that the next sentence speaks of *"the souls of those who had been beheaded because of their testimony for Jesus and because of the word of God."* The inference seems to be that the judgment of the nations as they stand before the Lord will have something to do with their treatment of Christ's own who faithfully testified to Christ and to the truth of His Word. Our Lord had previously said in Matthew 10, *"He who receives you receives me, and he who receives me receives the one who sent me. Anyone who receives a prophet because he is a prophet (the two witnesses of Rev. 11?) will receive a prophet's reward, and anyone who receives a righteous man because he is a righteous man will receive a righteous man's reward, And if anyone gives even a cup of cold water to one of these little ones because he is my disciple, I tell you the truth, he will certainly not lose his reward (Matt. 10:40-42).* That certainly explains what Jesus meant in Matthew 25 when he talks about the basis for judgment or reward: *"Whatever you did for one of the least of these brothers of mine, you did for me."* And the opposite is also true (verse 45).

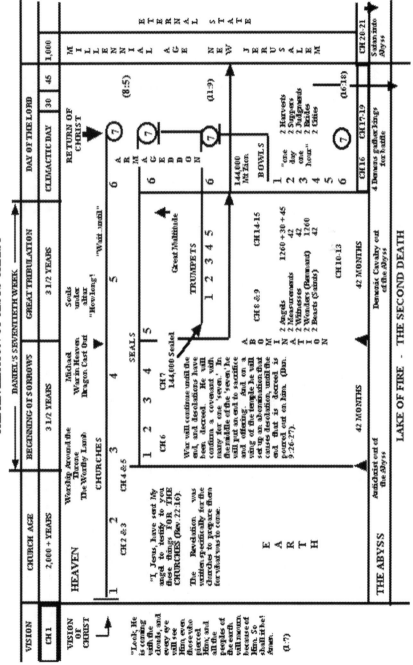

THE REVELATION OF JESUS CHRIST

THE SECOND COMING OF CHRIST – CLIMAX OF THE AGES

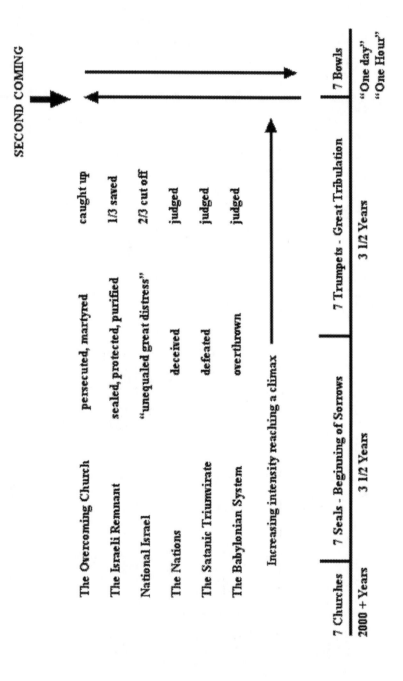

SECOND COMING

The Overcoming Church	persecuted, martyred	caught up
The Israeli Remnant	sealed, protected, purified	1/3 saved
National Israel	"unequaled great distress"	2/3 cut off
The Nations	deceived	judged
The Satanic Triumvirate	defeated	judged
The Babylonian System	overthrown	judged

Increasing intensity reaching a climax

| 7 Churches | 7 Seals - Beginning of Sorrows | 7 Trumpets - Great Tribulation | 7 Bowls |
| 2000 + Years | 3 1/2 Years | 3 1/2 Years | "One day" "One Hour" |

84

The Hour Glass Effect

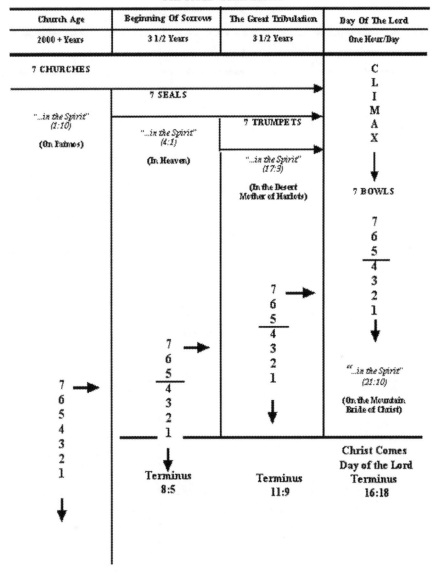

Church Age	Beginning Of Sorrows	The Great Tribulation	Day Of The Lord
2000 + Years	3 1/2 Years	3 1/2 Years	One Hour/Day

7 CHURCHES

7 SEALS

7 TRUMPETS

"...in the Spirit"
(1:10)

(On Patmos)

"...in the Spirit"
(4:1)

(In Heaven)

"...in the Spirit"
(17:3)

(In the Desert
Mother of Harlots)

C
L
I
M
A
X

7 BOWLS

7
6
5
4
3
2
1

"...in the Spirit"
(21:10)

(On the Mountain
Bride of Christ)

7
6
5
4
3
2
1

7
6
5
4
3
2
1

7
6
5
4
3
2
1

Terminus
8:5

Terminus
11:9

Christ Comes
Day of the Lord
Terminus
16:18

Three Climactic Terminal Statements

3 Termini	Text	Notes
1 **At The End Of** **The Seventh Seal** **(8:5)**	**From the Temple** **The Altar** **(Altar of Incense)** "Then the angel took the censer, filled it with fire from the altar, and hurled it on the earth and there came peals of thunder, rumblings, flashes of lightning and an earthquake" (8:5).	**The Climax of** **the Ages** This terminal statement is immediately preceded by the **sixth seal** which announces the celestial disturbances, the Day of the Lord, and **Armageddon** as the Lord comes. It parallels Rev. 19:11-18. Note the similarity of language.
2 **At The End Of** **The Seventh** **Trumpet** **(11:19)**	**From the Temple** **(The Ark of the Covenant)** "Then God's temple in heaven was opened, and within his temple was seen the ark of his covenant. And there came flashes of lightning, rumblings, peals of thunder, an earthquake and a great hailstorm" (11:19).	The seventh trumpet which announces *"you...have begun to reign"* *"your wrath has come"* *"judging the dead"* *"rewarding your servants"* *"destroying the destroyers"* ...is preceded by the **sixth trumpet** which announces the gathering of the mounted troops, 200 million, who slay 1/3 of mankind. This is certainly preparation for **Armageddon**.
3 **At The End Of** **The Seventh Bowl** **(16:17)**	**From the Temple** **(The Throne)** "The seventh angel poured out his bowl into the air, and out of the temple came a loud voice from the throne, saying, "It is done!" Then there came flashes of lightning, rumblings, peals of thunder and a severe earthquake" (16:17).	Just before this terminal statement, the sixth bowl brings us to **Armageddon**. *"Then they gathered the kings together to the place that in Hebrew is Armageddon"* (16:16). Note: The **seals, trumpets, and bowls** are progressively parallel, but not simultaneous.

Theme Chart

Armageddon
The World's Last Great Battle
When Does It Occur in the Revelation?

Occurrence	Text
1 At The Opening Of The Sixth Seal (6:12-17)	They called to the mountains and the rocks, 'Fall on us and hide us from the face of him who sits on the throne and from the wrath of the Lamb! For the great day of their wrath has come, and who can stand?
2 At The Sounding Of The Sixth Trumpet (9:13-19)	The number of the mounted troops was two hundred million. I heard their number.
3 At The Harvest Of The Earth (14:19-20)	They were trampled in the wine press outside the city, and blood flowed out of the press, rising as high as the horses' bridle for a distance of 1,600 stadia (180 miles).
4 At The Pouring Out Of The Sixth Bowl (16:16)	Then they gathered the kings together to the place that in Hebrew is called Armageddon.
5 At The Overthrow of Antichrist (17:14)	They will make war against the Lamb, but the Lamb will overcome them because he is Lord of lords and King of kings—and with him will be his called, chosen and faithful followers.
6 At The Destruction Of Babylon (18:8)	...in one day her plagues will overtake her: death, mourning and famine. She will be consumed by fire, for mighty is the Lord God who judges her.
7 At The Coming of The King of kings And Lord of lords (19:11)	I saw heaven standing open and there before me was a white horse, whose rider is called Faithful and True. With justice he judges and makes war.

Theme Chart

The Coming of Christ

"Look, he is coming with the clouds, and every eye will see him, even those who pierced him, and all the peoples of the earth will mourn because of him. So shall it be! Amen." (Revelation 1:7)

Occurrence	Text
1 **As the Last Seal Is Opened** **(6:16-17)**	Hide us from the face of him who sits on the throne and from the wrath of the Lamb! For **the great day of their wrath has come,** and who can stand?
2 **As the Last Trumpet is Sounded** **(11:18)**	The seventh angel sounded....**You have taken your great power and have begun to reign...The time** is come for judging the dead, and for rewarding your servants ...
3 **As the Israeli Remnant Believes** **(14:1)** **See Zech. 12:10**	...the **Lamb standing on Mount Zion** with the 144,000..
4 **As the Harvests of the Earth Take Place** **(14:16)**	So **he who was seated on the cloud** swung his sickle over the earth, and the earth was harvested." "The harvest is at the end of the age, and the harvesters are the angels.(Matthew 13:39).
5 **As the Bowls of Wrath** **are Poured Out,** **And As Babylon Falls** **(16:15-16;18:4; 19:2)**	**Behold, I come like a thief!** Blessed is he who stays awake and keeps his clothes with him, so that he may not go naked and be shamefully exposed. **Come out of her, my people,** so that you will not share in her sins, so that you will not receive her plagues.
6 **As the Marriage Supper Takes Place** **(19:7)**	**The wedding of the Lamb has come,** and his bride has made herself ready.
7 **As the Last Great Battle Is Fought** **(19:11)**	**I saw heaven standing open and there before** me was a white horse, whose rider is called **Faithful and** True. With justice he judges and makes war.......

Christ's Coming & The Day of the Lord
I Thessalonians 4:13-5:1-11

"Brothers, we do not want you to be ignorant....or to grieve" (4:13)
"...Now, brothers, about times and dates..." (5:1).

Unbelievers	Believers
1 **As To Their Understanding** "...ignorant about those who fall asleep (who have died)..." (4:13).	**1** **As To Their Understanding** "**We believe** that Jesus died and rose again and so we believe that God will bring with Jesus those who have fallen asleep (died) in him" (4:14).
2 **As To Their Expectation** "...grieve like ...men, who have no hope" (4:13).	**2** **As To Their Expectation** "According to the Lord's own word, we tell you that we who are still alive, who are left till the coming of the Lord, will certainly not precede those who have fallen asleep. For the Lord himself will come down from heaven, with a loud command, with the voice of the archangel and with the trumpet call of God, and the dead in Christ will rise first. After that, we who are still alive and are left will be caught up together with them in the clouds to meet the Lord in the air. **And so we will be with the Lord forever.** Therefore encourage each other with these words" (4:15-18).
3 **As To Their Preparedness** "...the day of the Lord will come like a thief in the night. While people are saying, 'Peace and safety,' destruction will come on them suddenly, as labor pains on a pregnant woman, and they will not escape" (5:2,3).	**3** **As To Their Preparedness** "**But you**, brothers, **are not in darkness so that this day should surprise you like a thief**" (5:4)
4 **As To Their Condition** "...belong to the night or to the darkness" (5:5)	**4** **As To Their Condition** "You are **sons of the light**" (5:5)
5 **As To Their Posture** "...are asleep" (5:6). "Those who sleep, sleep at night, and those who get drunk, get drunk at night" (5:7).	**5** **As To Their Posture** "So let us not be like others, who are asleep, but let us be **alert, and self-controlled**...Since we belong to the day, let us be self-controlled, putting on faith and love as a breastplate, and the hope of salvation as a helmet" (5:6,8).

Christ's Coming & The Day of the Lord
II Thessalonians 1:6--2:1-14
(continued)

Unbelievers	Believers
6 **As To Their Prospect** "...to suffer wrath" (5:9). "God is just: He will **pay back** trouble to those who trouble you...(2 Thes. 1:6) "**He will punish** those who do not know God and do not obey the gospel of our Lord Jesus. They will be punished with everlasting destruction and shut out from the presence of the Lord and from the majesty of his power on the day he comes to be glorified..." (2 Thes. 1:8-9).	**6** **As To Their Prospect** "For **God did not appoint us to suffer wrath** but to receive salvation through our Lord Jesus Christ. He died for us so that, whether we are awake or asleep, we may live together with him. Therefore encourage one another and build each other up, just as in fact you are doing" (1 Thes 5:9-10). "He will... **give relief** to you who are troubled, and to us as well. **This will happen when the Lord Jesus is revealed from heaven in blazing fire with his powerful angels....on the day he comes to be glorified in his holy people and to be marveled at among all those who have believed**" (2 Thes. 1:7, 10).
7 **How Will They Know?** **They won't!** "...and so all will be condemned who have not believed the truth but have delighted in wickedness" (2 Thes. 2:12)	**7** **How Will They Know?** "Concerning the coming of our Lord Jesus Christ and our being gathered to him, ...We ask you, brothers, not to become easily unsettled or alarmed by some prophecy, report or letter supposed to have come from us, saying that the day of the Lord has already come. Don't let anyone deceive you in any way, for that day will not come **until** the rebellion (apostasy) occurs and the man of lawlessness is revealed, the man doomed to destruction..." (2 Thes. 2:1-3). "...the lawless one will be revealed, whom the Lord Jesus will overthrow with the breath of his mouth and destroy by **the splendor of his coming**..." (v 8) "God chose you to be saved ....to share in the glory of our Lord Jesus Christ" (2:13-14).

Message To The Seven Churches
Revelation 2 & 3

	1 Ephesus 2:1-7	2 Smyrna 2:11-17	3 Pergamum 2:12-17	4 Thyatira 2:18-29	5 Sardis 3:1-6	6 Philadelphia 3:7-13	7 Laodicea 3:14-22
1 Church							
2 Christ	Holds 7 stars Walks among 7 lampstands	First & Last Was dead-now lives	Sharp two-edged sword	Eyes, blazing fire, Feet, burnished bronze	Holds 7 Spirits & 7 stars	Holy & True Hold Keys of David	The Amen The Witness The Ruler
3 Commendation What He sees and approves	Deeds, hard work, perseverance, intolerant of wicked men, tested teachers, endured hardships, steadfast	Afflicted, poor, slandered, persecuted, tested	True, steadfast, faithful unto death	Deeds, love, faith, service, perseverance, progress—doing more now than at first	Only a few with unsoiled garments	Deeds, an open door, kept His word, faithful to His name	
4 Condemnation What He sees and disapproves	Loveless Forsaken first love		Tolerated Balaam & Teaching of Nicolaitans	Tolerated a false prophetess, some being led into sexual sin, deeds will be punished	Wake up! Strengthen what remains! Deeds not complete in God's sight	A synagogue of Satan in their midst, made to acknowledge God's love for the church	Lukewarm, complacent, satisfied, spiritually blind
5 Counsel, Caution, Coming What they should do	Remember, Repent, Repeat I will come to you and remove	Be faithful even to death	Repent I will soon come	Repent Hold on to what you have until I come	Remember Repent Wake up I will come like a thief	I will keep you from the hour I am coming, hold on to what you have	Buy from me gold, white clothes, salve Repent Here I am!
6 Challenge To The Overcomers	Right to eat of the tree of life	Crown of life Not hurt by the second death	Some of the hidden manna, White stone with new name	Authority over the nations The morning star	Dressed in white Name in the Book of Life	Pillar in God's temple Name of God, the City of God, & Christ's new name written on him	Right to sit with Christ on His throne
7 Command To Hear							

He Who Has An Ear, Let Him Hear What The Spirit Says To The Churches!
His message to all is His message to each!

THE OVERCOMERS
Who Are They?

1
Who Are Challenged To Overcome?
Individuals In The Churches
"To him who overcomes..."

2
Who Are Said To Overcome?
The Saints

"They overcame him (Satan) by the blood of the Lamb and by the Word of their testimony; they did not love their lives so much as to shrink from death" (12:11, 17).

3
How Do They Overcome?

By refusing to worship the beast, his image, or to receive his mark—even if that refusal costs them their lives!

"And I saw the souls of those who had been beheaded because of their testimony for Jesus and because of the word of God. They had not worshiped the beast or his image and had not received his mark on their foreheads or their hands. They came to life and reigned with Christ a thousand years" (20:4

4
Who Is The Great Overcomer?
The Lamb

"..the Lamb will overcome them because He is Lord of lords and King of kings--

5
Who Overcome With Him?
His Faithful Followers

"..and with him will be his called, chosen and faithful followers" (17:14)

6
What Promises Are Made To Overcomers?
Promises That Relate to Reigning With Christ in The New Jerusalem

The Promises

Ephesus
I will give the right to eat from the tree of life, which is in the paradise of God (2:7).

Smyrna
...will not be hurt at all by the second death. (2:11).

Pergamum
I will give some of the hidden manna. I will also give him a white stone with a new name written on it, known only to him who receives it (2:17).

Thyatira
I will give authority over the nations...I will also give him the morning star (2:26, 27).

Sardis
...be dressed in white. I will never blot out his name from the book of life, but will acknowledge his name before my Father and his angels

Philadelphia
I will make a pillar in the temple of my God. Never again will he leave it. I will write on him the name of my God and the name of the city of my God, the new Jerusalem, which is coming down out of heaven from God; and I will also write on him my new name.

Laodicea
I will give the right to sit with me on my throne, just as I overcame and sat down with my Father on his throne.

7
The Ultimate Overcomers!

"He that overcomes will inherit all this, and I will be his God and he will be my son" (21:7).

Overview

The Seven-Sealed Scroll
Revelation 6:1-8:5

Seal	Horse	Rider	Symbol	Result
1st Seal Cherubim (6:1)	White	Conqueror	Bow Crown	Conquest
2nd Seal Cherubim (6:3)	Fiery Red	Remove Peace From Earth Make Men Slay Each Other	Sword	Internecine Strife
3rd Seal Cherubim (8:10,11)	Black	Holds Scales	Scales	Famine
4th Seal Cherubim (8:12,13)	Pale	Death	Sword Famine Plague Wild Beasts	Death Hades 1/4 Of Earth Affected
5th Seal (6:9)	Martyrs Under The Altar	Their Prayer: "How Long?"	Given White Robes	"Wait A Little Longer"
6th Seal (6:12)	Great Earthquake Celestial Disturbances	Men Hide In Terror	The Wrath of the Lamb	Day of The Lord
7th Seal (8:1)	Silence in Heaven for about 1/2 Hour			

The Seven Trumpet Judgments
Partial and Remedial
Revelation 8:6-11:19

Trumpet Angels	Nature of Plague	Area Affected	Extent	Result
1st Angel (8:7)	Hail & Fire Mixed With Blood	Earth Trees Green Grass	1/3 1/3 All	Burned Up
2nd Angel (8:8,9)	Huge Blazing Mountain	Sea Sea Creatures Ships	1/3 1/3 1/3	Turned To Blood Died Destroyed
3rd Angel (8:10,11)	Great Blazing Star Wormwood	Rivers & Streams	1/3	Turned Bitter Many Die
4th Angel (8:12,13)	Heavenly Bodies Struck	Sun Moon Stars	1/3 1/3 1/3	Turned Dark
5th Angel First Woe (9:1-12)	A Star-Angel Opens The Abyss Demonic Locusts	People Without The Seal of God	5 Months	People Tortured But Not Killed
6th Angel Second Woe (9:13-19)	Four Bound Angels Released A Vast Army	Mankind	1/3	Killed By Fire Smoke Sulfur
7th Angel Third Woe (10:6,7)	"The rest of mankind that were not killed by these plagues **still did not repent...**" (Revelation 9:20, 21). **No More Delay-- The Time Has Come!**			

Overview

The Seven Bowls Of Wrath
Revelation 15:1-16:21
"God's wrath is completed..." (15:1).

Bowl Angels	Nature Of The Plague	Area Affected	Extent	Result
1st Angel (16:2)	Ugly Painful Sores	Land	All Beast Worshipers	Sores Broke Out
2nd Angel (16:3)	Like Dead Men's Blood	Sea	Every Living Thing	Died
3rd Angel (16:4)	Blood	Rivers & Springs Of Water	All Those Who Shed Blood	Blood to Drink
4th Angel (16:8)	Scorching Heat	Sun	Unrepentant People	Seared By Intense Heat
5th Angel (16:10)	Darkness	Throne & Kingdom Of The Beast	Unrepentant People	Darkness Pains Sores
6th Angel 16:12	Waters Dry Up 3 Evil Spirits From Satanic Trio	Euphrates River	Whole World Summoned For Battle	Kings Gathered For Battle
7th Angel 16:17	It Is Done! Great Earthquake Hail	Air	Nothing Like It 100 Pound Hailstones	City Splits Cities Collapse Babylon Falls

SUGGESTED STRUCTURAL OUTLINE OF REVELATION

The Prologue—Jesus Is Coming Soon!

Chapter 1 The Sevenfold Introduction To Revelation

1. The Revelation
2. The Blessing
3. The Greeting
4. The Roles
5. The Doxology
6. The Coming
7. The Attestation

The Sevenfold Vision of the Sovereign Christ

1. His Head
2. His Eyes
3. His Feet
4. His Voice
5. His Right Hand
6. His Mouth
7. His Face

Chapters 2 & 3 The Sevenfold Letters to the Seven Churches

1. Ephesus
2. Smyrna
3. Pergamum

4. Thyatira
5. Sardis
6. Philadelphia
7. Laodicea

Chapter 4 The Seven Positions Around the Throne in Heaven

1. On the Throne
2. Surrounding the Throne
3. From the Throne
4. Before the Throne
5. Around the Throne
6. Center of the Throne
7. Encircling the Throne

Chapter 5 The Seven Sealed Scroll and the Worthy Lamb

Chapter 6 The Seven Seals—The Climactic Week of Years—An Overview

1. First Seal
2. Second Seal
3. Third Seal
4. Fourth Seal
5. Fifth Seal
6. Sixth Seal

The Great Tribulation—The Last Half of the Week of Years

Chapter 7 Two People Groups and The Time of Great Distress

The 144,00 Israeli Remnant
The Great Multitude of Gentile Believers

Chapter 8 The Seven Trumpet Judgments

7. Seventh Seal

Terminus Statement: The Time Is Near!

The Prayers of the Saints Offered Up To God

The Seven Trumpets Judgments God's Final Warning

Partial and Remedial

1. First Trumpet
2. Second Trumpet
3. Third Trumpet
4. Fourth Trumpet

Chapter 9

5. Fifth Trumpet
6. Sixth Trumpet

Chapter 10 The Time-Frame of the Great Distress
        Time, Times, and Half a Time

No More Delay!

Chapter 11 The Two Witnesses

42 months-The Times of the Gentiles Comes to An End
42 months-The Two Witnesses Hold Forth
The Second Woe Ends

7. Seventh Trumpet (3rd Woe)

Terminus Statement: The Time is Here!

Chapter 12 & 13 Seven Persons on the Final Stage—A Fuller View

1. The Woman
2. The Dragon
3. The Child
4. The Archangel Michael
5. The Beast Out of the Sea

6. The Beast Out of the Earth
7. The Lamb

The Bestial Treatment of the People of God

3 1/2 Years Israel Persecuted and the Remnant
    Protected
3 1/2 Years The Saints Persecuted

Chapter 14 The **Great Tribulation Is Over!**

The 144,000 With the Lamb on Mount Zion
The Great Multitude in Heaven Singing the Welcoming
    Song of Redemption

The Seven Administrative Angels
A Preview of the Approaching Climax
The Final Countdown

Warnings

1. First Angel
2. Second Angel
3. Third Angel

The First Harvest

4. Fourth Angel
5. Fifth Angel

The Second Harvest

6. Sixth Angel
7. Seventh Angel

Chapter 15 The **Victorious Saints In Heaven**

The Seven Angels Prepare to Pour Out The Bowls of Wrath

Chapter 16 The Day of the Lord: The Seven Bowls of Wrath.
   An Overview

1. First Bowl
2. Second Bowl
3. Third Bowl
4. Fourth Bowl
5. Fifth Bowl
6. Sixth Bowl
7. Seventh Bowl

Terminus Statement: It Is Done!

Chapter 17 & 18 A Fuller View: Mystery Babylon
   the Great Destroyed

The Unholy Alliance
The Great City—No More!

Chapter 19 The Climax of the Ages—The Great
   Unveiling—Second Coming of Christ!

The Hallelujah Chorus
The Marriage Supper of the Lamb
The Rider on the White Horse
The Great Supper of God
Defeat and Judgment of the Two Beasts
Defeat of the Nations

Chapter 20 The Kingdom Comes—The 1,000 Year Reign

Before the 1,000 Years

Satan Bound
Judgment Thrones
First Resurrection

During the 1,000 Years

The Saints Reign With Christ

After the 1,000 Years

The Second Resurrection
Satan's Release and Final Doom
The Final Judgment & The Second Death

Chapter 21 Everything New in The New Age. An Overview.

1. New Heaven
2. New Earth
3. New Closeness
4. New City
5. New Proximity
6. New Conditions
7. Everything New!

Terminus Statement: It Is Done!

Chapter 22 Fuller View: Sevenfold Description of the Bride, the New Jerusalem

Negative:
1. No Temple (Man Made)
2. No Natural Light Needed
3. No Closing of the Gates
4. No Unclean Thing
5. No Curse
6. No Night
7. No Artificial Light

Positive:
1. Perfect Worship
2. Perfect Government
3. Perfect Service
4. Perfect Vision
5. Perfect Likeness
6. Perfect Illumination
7. Perfect Blessedness

Epilogue Sevenfold Conclusion-Jesus Is Coming Soon!

1. Behold, I am coming soon!
2. Behold, I am coming soon!
3. The Spirit and the bride say, "Come!"
4. Let him who hears say, "Come!"
5. Whoever is thirsty, let him come!
6. Yes, I am coming soon!
7. Come, Lord Jesus!

PART 3

THE BOOK
OF REVELATION WITH
COMMENTARY

CHAPTER 1

INTRODUCTION

I have this sense that the average Christian tends to skirt the Book of Revelation. It seems so incomprehensible. Being largely a book of imagery, to read it is to step into a strange, unfamiliar world of angels and demons, of lambs, lions, horses and dragons. Seals are broken, trumpets sound and resound and the contents of seven bowls are poured out on the earth. Two particularly malicious beasts appear, one emerging out of the sea with ten horns and seven heads, and the other rising from the earth, with a lamb's horns and a dragon's voice. There is thunder, lightning, hail, fire and smoke. It all seems very weird and mysterious.

Actually, this kind of written apocalpyse was no novelty in Jewish pre-Christian literature; there are examples of this class of writing within the canon of the Old Testament, and besides these, eight or nine extant apocalyptic works could be enumerated which were a bit earlier than the Apocalypse of John, and a few nearly contemporary with it. These writings without exception used assumed names for their writings, never using their own. Unlike them, John used his own name, and underlines the fact that he received his message directly from Christ through his angel and not at second hand.

The book, then, claims to be a divine revelation of the Sovereign, soon returning Christ, given by God to His servants. Furthermore, one of several triads that appear in this first chapter of the Revelation promises special blessing to the one who reads this book, those who hear it, and those who obey or take it to heart. And it adds at the end solemn warnings about those who tamper with its contents, either adding to or detracting from its message. We would be foolish to either ignore it or neglect it!

1. The Title or Prologue

1:1 The revelation of Jesus Christ, which God gave him to show his servants what must soon take place. He made it known (signified) by sending his angel to his servant John,

"Revelation" apocalypse . . . means an unveiling or disclosure. It is a prophetic letter having all the formal characteristics of a letter, like the letters of Paul, and is the longest letter in the New Testament.

"signified" The revelation is said to be signified to John by an angel with Jesus mediating. The term carries the idea of making known by some sort of sign, and therefore is appropriate to designate the symbolic portrayal of events in the book.

"Soon take place" John is stressing how the events surrounding the unveiling of Christ will take place (quickly) rather than when (proximity). In Matthew 24:36, Jesus states that only the Father knows the when, the moment of His coming. Here in Revelation, John is given a proleptic view of the future (as if the events described had already occurred or were soon to occur.) God will now unfold what, in His wisdom, he has planned before hand.

"His angel" Twice John is cautioned not to worship the angel that is guiding him (19:10; 22:9). This gives us some idea of the importance of the angel in John's experience.

Note the triadic structure:

- ➢ God gave it to Christ . . . ultimate Source
- ➢ Christ showed it to John via an angel . . . mediate Source
- ➢ John testified to the churches . . . the immediate source

The theme of Angels can be seen throughout the book of Revelation:

- ➢ 7 Church angels
- ➢ Myriad angelic chorus
- ➢ 4 Throne and Seal angels
- ➢ 7 Trumpet angels
- ➢ 7 Harvest angels
- ➢ 7 Bowl angels
- ➢ 7 Climactic angels

1:2 who testifies to everything he saw—that is, the word of God and the testimony of Jesus Christ.

We shall be seeing what we see and hearing what we hear through the eyes and ears of John. He writes only what he is told to write. *"the testimony of Jesus is the spirit of prophecy" (19:10).* John, the beloved one, was a servant, apostle, evangelist, and prophet of the Lord, perhaps the last surviving apostle.

The phrase *"word of God and the testimony of Jesus Christ"* is an integrating theme throughout the book of Revelation. It involves not only being true to Him and His Word, but a willingness to suffer, if need be, to be a faithful witness

➤ Why John was suffering 1:9
➤ Why the martyrs were slain 6:9
➤ Why the two witnesses were slain 11:7
➤ How the saints overcame 12:11
➤ Why the saints were persecuted 12:17
   Why the woman was drunk with the blood of the saints 17:6
➤ Why the saints were martyred 20:4

Jesus said, *"And this gospel of the kingdom will be preached in the whole world **as a testimony** to all nations, and **then the end will come**" (Matt. 24:14).*

It is precisely for this reason that the saints are persecuted. Their testimony is a testimony sealed by death. "The gospel of the kingdom" is *"Repent, for the kingdom of God is at hand."*

2. The Blessing

1:3 Blessed is the one who reads the words of this prophecy, and blessed are those who hear it and take to heart what is written in it, because the time is near.

Revelation is preeminently a book of worship, and the reading of it in public worship is here commended. There are seven beatitudes that form a thread through Revelation, and pronounce blessing on those who are obedient and faithful followers of Christ regardless of the severity of their trials. They end up enjoying access to the glories of the New Jerusalem.

This first beatitude indicates one must be both a hearer and a doer. James says the same thing, *"Do not merely listen to the word, and so deceive yourselves. Do what it says" (James 1:22).* (See theme chart)

The blessing here is much like the words of Jesus in Luke 11:28, *"Blessed . . . are those who hear the word of God and keep it!"*

The Seven Beatitudes in Revelation

➤ The blessedness of reading, hearing, and obeying the words of this prophecy (1:3)
➤ The blessedness of those who die in the Lord (14:13)
➤ The blessedness of the watchful pilgrim (16:15)
➤ The blessedness of the wedding feast (19:9)
➤ The blessedness of those whom the second death cannot touch (20:6)
➤ The blessedness of the one who keeps the words of this prophecy (22:7)
➤ The blessedness of those who have access to the City (22:14)

"The words of this prophecy" is another integrating theme throughout the book. Although the apocalyptic nature of Revelation is obvious and symbols abound, a literal understanding is still possible, because Daniel's prophecy foretells a week of years in the future that will initiate the climactic events at the end of the age. That prophecy gives the framework for chapters 7 through 13 of Revelation, especially the last half of this seven year period.

➤ Reading and heading the words of this prophecy (1:3)
➤ The prophetic words of Christ, the Faithful Witness (2:1—repeated seven times)
➤ The prophetic words are trustworthy and true (19:9; 21:5; 22:6)
➤ The one who keeps the prophetic words is blessed (22:7). His servants keep the prophetic words (22:9)
➤ Prohibition against sealing up the prophetic words (22:10)
➤ Prohibition against adding to the prophetic words (22:18)
➤ Prohibition against subtracting from the prophetic words (22:19)

This theme stresses the solemn importance of heeding God's Word. His word here in the Revelation should be to us like the burning bush experience was to Moses in the desert. *"Take off your sandals, for the place where you are standing is holy ground" (Exodus 3:5)*

"The time is near" Peter, speaking at Pentecost, indicated that we are in the "last days" or the age of the Spirit. The next event on God's agenda would be the kingdom age. From John's perspective, the vision he is now to see is "near."

3. The Greeting

1:4 John, to the seven churches in the province of Asia:

John assumes that his readers know who he is. Irenaeus cited him as "John, the Lord's disciple." Church tradition is heavy in favor of John the apostle, and the timing of the writing is probably at the end of the reign of Domitian around 96 A.D. The Preterist School protests this late date. But if Christ's coming is the climax of the age, then it is important to begin there, and work backwards. What immediately precedes His coming is Daniel's Seventieth Week, with the greater emphasis on the final 3 1/2 years of that week of years. (Revelation chapters 7-14 constitute the bookends of The Great Tribulation).

The seven churches formed a circle in Asia moving clockwise north from Ephesus and coming around full circle from Laodicea. It has been suggested that these cities were a postal route serving geographic centers.

The number seven, frequently used in Revelation, denotes fullness of quality while the number 10 speaks of fullness of quantity "manyness".

The message of this book appears to be a wake-up call to Christians who are unaware that there is impending danger ahead. Its message, therefore, continues to be relevant for the church of today. Just as Paul's seven letters are certainly for us, so these seven letters of our Lord to the churches here addressed are for us today also.

Grace and peace to you from him who is, and who was, and who is to come, and from the seven spirits before his throne,

1:5 and from Jesus Christ,

"Grace and peace" summarize all that God has done for us in Christ.

Note the triadic structure:

➤ From the Father (He is eternally present, eternally existent, without beginning or end. Therefore, we need not fear an uncertain future.)

> Him who is
> Him who was
> Him who is to come

➤ From the Seven Spirits
➤ From Jesus Christ

This is surely a reference to the Triune God, Father, Holy Spirit, and Son. The unusual order here may suggest the order of the heavenly Tabernacle of which the earthly one was a copy. (The Holy of Holies, the Throne of the Father, The Holy Place lighted by the Seven-branched Menorah, and the Outer Court with the Altar of Redemption.) The order indicates also that John has more he wants to say about the Son.

The seven "Spirits" could be a reference to the seven churches in which the Holy Spirit operates. The churches are pictured as a seven-branched Menorah. In this context, the Seven Spirits seems to be a reference to the Holy Spirit in His manifold operations. The Old Testament Menorah was a seven-branched candelabrum, and the oil that supplied the lamps symbolized the supply of the Holy Spirit. Here, then, it is the Holy Spirit speaking to and working in the several churches. *"He who has an ear let him hear **what the Spirit says** to the churches."* (A word of admonition to all seven churches).

Zechariah's reference to the Holy Spirit is certainly in view here.

> *"Not by might nor by power, but by My Spirit," says the Lord of hosts. (Zech. 4:6). "These seven are the eyes of the Lord, which range throughout the earth" (Zech. 4:10).*

Or notice how Isaiah describes the sevenfold operation of the Spirit. *"The Spirit of the Lord will rest on him—the Spirit of wisdom and of understanding, the Spirit of counsel and of power, the Spirit of knowledge and of the fear of the Lord" (Isaiah 11:2).*

Some have identified the seven Spirits with the seven archangels or "angels of the presence." This is unlikely since the seven archangels are never mentioned in Scripture even though identified in Jewish literature. Scripture mentions only two, Michael and Gabriel.

"Before the throne" God's throne is mentioned 46 times in the book. The universal rule of God is stressed throughout.

4. The Roles

who is the faithful witness, the firstborn from the dead, and the ruler of the kings of the earth.

Note again the triadic structure:

- ➤ Faithful Witness
- ➤ Firstborn from the Dead
- ➤ Ruler of the Kings of the Earth

Here Jesus is seen in his threefold prophetic office of Prophet, Priest, and King. In other words, He is the Revelator, Redeemer, and Ruler

1. Faithful Witness (Prophet)

Throughout the Gospels, Jesus repeatedly uses the expression, *"I tell you the truth . . . "*He not only spoke the truth, the very words the Father gave Him to speak, but He Himself was the embodiment of the Truth he spoke. This is borne out here in the Revelation, *"These are the words of him . . . "* prefaces each message to the several churches, and they are reminded that *"they are the words of the Amen, the faithful and true witness, the ruler of God's creation" (3:14)*. As the book draws to a close there is again the reminder, *"Write this down, for these words are trustworthy and true" (21:5)*, and again the angel underscores this for John, *"These words are trustworthy and true" (22:6)*. Two of the names given to the rider on the white horse in chapter 19 are *"Faithful and True" (v 11)*. And because they are a message from the Faithful, Trustworthy, True One, they are to be obeyed, *"Blessed is he who keeps the words of the prophecy in this book" (22:7)*.

2. Firstborn from the Dead (Priest)

In the Pentateuch, we have the longing for a *priest* who would intercede and mediate between God and man. The Levitical priesthood was temporary. In the New Testament, Christ is the eternal Melchizedekan Priest who intercedes and mediates for His own forever. And He is not only the Priest who offers the sacrifice, but He Himself is the Sacrifice that is offered. Paul, in defining the Good News in the opening verses of I Corinthians, speaks of Christ's death, burial and resurrection. A little later in this great resurrection chapter Paul writes of Christ as the "firstfruits," *"But Christ has indeed been raised from the dead, **the firstfruits of those who have fallen asleep**. (or who have died) . . . But each in his own turn: Christ, **the firstfruits;** then, **when he comes**, those who belong to him. **Then the end will come,** when he hands over the kingdom to God the Father after he has destroyed all dominion, authority and power. For he must reign until he has put all his enemies under his feet. The last enemy to be destroyed is death"* (15:20, 23-26). In Romans, Paul speaks of Christ as being the "firstborn" of a whole new creation that would reflect His divine image, *"For those God foreknew he also predestined to be conformed to the likeness of his Son, that he might be **the firstborn** among many brothers"* (8:29). Or yet again, in Colossians 1:18, he writes, *"And He is the head of the body, the church; he is the beginning and **the firstborn from among the dead,** so that in everything he might have the supremacy"* (1:18).

God has given Him supremacy, the first place in all creation signifying priority and sovereignty. Because He lives, we shall live also.

> . *"I will also appoint him **my firstborn**, the most exalted of the kings of the earth"* (Psalm 89:27).

3. Ruler (King)

> *"All authority has been given to me in heaven and earth"* (Matthew 28:18).

> *"He was given authority, glory and sovereign power; all peoples, nations and men of every language worshiped him. His dominion is*

*an everlasting dominion that will not pass away, and his kingdom
is one that will never be destroyed" (Daniel 7:14).*

In the historical books, there is the longing for a *king*, and a temporal ruler is given to replace Samuel and the Theocratic rule. Saul is rejected, and David is chosen with whom an everlasting, unconditional covenant was made that his throne would last forever. Thus the significance of the following references in Revelation, *". . . the Lion of the tribe of Judah, the Root of David . . . " (5:5), and "King of kings and Lord of lords" (19:16, and still further, "I am the Root and Offspring of David, and the bright Morning Star" (22:16).*

He will set up his kingdom, rule from David's throne in the New Jerusalem over a renovated earth and a renewed people, establishing universal peace, justice and righteousness.

In Christ's first advent, he perfectly fulfilled these prophetic roles in Himself. In Luke, He is the Prophet, who both speaks the Truth and is the Truth He speaks. In Mark, He is the Priest, who both offers the sacrifice and is the sacrifice He offers. In Matthew, He is the King, who rules over a kingdom of grace, but will rule over a kingdom of glory. In the last day, all will find their ultimate and complete fulfillment.

By this threefold designation, Jesus, through John, encourages the readers not to fear what might be ahead for them, because by His death and resurrection He has shown the way to victory.

5. The Doxology

To him who loves us and has freed (loosed) us from our sins by his blood,

1:6 and has made us to be a kingdom and priests to serve his God and Father-to him be glory and power (dominion) for ever and ever! Amen.

Note the triadic structure:

➢ To Him who loves us (note the present tense)
➢ To Him who freed us (by the payment of a ransom)
➢ To Him who made us a kingdom and priests

The members of His body, the Church, are to fulfill the same roles as man was meant to have from the very beginning, and which our Lord, the Representative Man fulfills: Prophet, Priest and King.

> *"You are worthy to take the scroll and to open its seals, because you were slain, and with your blood you purchased men for God from every tribe and language and people and nation. You have made them **to be a kingdom and priests** to serve our God, and they will reign on the earth" (Revelation 5:9-10).*

> *"Blessed and holy are those who have part in the first resurrection. The second death has no power over them, but they will be **priests of God** and of Christ and **will reign with him for a thousand years"** (Revelation 20:6).*

> *"And **I confer on you a kingdom,** just as my Father conferred one on me, so that you may eat and drink at my table in my kingdom and sit on thrones, judging the twelve tribes of Israel" (Luke 22:29-30).*

It is important to note that those who are purchased by God *"from every tribe and language and people and nation"* will reign with Christ.

➤ On the earth
➤ For a thousand years
➤ From the New Jerusalem (3:12)

> *"As you come to him, the living Stone—rejected by men but chosen by God and precious to him—you also, like living stones, are being built into a spiritual house to be **a holy priesthood,** offering spiritual sacrifices acceptable to God through Jesus Christ" (I Peter 2:4-5).*

An equivalent phrase is used of Israel in the Old Testament, but participation in the divine blessing is always conditioned upon faith and obedience. *"Now if you obey me fully and keep my covenant, then out of all nations you will be my treasured possession. Although the whole earth is mine, you will be for me **a kingdom of priests and a holy nation.** " (Exodus19: 5-6).*

Does this suggest that the Church is the successor to Israel? No, only that God's principle for His believing people has always been by grace through faith apart from works, and His purpose is unchanging.

6. The Unveiling

1:7 Look, he is coming with the clouds, and every eye will see him, even those who pierced him; and all the peoples of the earth will mourn because of him. So shall it be! Amen.

"So shall it be! Amen"—doubly affirmed!

Note the triadic structure once again:

- ➤ Every eye shall see him
- ➤ Even those who pierced him
- ➤ All the peoples of the earth will mourn because of him

In Zechariah's prophecy, it is Israel that leads the mourning. Israel will mourn in repentance. This will mark the time when the remnant will finally believe and participate in the New Covenant promise. The unbelieving world will mourn, because their judgment is imminent.

> *"They will look on me, the one they have pierced, and **they (Israel) will mourn for him** as one mourns for an only child, and grieve bitterly for him as one grieves for a firstborn son" (Zechariah 12:10).*

> John, as an eye witness to Jesus' crucifixion, sees a partial fulfillment of this when the soldier pierced His side as He hung on the cross (John 19:37).

> His Cloud Coming

> *"In my vision at night I looked, and there before me was one like a son of man, **coming with the clouds of heaven.** He approached the Ancient of Days and was led into his presence" (Daniel 7:13).*

*"At that time the sign of the Son of Man will appear in the sky, and all the nations of the earth will mourn. They will see the Son of Man coming on **the clouds of the sky,** with power and great glory" (Matthew 24:30)*

*"In the future you will see the Son of Man sitting at the right hand of the Mighty One and **coming on the clouds of heaven"** (Matthew 26:64)*

*"I looked, and there before me was a white cloud, **and seated on the cloud** was one' like a son of man' with a crown of gold on his head and a sharp sickle in his hand" (Revelation 14:14).*

The cloud referred to may well be the glory-cloud, the Shekinah, dazzling in its brightness, which led Israel through the wilderness and overshadowed the Tabernacle and the Temple. At the Transfiguration, God spoke of his pleasure in the Son from *"a bright cloud."*

We believe Revelation pictures Christ's coming as singular . . . one climactic coming at the end of the age. Seven "comings" (which are really one coming) can be discerned in the Revelation.

- ➤ As the last seal is opened (6:16-17)
- ➤ As the last trumpet is sounded (11:18)
- ➤ As the Israeli remnant believes (14:1—see also Zech. 12:10)
- ➤ As the harvest of the earth takes place (14:16)
- ➤ As the bowls of wrath are poured out, and as judgment falls on Babylon (16:15-16; 18:4; 19:2)
- ➤ As the marriage supper takes place (19:7)
- ➤ As the last great battle is fought (19:11; 20:4)

7. The Attestation

1:8 "I am Alpha and Omega," says the Lord God, "who is, and who was, and who is to come, the Almighty."

Note still again the triadic structure:

➢ Alpha and Omega

> Who is
> Who was
> Who is to come

➢ The Lord God
➢ The Almighty (All-Ruler, Who has all power and rules over everything)

Alpha and Omega are the first and last letters of the Greek alphabet. But the term also means that God is everything in between—He is the sovereign Lord of all history. Thus, the term stands for totality, embracing all, transcending all.

> *"Who has performed and accomplished it, calling forth the generations from the beginning? I, the Lord,* **am the first, and with the last***. I am He" (Isaiah 41:4)*

> *"This is what the LORD says—Israel's King and Redeemer, the LORD Almighty: I am* **the first and I am the last***; apart from me there is no God" (Isaiah 44:6).*

> *"I am He; I am* **the first and I am the last***" (Isaiah 48:12).*

John's Vision of The Risen, Sovereign Lord

1. Who John Was.

1:9 I, John, your brother and companion (partaker, fellow sharer) in the suffering and kingdom and patient endurance that are ours in Jesus,

➢ Suffering (tribulation as a result of being faithful to the Lord)
➢ kingdom (the promised blessing to the faithful at His coming)
➢ patient endurance (what is needed by the faithful to survive)

119

> "**Be patient**, then, brothers, until the Lord's coming. See how the farmer waits for the land to yield its valuable crop and **how patient he is** for the autumn and spring rains. You too, **be patient and stand firm**, because the Lord's coming is near" (James 5:7-8).

> "May the Lord direct your hearts into God's love and Christ's **perseverance** (or in the patient waiting for Christ)" (2 Thessalonians 3:5)?

2. Where John Was.

. . . was on the island of Patmos because of the word of God and the testimony of Jesus.

John seems to be on Patmos because he openly was giving witness to His Lord, and thus sent there by Rome as an exile. Eusebius writes that John was released about AD 96-98 and returned to Ephesus.

For a persecuted church, the key responses are not self-defense or escape, but . . .

➢ A bold witness
➢ Standing firm to the end
➢ Perseverance
➢ Patient endurance
➢ Faithfulness
➢ Wisdom
➢ A willingness to die if necessary

3. What John Heard.

1:10 On the Lord's Day I was in the Spirit, and I heard behind me a loud voice like a trumpet,

The loud voice was probably Christ's angel. Note the triadic structure:

➢ On Patmos

➢ On the Lord's Day
➢ In the Spirit

Being *"in the Spirit on the Lord's day"* for each of us is a prerequisite for getting a message from God. There are four uses of the phrase *"in the Spirit"* and they might offer one method of outlining the book: 1:10; 4:2; 17:3 and 21:10.

➢ Heading
➢ Introduction to Letter
➢ "in the Spirit" on Patmos
➢ "in the Spirit" to heaven
➢ "in the Spirit" to the desert
➢ "in the Spirit" to the mountain
➢ Conclusion to Letter

1:11 which said: "Write on a scroll what you see and send it to the seven churches: to Ephesus, Smyrna, Pergamum, Thyatira, Sardis, Philadelphia and Laodicea.

The whole of the Revelation is a letter, and here is the beginning of the Letter. It is written to seven churches which are in Asia, more specifically Asia-Minor, roughly equivalent to the area which includes modern day Turkey. It is written to these particular churches, because they were the ones that had been under John's jurisdiction and for which he had been responsible during his service in Ephesus. They are also representative. In them are found the characteristic strengths and weaknesses of all churches. They are living churches in a dying and decaying world, and the message our Lord gives to them is the same message that applies to the church of today and the church at the end of the age. Although His words had special reference to events familiar to that age and those churches, it is a message for the end of the age, and churches in existence when the final curtain of the world's drama falls. It is important to note that the entire message of the Revelation was written to and for the churches. And the reason for this is to prepare them for that which is to come. A concluding statement in chapter 22 confirms this, *"I Jesus, have sent My angel to testify to you these things for the churches (22:16).* Christ's coming will have a special impact on the churches, and individual members are challenged by our Lord to overcome and to persevere even to the point of death. That which they are to overcome is the beast (antichrist), the receiving of his mark, and the worshiping of his image—even if that refusal costs them their lives. They are said to overcome him *"by the blood of the Lamb and by the word of their testimony" (12:11)*. When the pressure of a hostile, unbelieving world becomes unbearable, Christ returns with power and great glory to deliver His people, calling them up to be with Him just before the awesome wrath of God is poured out on antichrist, the false prophet, and those who worship and follow them.

4. What John Saw

1:12 I turned around to see the voice that was speaking to me. And when I turned I saw seven golden lampstands,

He saw a candelabrum bearing seven lamps, like that in the tabernacle (Exodus 25:36). Solomon's temple had five lampstands on the right side and five on the left before the oracle (I Kings 7:49). Zechariah's vision again comes to mind.

> *"I see **a solid gold lampstand** with a bowl at the top and seven lights on it, with seven channels to the lights." (Zechariah 4:2).*

1:13 and among the lampstands was someone "like a son of man," dressed in a robe reaching down to his feet and with a golden sash around his chest.

> *"In my vision at night I looked, and there before me was **one like a son of man**, coming with the clouds of heaven" (Daniel 7:13).*

> *"I looked, and there before me was a white cloud, and seated on the cloud was one **"like a son of man"** with a crown of gold on his head and a sharp sickle in his hand" (Revelation 14:14).*

> *"Here is the man whose name is the Branch, and he will branch out from his place and build the temple of the Lord. It is he who*

*will build the temple of the Lord, and **he will be clothed with majesty** and will sit and rule on his throne. And he will be a priest on his throne" (Zechariah 6:12-13).*

The long flowing robe suggests the office of the high priest (Exodus 28:4; 29:5).

The phrase *"Son of Man"* means like a man or a human being. It is a favorite designation our Lord uses for himself in all of the Gospels. The phrase is also used for the prophet Ezekiel.

On the Lord's Day, John was worshiping, and suddenly he heard a trumpet like voice behind him. He must have almost jumped out of his skin when he heard it command him to write out what he would be given, and send it to the seven churches in Asia-Minor. When He turns he sees this glorious person standing in the midst of what appeared to be seven menorahs or lampstands, or one giant menorah with seven lampstands like branches. In the midst of them is "someone like the son of man," someone in human form dressed in a robe reaching down to his feet, a mark of honor and dignity. The sevenfold description that follows is impressionistic. John strains to describe in mere words the awesomeness of what he sees.

A Sevenfold Description of The Sovereign Christ

1. His Head

1:14 His head and hair were white like wool, as white as snow,

> *"As I looked, thrones were set in place, and the Ancient of Days took his seat. His clothing was as white as snow; **the hair of his head was white like wool**" (Daniel 7:9).*

It is not necessary to say that John borrowed his language from Daniel. John has his own glimpse of the Sovereign Lord, and describes it in similar language.

2. His Eyes—penetrating insight and his eyes were like blazing fire.

> "... his eyes were **flaming torches** ... " *(Daniel 10:6)*

3. His Feet—insufferably brilliant

1:15 His feet were like bronze glowing in a furnace,

> "His arms and legs like the gleam of **burnished bronze** ... " *(Daniel 10:6).*

4. His Voice—majestic, resistless and his voice was like the sound of rushing waters.

> "I saw the glory of the God of Israel coming from the east. **His voice was like the roar of rushing waters,** and the land was radiant with his glory" *(Ezekiel 43:2).*

> "His voice was **like the sound of a multitude**" *(Daniel 10:6).*

5. His Right Hand

1:16 In his right hand he held seven stars,

According to verse 20, these are seven angels.

6. His Mouth—powerful and reproving and out of his mouth came a sharp double-edged sword.

> "He will strike the earth with **the rod of his mouth;** with the breath of his lips he will slay the wicked. Righteousness will be his

*belt and faithfulness the sash around his waist" (Isaiah 11:4-5). "He made my mouth like **a sharpened sword . . . "** (Isaiah 49:2).*

*"For the word of God is living and active. Sharper than **any double-edged sword,** it penetrates even to dividing soul and spirit, joints and marrow; it judges the thoughts and attitudes of the heart" (Hebrews 4:12).*

7. His Face

His face was like the sun shining in all its brilliance.

*"His body was like chrysolite, **his face like lightning** . . . " (Daniel 10:6).*

John Is Comforted

1:17 When I saw him, I fell at his feet as though dead. Then he placed his right hand on me and said: "Do not be afraid. I am the First and the Last.

The effect on John was stunning and paralyzing. He fell as one dead at the feet of this Glorious One. Like Isaiah of old, John became aware of his own unworthiness and sinfulness and he was utterly overwhelmed with the splendor of this heavenly Person. Then comes one of the most tender passages in Scripture. *". . . and He placed His right hand on me . . . "* The right hand of His majesty is also the right hand of His mercy. How like the Lord to touch His dear friend, John! He did that so often during the days of His ministry on earth, the blind, the beggars, the babes, the broken. The Jesus of Galilee is the Christ of Glory. The hand that holds the seven stars is the same nail-pierced hand that was extended in love and invitation. The eyes of flaming fire are the eyes that wept over Jerusalem and at the tomb of Lazarus.

Daniel's experience left him terrified, exhausted and ill (Daniel 8:17, 27). Also listen to the impression God's glory made on the prophet Ezekiel,

> *"This was the appearance of the likeness of the glory of the Lord. When I saw it, I fell facedown, and I heard the voice of one speaking" (Ezekiel 1:28).*

1:18 I am the Living One; I was dead, and behold I am alive forever and ever! And I hold the keys of death and Hades."

> *"Then I praised the Most High; I honored and glorified **him who lives forever."** (Daniel 4:34).*

> *"For we know that since Christ was raised from the dead, **he cannot die again;** death no longer has mastery over him. The death that he died, he died to sin once for all; but the life he lives, he lives to God" (Romans 6:9-10).*

Again, note the Triadic Structure:

- ➤ I am the First
- ➤ I am the Last
- ➤ I am the Living One
- ➤ I was dead
- ➤ I am alive forever and ever
- ➤ I hold the keys

Jesus has the power to give life and also to take it away!

John Is Commissioned

1:19 "Write, therefore, what you have seen, what is now and what will take place later.

Note the triadic structure:

- ➤ What you have seen (past)
- ➤ What is now (present)
- ➤ What will take place later (future)

This threefold statement is simple, but could afford us an outline to the book:

> ➢ "What you have seen"—the inaugural vision in chapter 1,
> ➢ "What is now"—the message to the churches, and
> ➢ "What will take place later"—everything from chapter 4 on.

John Is Clarified

1:20 The mystery of the seven stars that you saw in my right hand and of the seven golden lampstands is this: The seven stars are the angels of the seven churches, and the seven lampstands are the seven churches.

So . . . 7 stars=7 angels of the 7 churches; 7 lampstands=7 churches

For consistency in interpretation, the "angels" here are very likely angels, and not earthly messengers or ministers of the churches as some suggest. The angelic administrators appear frequently throughout the book.

CHAPTER 2

THE SEVENFOLD MESSAGE TO THE SEVEN CHURCHES

John was commanded, *Write on a scroll what you see and send it to the seven churches: to Ephesus, Smyrna, Pergamum, Thyatira, Sardis, Philadelphia and Laodicea." (1:11). Also, "Write what you have seen, what is now and what will take place later." (1:19).* This last verse indicates three divisions of the subject matter. While our discussion will deal mainly with chapters two and three, it is interesting to note that in the last division—*"what must take place after this"*—the phrase is repeated in the first verse of chapter four, indicating that here "the things which must take place after this", begin in chapter four. The question at once arises, What do the candlesticks (lit., lampstands) represent? In answer to this question, observe:

1. They represent seven churches in actual existence. There were other churches in Asia, but these seven were chosen for a particular purpose. But bear in mind that these seven churches were in actual existence at the time the Apocalypse was written.

2. They represent seven different types of churches which exist through the present dispensation. There always has been, and still is, the Ephesus type of churches—the church which could be commended for its labor and patience, but has lost its first love. The Smyrna church was a persecuted church, which has been the case through the years in various parts of the world. And so with the other churches which are found to exist through the present church age.

3. They represent seven types of individuals in the church. In an average congregation can be found members who have lost their

first love as was true with the church of Ephesus. And on through the succeeding churches there are individual members who display the characteristics of the various churches. In chapter 3 and verse 20 we read, *"I stand at the door and knock. If anyone hears my voice and opens the door, I will come in and eat with him, and he with me."* This is very individualistic and personal.

4. There are to be discerned certain characteristics in these letters that correspond with various periods of church history. It should be borne in mind that these are not very precise, but some have tried to make the case that these churches are prophetic of various periods in the history of the church.

5. The number seven indicates completeness. There were other churches in Asia, but God selected these seven apparently to cover the whole period of church history.

The progress of evil in the succeeding churches indicates that these particular churches were selected to depict the history of the church so long as the development of evil in the church is possible. What was hated by the church of Ephesus (2 :6) is held by the church of Pergamos. And we note that what Ephesus and Smyrna judged evil Pergamos endured, Thyatira adopted it, and Sardis was dead in the presence of it. Laodicea is pictured as a church were Christ stands on the outside (3 :20).

6. The continuous character of the promises given. The continuous character of the promises given warrants an expectation far beyond that limited to the then existent seven churches of Asia.

We are distinctly told that the Apocalypse is a book of prophecy (1:3; 22:7, 10, 18-19). If the Apocalypse is a book of prophecy, then why are chapters 2-3 not prophetic? Being in a book of prophecy, it is only reasonable to suppose that Chapters 2-3 are prophetic, and therefore give us a prophetic view of the church.

In 1:19 John was commanded to *"write the things which thou hast seen, and the things which are, and the things which shall be hereafter"* (literally, after these things). Here we have indicated three divisions of the Apocalypse. In 1:11, "the seven churches which are," shows that these churches cover the period indicated by the things "which are," and therefore cover the whole church age.

Revelation 1:19 gives three divisions of the Apocalypse. In 4:1 John is shown the things which must be hereafter. Since 4:1 marks the beginning of the period described as "after these things," it is only reasonable to conclude that chapters 2-3 cover the period between the things which John had seen, recorded in chapter 1, and the things which shall "be after these things," and therefore cover the present church age.

It might be objected that if we have the entire history of the church set forth, or covered, in chapters 2-3, what about the imminency of Christ's return? It is definitely stated in the Apocalypse that the things revealed "must shortly come to pass" (1:1); "for the time is at hand" (1:3); behold, I come quickly" (3:11); and, "surely I come quickly" (22:20). It is not uncommon for the Scripture to place side by side events widely separated in time, or to speak of events which were at the time of writing far distant in the future as near at hand. It might be understood from I Peter 1:11 that the Old Testament prophets did not see the period between Christ's coming in humiliation and His coming in glory. A like interval of time is intimated in Acts 15:16. Isaiah 61:1-2 gives the two advents of Christ in one view. Ezekiel 26:12 reads as though the things there related were accomplished in a short time. Yet, we know from history there were 250 years between the destruction of the pleasant houses and the laying of the stones, and timbers, and dust in the midst of the waters.

It should be observed that the first section of the Apocalypse (chapter 1) does contain things which shortly came to pass, and their time was at hand. The history of the churches of chapters 2-3 began to be fulfilled in John's own day. We have an expression in Luke 18:8, where long delay is implied. The expressions in the Apocalypse are in harmony with the general teaching of the Scripture that the Lord would soon return, and rightly so, for the return of the Lord—regardless of how distant from the time the Apocalypse was written—was, and is, the next major prophetic event.

While our Lord did teach the expectancy of His return, He also gave a few hints that there might be some time before that event. After relating some of the events which are to occur during the present age, Jesus stated, *"But **the end is not yet"** (Matt. 24 :6), "But the end shall not be yet" (Mark 13:7), "But the end is not by and by" (Luke 21:9)*. Christ *"added and spoke a parable, because he was nigh to Jerusalem, and because they thought that the kingdom of God **should immediately appear"** (Luke 19:11)*. If Pentecost was to be the coming of the kingdom, this parable is without point, and indicates that the kingdom was not near. *"For the kingdom of heaven is as* *a man traveling into a far country . . . . **After a long time** the lord of those servants cometh" (Matt. 25:14-19).* "After a long time" embraces the whole period intervening between the first and second coming of Christ.

It has been said of Jesus that, whenever he met any one, it was as though that person were an island around which Jesus sailed until he saw where the real problem was—and then he landed. He did that with the rich young ruler and landed on the money question. He did that with the woman of Samaria and landed on the family question. He did that with Zacchaeus and landed on the problem of honesty. There was a personal penetration in Jesus' dealings, a clairvoyant realism in getting at what was really the matter with the individuals he touched, which made him terrible to any one who did not wish to be brought face to face with himself.

If Jesus came to our church and did what He did when he addressed the churches of Asia-Minor, one thing would immediately begin to happen. Were Jesus dealing with us here today, for example, we would cease being a crowd and would become individuals. He would so look at us as individuals that we could not forebear so looking at ourselves. We might resent and resist it—we probably would—but unless we ran away from him we could not escape him. Again and again he would sail around our lives until he saw where the real problem was and then he would land.

Jesus called people to repentance. *"Repent; for the kingdom of heaven is at hand."* Look to yourself. Repent—change your mind—clean up your own life. This indicates that the first responsibility of every man is himself. There is no sin whose central responsibility is not inside individuals. Thus these messages to the churches find us where we live, and call us to conviction.

The message to the churches seems to have a near and far application. His message to each church is also His message to all the churches. *"Let him hear what the Spirit says to the churches."* This certainly would apply to the churches then, but also to the church universal.

Many have recognized that each message has seven parts. I would suggest the following elements:

> ➢ Church
> ➢ Character of Christ
> ➢ Commendation

➤ Condemnation
➤ Counsel, Caution, Coming
➤ Command to Hear
➤ Challenge to the Overcomer

1
The Church in Ephesus

1. Church

2:1 To the angel of the church in Ephesus write:

The ancient city of Ephesus was in the western part of Asia Minor, also called Anatolia, which today forms part of the Republic of Turkey. It is located near the historical town of Selcuk (Seljuk). The ruins are not far from the port city of modern Kusadasi, a resort town on the shores of the Aegean. Ancient Ephesus used to be a seaport town, but silt filled the bay carried there by the waters of the Menderes river. The temple of Artemis in Ephesus was known as one of the seven wonders of the ancient world. Paul ministered in this city for a number of years, and also wrote a letter to the congregation here (probably an encyclical letter). John lived and ministered here, and probably had some jurisdiction or oversight of the seven churches to which he is commanded to write. Tradition says that Mary, the mother of Jesus, lived here with John, and the site of the Church of St. Mary can be visited today.

2. Character of Christ

2:1 These are the words of him who holds the seven stars in his right hand and walks among the seven golden candlesticks:

Through his angelic mediators, the Living Christ oversees each church, but is also immediately present in their midst. He "walks" among the churches, and is knowledgeable as to their doings, and the spirit that motivates their actions.

3. Commendation

2:2 I know your deeds, your hard work and your perseverance. I know that you cannot tolerate wicked men, that you have tested those who claim to be apostles but are not, and have found them false.

He is ever mindful of what they are going through. "I know" is the repeated expression of his abiding interest in their affairs.

"We continually remember your work produced by faith, your labor prompted by love, and your endurance inspired by hope in our Lord Jesus Christ" (I Thessalonians 1:3). The reference in I Thessalonians includes the little triad of faith, love, and hope that this passage addressed to the Ephesian church here omits. Later Jesus is to tell them that they were doing what they were doing without the dynamic of love. They were sort of going through the motions. They were working, even working hard, yes, even persevering in their labors, but that which makes even the hardest task lighter was missing, faith, hope, and love. Faith activates, hope anticipates, and love motivates.

They had also learned to spot phonies. Lying, or pretending you are something you are not is a sin that is mentioned frequently in Revelation.

2:3 You have persevered and have endured hardships for my name, and have not grown weary.

"All men will hate you because of me, but he who stands firm to the end will be saved" (Matthew 10:22). An unflagging, patient endurance, motivated by love for Christ, is the only thing that will enable us to keep going when we feel like giving up and giving in.

4. Condemnation

2:4 Yet I hold this against you: You have forsaken your first love.

First love is the love of fidelity, the love of simplicity, and the love of purity. Earlier, Jesus warns that in the last days the love of most will grow cold. *"Because of the increase of wickedness, the love of most will grow cold, but he who stands firm to the end will be saved" (Matthew 24:12-13).*

> *"I remember the devotion of your youth, how as a bride you loved me . . . " (Jeremiah 2:1).*

Loss of first love may not only mean a failure to love the Lord, but also a failure to continue helping and serving one another in love as at first.

5. Counsel, Caution, Coming

2:5 Remember the heights from which you have fallen! Repent and do the things you did at first.

> ➤ **Remember**. Remember how you loved Christ as a young believer when you were the happiest person in the world, and before you met too many others who disappointed you.
> ➤ **Repent**. Turn, confess, go back and ask God to fill your heart with His love through the Spirit.
> ➤ **Repeat**. Do again the first works as you used to do them as a labor of love, and not out of sense of duty.

2:5 If you do not repent, I will come to you and remove your lampstand from its place.

The 3 R's above, if not observed, can lead to this fourth "R" at our Lord's coming.

> ➤ **Remove**. It is revival or removal. There can be no light without Love.

2:6 But you have this in your favor: You hate the practices of the Nicolaitans, which I also hate.

The Nicolaitans were a heretical sect that evidently believed and taught that spiritual liberty gave them the right to practice idolatry and immorality. Liberty often leads to license.

6. Command to Hear

2:7 He who has an ear, let him hear what the Spirit says to the churches.

"Ears to hear and eyes that see—the Lord has made them both" (Proverbs *20:12).* This ancient proverb is not so much a commentary on God's *creativity* as it is on man's *responsibility.* The Scriptures say over and over again that man has a severe visual and auditory problem. He hears, but he doesn't hear with understanding. He sees, but he doesn't see with discernment. He lacks insight. Our Lord said the same thing to his disciples in Matthew 13 in relationship to hearing the Word. *"He who has ears, let him hear"* (13:9). As someone has said, "We must do more than hold the truth; the truth must hold us."

7. Challenge to Overcomers

To him who overcomes, I will give the right to eat from the tree of life, which is in the paradise of God.

Here John identifies Paradise with the New Jerusalem, the restoration of the pre-fall conditions of fellowship between God and man. This promise applies to any repentant sinner, even a dying thief! *"Jesus answered him (the thief), 'I tell you the truth, today you will be with me in paradise'"* (Luke 23:43).

> *"On each side of the river stood the tree of life, bearing twelve crops of fruit, yielding its fruit very month"* (Revelation 22:2)

> *"Blessed are those who wash their robes, that they may have the right to the tree of life and may go through the gates into the city"* (Revelation 22:14).

The one who overcomes loves the Lord more than His own life, and will offer that life up if necessary to show his love and loyalty. *"They did not love their lives so much as to shrink from death"* (Revelation 12:11). Because of this, the Lord promises not just life, but life abundant and life eternal that far surpasses any earthly pain or privation. The apostle put it all in perspective when he wrote, *"For our light and momentary troubles are achieving for us an eternal glory that far outweighs them all" (2 Corinthians 4:17).* It is always a good thing for us who seek to live out our Christian faith here below to keep the present balanced by the future, to see the temporal in the light of the eternal, to know that the unbearable "now" is made bearable by the indescribable "then.

2
The Church in Smyrna

1. Church

2:8 To the angel of the church in Smyrna write:

Smyrna was an important port city about 35 miles northwest of Ephesus (modern Ismir). This city was wealthy, sophisticated, beautiful, and politically astute. She had always managed to align herself with all the correct political parties in Rome. Smyrna was one of the first cities in the region to build a temple to the emperor. It was a source of civic pride, but a disaster for believers. The imperial cult was not against the worship of other gods—old or new. So long as it was not reflected on the political stage, pagans did not mind whatever Christians believed or practiced. Actually, all anyone had to do was burn a pinch of incense to Caesar, declaring him Lord, and all would be well. Christians could not do this, of course, and it brought them a world of hurt. A number of years later, Polycarp, one of the early Church fathers, was put to death in Smyrna. When arrested, the efforts of the proconsul to persuade him to take an oath to the emperor and curse Christ were useless. Polycarp is reported to have answered, "For eighty and six years I have been His servant and He has never done me wrong. How can I blaspheme my king, who has saved me." He was sentenced to death by burning. At his own request he was not lashed to a stake but his hands were tied behind his back. He met death with a look of joy on his face. As the flames licked at his body, he prayed his great prayer of committal: "I thank Thee that Thou has graciously thought me worthy of this day and this hour, that I may receive a portion in the number of the martyrs, in the cup of Thy Christ." That was the kind of stuff the believers were made of in Smyrna.

2. Character of Christ.

2:8 These are the words of him who is the First and the Last, who died and came to life again.

Christ, the Eternal One, came out of eternity into time, and laid down His life for us. But He is alive forevermore! He, more than any other, can know the depth of our suffering, and show us the way to overcoming victory. He is our eternal immovable, unchanging rock. Most men live and die; Christ died and lived! If we must experience death, even violent death, he experienced death and conquered it.

3. Commendation

2:9 I know your afflictions and your poverty—yet you are rich! I know the slander of those who say they are Jews and are not, but are a synagogue of Satan.

Again His intimate knowledge of them is shown.

> ➤ I know your tribulation (the word could be translated *pressure*, like a heavy boulder crushing the very life out of you). Sometimes the difficulties we face are relentless, bearing down on us, never going away. This is not so much inward pressure, but outward. It comes from those bent on doing us bodily harm, inflicting pain.
> ➤ I know your poverty. Their poverty is severe. These believers not only had very little; they were destitute. They possessed nothing having suffered "the loss of all things."
> ➤ I know how ridiculed and reviled you are.

Pressure, poverty, persecution, maybe even prison—such was the lot of these saints in Smyrna. But the Lord knew and understood.

Their slanderers seem to be Jewish, active in the local synagogue, but threatened by the open faith of the Christians here. They seemed to be Satanically motivated to slander Christ's followers. Paul tells us about the true Jew.

> *"A man is not a Jew if he is only one **outwardly**, nor is circumcision merely outward and physical. No, a man is a Jew if he is one **inwardly**; and circumcision is circumcision of the heart, by the Spirit, not by the written code. Such a man's praise is not from men, but from God" (Romans 2:28-29). "For not all who are descended from Israel are Israel . . . it is **the children of the promise** who are regarded as Abraham's offspring" (Romans 9:6, 8).*

Jesus addressed the religious leaders who claimed to be children of Abraham and children of God, and said, *"If your were Abraham's children, then you would do the things Abraham did . . . If God were your Father, you would love me, for I came from God. (John 8:39, 42).* How sad that God's elect people failed to receive Him when He came.

Yet in spite of their severe poverty, the Lord called them rich. A young Frenchman in a German concentration camp during the Second World War wrote, "It is only when everything but God is gone that one learns that God alone is enough." The psalmist said it first, *"Whom have I in heaven but you? And earth has nothing I desire besides you"* (73:25).

Listen to how the apostle James puts it, *"God has chosen those who are poor in the eyes of the world to be rich in faith and to inherit the kingdom promised those who love Him"* (James 2:5).

4. Condemnation (None)

5. Counsel, Caution, Coming

2:10 Do not be afraid of what you are about to suffer. I tell you, the devil will put some of you in prison to test you, and you will suffer persecution for ten days. Be faithful even to the point of death, and I will give you the crown of life.

> *"Blessed is the man who perseveres under trial, because when he has stood the test, **he will receive the crown of life** that God has promised to those who love him" (James 1:12).*

> *"Please test your servants **for ten days** . . . So he agreed to this and tested them for ten days" (Daniel 1:12).*

6. Command to Hear

2:11 He who has an ear, let him hear what the Spirit says to the churches.

Please notice that the Spirit's message comes to each (let him), but it is also for all (the churches).

7. Challenge to Overcomer

He who overcomes will not be hurt at all by the second death.

> *"Blessed and holy are those who have part in the first resurrection. **The second death** has no power over them, but they will be priests of God and of Christ and will reign with him for a thousand years"* *(Revelation 20:6)*

Question: Reign with Him from where? Other references seem to point to the New Jerusalem. Since the city and its people (the Church—the Lamb's Bride) are synonymous, this would be true. We have already been told that they will reign *"on the earth."*

> *"Then death and Hades were thrown into the lake of fire. The lake of fire is **the second death**. If anyone's name was not found written in the book of life, he was thrown into the lake of fire"* *(Revelation 20:14-15).*

3
The Church in Pergamum

1. Church

2:12 To the angel of the church in Pergamum write:

At the time of John's writing, Pergamum was one of the largest cities in the region. Its wealth, number of temples and their beauty were eclipsed only by those of Ephesus. Along with Ephesus and Smyrna, it was one of the earliest cities where the Roman imperial cult was established. The Asclepion of Pergamum was the most important medical center of the Roman Empire. Asclepius was the healer-god, and the center attracted patients from distant corners of the world.

2. Character of Christ

These are the words of him who has the sharp, double-edged sword.

The author of Hebrews writes,

> *"The word of God is living and active. Sharper than any **double-edged sword**, it penetrates even to dividing soul and spirit, joints and marrow; it judges the thoughts and attitudes of the heart. Nothing in all creation is hidden from God's sight. Everything is uncovered and laid bare before the eyes of him to whom we must give account."*

This certainly is the best commentary on what these words mean here. He knows all. Nothing is hidden. All will be held accountable to Him.

3. Commendation

2:13 I know where you live—where Satan has his throne. Yet you remain true to my name. You did not renounce your faith in me, even in the days of Antipas, my faithful witness, who was put to death in your city—where Satan lives.

"I know where you live . . ." To the Ephesians He said, *"I know what you do."* To the believers in Smyrna he wrote, *"I know what you endure."* Now he says, *"I know where you live."* These Pergamene Christians lived in this city, and it was oppressive (where Satan has his throne). They weren't able to pack up and move elsewhere where it was easier to be a Christian. No, they had to keep living there where they felt exposed to continuous pressure, which should remind us that many live in situations that are far

from easy, in homes where it is difficult to stand up for Christ without ridicule, or in places of work where God is constantly blasphemed. When Jesus had restored the madman of Gerasa to sanity, the man wanted to follow Jesus, but Jesus didn't allow it. He said, *"Go home to your friends, and tell them how great things the Lord has done for you."* Going home, and living for the Lord there can be one of the hardest things some are called on to do, among family, friends, and neighbors.

The conflict was not between good and evil, but between truth and error. And they were standing true, holding fast to His name and holding on to the truth. One way we can show our love for Christ is by our loyalty to Him in enduring suffering if need be. Another is by standing firm, not renouncing our faith, holding to the truth, no matter what. Love and truth are always held together in perfect balance by Scripture. Someone has well said, "Love becomes sentimental if it is not strengthened by truth, and truth becomes hard if it is not softened by love.

We do not know who this man Antipas was, but the fact that he is specifically mentioned points to the fact that extreme persecution issuing in martyrdom was not yet that common in Asia-Minor. Tradition says that he was one of the spiritual leaders of the Pergamene congregation, and was martyred by being roasted alive in a brazen bull.

4. Condemnation

2:14 Nevertheless, I have a few things against you: You have people there who hold to the teaching of Balaam, who taught Balak to entice the Israelites to sin by eating food sacrificed to idols and by committing sexual immorality.

> *"They have left the straight way and wandered off to follow the way of Balaam son of Beor, who loved the wages of wickedness. But he was rebuked for his wrongdoing by a donkey—a beast without speech—who spoke with a man's voice and restrained the prophet's madness"* (2 Peter 2:15-16).

Because of the money Balak offered him, Balaam sought to curse Israel, but God would not allow it. Balaam accomplished his purpose eventually by enticing Israel's men to commit immorality with the daughters of Moab, thus bringing the wrath of God upon them.

2:15 Likewise you also have those who hold to the teaching of the Nicolaitans.

Many believe that the Nicolaitans in the church were the New Testament counterpart of the Old Testament Balaamites, i.e. referring to the same teachers. The Nicolaitans, as noted above, were suggesting that the liberty with which Christ had set them free was liberty to sin. There is a subtlety to modern programming on TV. We used to be shocked with the things we now take for granted. We watch while those on the screen scoff at the things of God, debunk faithfulness in marriage, advocate free sexual expression under the cloak of love, and promote divorce for any and all reasons. Satan is alive and well today in every non-Christian religion and philosophy, and in every attempt to divert to others the honor that is due only to Christ. This is the spirit of antichrist. This is the work of the Evil One.

5. Counsel, Caution, Coming

2:16 Repent therefore! Otherwise, I will soon come to you and will fight against them with the sword of my mouth.

Again we see a reference to Christ's coming. If they will not engage the enemy, then He will. The kingdom of Satan retreats only as the kingdom of God advances.

6. Command to Hear

2:17 He who has an ear, let him hear what the Spirit says to the churches.

7. Challenge to Overcomer

To him who overcomes, I will give some of the hidden manna. I will also give him a white stone with a new name written on it, known only to him who receives it.

*"The nations will see your righteousness, and all kings your glory; you will be called by **a new name** that the mouth of the Lord will bestow" (Isaiah 62:2). ". . . to them I will give within my temple and its walls a memorial and a name better than sons and daughters; I will give them **an everlasting name** that will not be cut off" (Isaiah 56:5).*

4
The Church in Thyatira

1. Church

2:18 To the angel of the church in Thyatira write:

Little is known about this city, but this letter is one of the longest of the seven, and has proven difficult to interpret. It was situated on the south bank of the Lycus in the long valley which connected the Caicus and Hermus valleys. Seleucus I founded it as a military outpost to guard one of the approaches to his empire. The city was known for its pagan trade-guilds and the church here felt their strong pressure. In Acts 16:14, a woman named Lydia is said to be from this city, a seller of purple goods. who owned a home in Philippi.

2. Character of Christ

These are the words of the Son of God, whose eyes are like blazing fire and whose feet are like burnished bronze.

The description here is taken from the initial vision of chapter 1 (1:14-15). Christ's eyes are seen as penetrating—all perceiving. His feet or legs looked like burnished brass, and convey the impression of splendor and strength.

3. Commendation

2:19 I know your deeds, your love and faith, your service and perseverance, and that you are now doing more than you did at first.

He knows that their ministry and patience spring from the motive power of love and faith, and they were continually increasing.

4. Condemnation

2:20 Nevertheless, I have this against you: You tolerate that woman Jezebel, who calls herself a prophetess. By her teaching she misleads my servants into sexual immorality and the eating of food sacrificed to idols.

"That Jezebel of a woman" The name of the Old Testament queen of Ahab was given to someone in this church to show her odious practice of misleading God's servants to sin much as the Jezebel of old. led the people to the worship of Baal. The worship of Baal was marked by idolatry and cultic prostitution. (I Kings 16:31).

5. Counsel, Caution, Coming

2:21 I have given her time to repent of her immorality, but she is unwilling.

2:22 So I will cast her on a bed of suffering, and I will make those who commit adultery with her suffer intensely, unless they repent of her ways.

2:23 I will strike her children dead. Then all the churches will know that I am he who searches the hearts and minds, and I will repay each of you according to your deeds.

The opportunity for repentance suggests that this woman is a member of the church. She attempts to influence the other members in the church to be tolerant of, or even participate in, the pagan practices associated with the trade guilds. The punishment was about to be meted out by her being cast into a bed, probably a bed of sickness and pain. Those who follow her pernicious doctrine will be stricken dead.

"All the churches will know." This indicates that all the letters were intended for all the churches not just for the one addressed.

> *"I the Lord search the heart and examine the mind, to reward a man according to his conduct, according to what his deeds deserve"* *(Jeremiah 17:10).*

2:24 Now I say to the rest of you in Thyatira, to you who do not hold to her teaching and have not learned Satan's so-called deep secrets (I will not impose any other burden on you):

The antinomian (against law) libertine doctrine taught that the only way to defeat Satan is to enter his stronghold, i.e., experience the evil you are trying to overcome.

2:25 Only hold on to what you have until I come.

6. Challenge to Overcomer

2:26 To him who overcomes and does my will to the end, I will give authority over the nations.

2:27 He will rule them with an iron scepter; he will dash them to pieces like pottery just as I have received authority from my Father.

> *You are my son, today I have begotten you"* *(Psalm 2:7).*

> *"You will rule them with an iron scepter; you will dash them to pieces like pottery"* *(Psalm 2:9). "He will rule them with an iron scepter"* *(Revelation 19:15).*

> *"It will break in pieces like pottery, shattered so mercilessly that among its pieces not a fragment will be found for taking coals from a hearth or scooping water out of a cistern"* *(Isaiah 30:14).*

2:28 I will also give him the morning star.

> *"I, Jesus, have sent my angel to give you this testimony for the churches. I am the Root and the Offspring of David, and **the bright Morning Star**" (Revelation 22:16)*

7. Command to Hear

2:29 He who has an ear, let him hear what the Spirit says to the churches.

CHAPTER 3

THE SEVENFOLD MESSAGE TO THE SEVEN CHURCHES PART 2

5
The Church in Sardis

1. Church

3:1 To the angel of the church in Sardis write:

Sardis was situated almost directly south of Thyatira, in the direction of Smyrna and the sea. It was once the proud capital of the ancient kingdom of Lydia. It was also an important center of the woolen industry.

2. Character of Christ

3:1 These are the words of him who holds the seven spirits of God and the seven stars.

3. Commendation (see verse 4)

4. Condemnation

3:1 I know your deeds; you have a reputation of being alive, but you are dead.

3:2 Wake up! Strengthen what remains and is about to die, for I have not found your deeds complete in the sight of my God.

5. Counsel, Caution, Coming

3:3 Remember, therefore, what you have received and heard; obey it, and repent. But if you do not wake up, I will come like a thief, and you will not know at what time I will come to you.

Their readiness depended on their wakefulness. *"Come like a thief"* is used frequently to describe the coming of the Lord or the Day of the Lord.

3:4 Yet you have a few people in Sardis who have not soiled their clothes. They will walk with me, dressed in white, for they are worthy.

"Hating even the clothing stained by corrupted flesh" (Jude 23).

6. Challenge To Overcomer

3:5 He who overcomes will, like them, be dressed in white. I will never blot out his name from the book of life, but will acknowledge his name before my Father and his angels.

"May they be blotted out of the book of life and not be listed with the righteous" (Psalm 69:28).

"But now, please forgive their sin—but if not, then blot me out of the book you have written" (Exodus 32:32).

"However do not rejoice that the spirits submit to you, but rejoice that your names are written in heaven" (Luke 10:20).
". . . the church of the firstborn, whose names are written in heaven" (Hebrews 12:23).

"Whoever acknowledges me before men, I will also acknowledge him before my Father in heaven. But whoever disowns me before men, I will disown him before my Father in heaven" (Matthew 10:32-33).

7. Command To Hear

3:6 He who has an ear, let him hear what the Spirit says to the churches.

6
The Church in Philadelphia

1. Church

3:7 To the angel of the church in Philadelphia write:

Ancient Philadelphia is modern Alashehir. One small square in the heart of the city marks the ancient site of Philadelphia. Ironically, through the gates of the ruins of St. John's church can be seen an Islamic mosque. In ancient times it was an important commercial city conveniently located as the gateway to the high central plateau of the province. Philadelphia means "brotherly love" and commemorates the loyalty and devotion of Attalus II to his brother Eumenes II.

2. Character Of Christ

3:7 These are the words of him who is holy and true, who holds the key of David. What he opens no one can shut, and what he shuts no one can open.

This was said of Eliakim son of Hilkiah. *"I will place on his shoulder the key to the house of David; what he opens no one can shut, and what he shuts no one can open" (Isaiah 22:22).* The key is the key of authority to minister in the name of or place of the king.

3. Commendation

3:8 I know your deeds. See, I have placed before you an open door that no one can shut. I know that you have little strength, yet you have kept my word and have not denied my name.

> *"For I gave them the words you gave me and they accepted them"* *(John 17:8).*

The open door here may be the open door of opportunity presented to these believers to carry the gospel to the eastern provinces. Attalus II had founded Philadelphia for this very purpose, to carry Hellenistic culture to the "barbarians" of the east.

4. Condemnation

3:9 I will make those who are of the synagogue of Satan, who claim to be Jews though they are not, but are liars—I will make them come and fall down at your feet and acknowledge that I have loved you.

> *"Since you are precious and honored in my sight, and because I love you . . . " (Isaiah 43:4).*

> *"They will bow down before you with their faces to the ground; they will lick the dust at your feet. Then you will know that I am the Lord; those who hope in me will not be disappointed" (Isaiah. 49:23)*

It is probable that Christians had been barred from the Jewish synagogue, and that the Lord was saying to them that He personally would open the door for them, and compel their detractors to recognize His love for them. These false Jews may have been Judaizing Gentiles as Ignatius later suggests (Ignatius, *To the Philadelphians*).

> *". . . protect them by the power of your name—the name you gave me—so that they may be one as we are one . . . While I was with them, I protected them and kept them safe by that name you gave me . . . My prayer is not that you take them out of the world but*

that you protect them from the evil one. May they be brought to complete unity to let the world know that you sent me and have loved them even as you have loved me" (John 17:11-12, 15, 23)

5. Counsel, Caution, Coming

3:10 Since you have kept my command to endure patiently, I will also keep you from the hour of trial that is going to come upon the whole world to test those who live on the earth.

Revelation 3:10 is considered by pre-tribulationists to be a watershed verse that proves that the church will be removed from the earth before the time of tribulation comes on the world.

However, there is very little agreement among Greek scholars as to how to best translate the phrase *"I also will keep you from the hour of temptation."* Each scholar seems to use the phrase to support their particular bias.

John 17:15 is the only precise grammatico-lexical parallel to Rev. 3:10. In our Lord's prayer there is no idea of removal bodily from the evil world but of preservation from the power of evil even when they are in its very presence. *"My prayer is not that you take them out of the world but that you protect them from the evil one."*

This suggests that Rev. 3:10 may not necessarily mean "take out of the world" by rapture, but that it might simply mean preservation and deliverance in and through the time of trial.

It must also be proven that "**the hour** of tribulation" applies to the entire 70th week of Daniel or 7 years. It may well refer to the "hour" of the Lord's outpoured wrath on the earth in the Day of the Lord, and in the bowl judgments. Jesus refers to his coming as that "day" or "hour." Revelation speaks of the Day of the Lord as being "one day or hour" (18:8, 9; 18:19).

Also, the latter phrase of Revelaltion 3:10 cannot be separated from that which precedes it where John says, *"Since you have kept my command to endure patiently . . . "* There is a definite cause and effect relationship here. The word "patience" consistently conveys the idea of *endurance in the midst of adversity*. It means to persevere, stand firm against all that might come. Luke 21:16-19 conveys the same thought, *"You will be betrayed even by parents, brothers, relatives and friends, and they will put some of you to death. All men will hate you because of me. But not a hair of your head will perish.* **By standing firm** *you will gain life."* (See other instances in I Thess. 1:3, 6; 2 Thess. 1:4; Rev. 13:10; Heb. 6:13; 11:13; Rev. 14:9-12)

So "patience" conveys the idea of endurance in the midst of affliction. It describes a time of tribulation at the end of the age in which patient endurance is called for. And such faithfulness and loyalty will be rewarded, *"I also will keep you from the hour of trial that is coming on* **the whole world.***"* Paul writes in I Thessalonians 5:9, *"For God did not appoint us to suffer wrath but to receive salvation though our Lord Jesus Christ."* And that describes the Wrath of God at the Day of the Lord from which the church shall surely be spared at the coming of Christ and just before or as the bowls are poured out on an unbelieving world and the throne of Antichrist. The Great Tribulation is not specifically an outpouring of God's wrath, but of Satan's wrath and that of his man of lawlessness, the Antichrist. The purpose of the Trumpet judgments seems to be partial and thus remedial. God offers one more chance for a rebellious and unbelieving world to repent before His wrath is poured out.

3:11 I am coming soon. Hold on to what you have, so that no one will take your crown.

6. Challenge To Overcomer

3:12 Him who overcomes I will make a pillar in the temple of my God. Never again will he leave it. I will write on him the name of my God and the name of the city of my God, the new Jerusalem, which is coming down out of heaven from my God; and I will write on him my new name.

"And I will dwell in the house of the Lord forever" (Psalm 23:6).

Note the triadic structure:

➢ the name of my God
➢ the name of the city of my God (the Church Triumphant)
➢ my new name

". . . to them I will give within my temple and its walls a memorial and a name better than sons and daughters; I will give them an

everlasting name that will not be cut off" (Isaiah 56:5). Names reveal character. Christ's new name symbolizes His redemptive work—celebrated also by the "new song." Ezekiel refers to "the new Jerusalem" in this way: *"and the name of the city from that time on will be: The Lord is there" (Ezekiel 48:35)*.

7. Command To Hear

3:13 He who has an ear, let him hear what the Spirit says to the churches.

7
The Church Of Laodicea

1. Church

3:14 To the angel of the church of Laodicea write:

2. Character of Christ

3:14 These are the words of the Amen, the faithful and true witness, the ruler of God's creation.

> *". . . the God of Amen (truth)" (Isaiah 65:16)*.

3. Commendation (none)

4. Condemnation

3:15 I know your deeds, that you are neither cold nor hot. I wish you were either one or the other.

3:16 So, because you are lukewarm—neither cold nor hot—I am about to spit you out of my mouth.

3:17 You say, 'I am rich; I have acquired wealth and do not need a thing.' But you do not realize that you are wretched, pitiful, poor, blind and naked.

> *Ephraim boasts, "I am very rich; I have become wealthy . . . "*
> *(Hosea 12:8).*

5. Counsel, Caution, Coming

3:18 I counsel you to buy from me gold refined in the fire, so you can become rich; and white clothes to wear, so you can cover your nakedness; and salve to put on your eyes, so you can see.

3:19 Those whom I love I rebuke and discipline. So be earnest, and repent.

> *"My son, do not despise the Lord's discipline and do not resent his*
> *rebuke, because the Lord disciplines those he loves, as a father the*
> *son he delights in" (Proverbs 3:11, 12).*

3:20 Here I am! I stand at the door and knock. If anyone hears my voice and opens the door, I will come in and eat with him, and he with me.

In relation to the references about Christ's coming, a progression can be seen:

- ➢ I will come to you and remove your lampstand
- ➢ Hold to what you have until come
- ➢ Wake up. I will come like a thief, and you will not know at what time I will come to you
- ➢ I am coming soon. Hold on to what you have.
- ➢ Here I am!!

6. Challenge To Overcomer

3:21 To him who overcomes, I will give the right to sit with me on my throne, just as I overcame and sat down with my Father on his throne.

> *"When the Son of Man comes in his glory, and all the angels with him, he will sit on his throne in heavenly glory. All the nations will be gathered before him, and he will separate the people one from another as a shepherd separates the sheep from the goats"* (Matthew 25:31-32).

> *"Do you not know that the saints will judge the world? Do you not know that we will judge angels"* (I Corinthians 6:2, 3).

> *"I saw thrones on which were seated those who had been given authority to judge. And I saw the souls of those who had been beheaded because of their testimony for Jesus and because of the word of God. They had not worshiped the beast or his image and had not received his mark on their foreheads or their hands. They came to life and reigned with Christ a thousand years. This is the first resurrection."* (Revelation 20:4-6). 7.

7. Command To Hear

3:22 He who has an ear, let him hear what the Spirit says to the churches.

CHAPTER 4

THE THRONE OF GOD
CENTER OF THE UNIVERSE

4:1 After this I looked, and there before me was a door standing open in heaven. And the voice I had first heard speaking to me like a trumpet said, "Come up here, and I will show you what must take place after this."

"The heavens were opened and I saw visions of God" (Ezekiel 1:1).

In chapter 1 we saw the sevenfold description of the Living Sovereign Lord of Glory, and in the next two chapters, He is seen walking in the midst of Seven Churches and giving to each of them a sevenfold message relating to His soon return. He tells them what they are doing right, what they are doing wrong, and what to do about it.

When we come to chapters 4 and 5, John the Seer, sees a door open in heaven. Just in passing, it might be well to mention that the final message to the church in Laodicea pictured Christ before a closed door. They had closed the door of their lives to Christ. Here we have an open door to John. Would it be appropriate to say that a closed door to Him down here means a closed door to that person up there, and an open door to Him down here means an open door to that person in heaven?

John is bid to enter the door—"Come up here . . ." Isn't it interesting how close heaven is to earth when viewed in this way? It is not a place far off there somewhere. It is a place very near, perhaps nearer than we realize—and it becomes even nearer and dearer the more our loved ones gather there. There John's attention is riveted on a great throne. This throne is mentioned 17 times in these two chapters, and is mentioned throughout the book in every chapter except chapters 1, 8, and 9. So it is very important to the scheme of the book. Handel was asked how he had come to write the magnificent music to the *Messiah,* and he replied: *"I saw the heavens opened and God upon His great white throne."* Here is the focal point of the vision and the very center of the Universe.

It is argued by pretribulationists that the experience described by John is a symbol of the rapture of the Church. It is asserted that the trumpet, the voice, heaven, and the Spirit, as well as John being caught up lend themselves to a symbolical representation of "rapture". Further they say that the phrase *"after these things"* points to the end of the present Church age, and the resumption of God's dealings with Israel. The 24 elders mentioned in 4:4 are seen to be the raptured, glorified saints.

But there is really no proof that the "rapture" is in view here at all. It seems to portray in normal, literal language John's own experience of being "in the Spirit" and transferred to a new sphere of observation where he views what will take place in the future from a heavenly perspective. The phrase "after these things" simply signals a sudden change in the content of John's vision, certainly not a change of ages or dispensations (7:1; 7:9; 15:5; 18:1). Only one who is specifically seeking to place the rapture of the church before Daniel's Seventieth Week would locate it here.

It is also argued that since the word "church" does not occur from chapter 4 to19, it must have been removed by rapture. But after saying that the letter was addressed to the churches, it is unnecessary to repeat the word. Notice some of the passages where the Church is in view.

1. 5:9 The Heavenly Worship Team's Song of Redemption. This is not **their** personal testimony as the King James Version suggests. In other words, these elders are not representative of the Church in heaven, but a high order of angelic beings that lead, along with the quartet of Four Living Creatures, the heavenly worship. The better rendering would be *"You are worthy to take the scroll and to open its seals, because you were slain, and with your blood you purchased **men** for God from every tribe and language and people and nation. You have made **them** to be a kingdom and priests to serve our God, and **they** will reign on the earth."* Please note that the New American Standard version and the New International Version are the more consistent reading of this text. *"They will*

reign on the earth" necessitates that the antecedents agree—not "us, us and we" but "men, them, and they."

2. 5:10 *"A kingdom and priests"* Note Peter's words in I Peter 2:9, *"You are a chosen people, a royal priesthood, a holy nation, a people belonging to God . . . "*

3. 6:9 The Martyrs Under the Altar. *"I saw the souls of those who had been slain because of the word of God and the testimony they had maintained."*

4. 7:9 The Great Multitude. *"These are they who have come out of the great tribulation; they have washed their robes and made them white in the blood of the Lamb."* It also says that they are *"from every nation, tribe, people and language"* which agrees with the description in 5:9 above.

5. 11:18 The Seventh Trumpet. *"The time has come for . . . rewarding your servants (bondservants) the prophets and your saints and those who reverence your name . . . "*

6. 12:10-11 The Overcomers. *"Our brothers"* *"They overcame him by the blood of the Lamb and by the word of their testimony; they did not love their lives so much as to shrink from death."* (See 6:9 above)

7. 12:17 The Rest of Her Offspring. *"Those who obey God's commandments and hold to the testimony of Jesus."*

8. 13:7, 10, 14:12; 18:20. The Saints. *"He was given power to make war against the saints and to conquer them* (in context, those whose names are written in the book of life)" *"This calls for patient endurance and faithfulness on the part of the saints." "This calls for patient endurance on the part of the saints who obey God's commandments and remain faithful to Jesus." "Rejoice, saints and apostles and prophets!"*

THE SEVEN POSITIONS AROUND THE THRONE

1
On The Throne

Yahweh

4:2 At once I was in the Spirit, and there before me was a throne in heaven with someone sitting on it.

4:3And the one who sat there had the appearance of jasper and carnelian. A rainbow, resembling an emerald, encircled the throne.

It would be appropriate for us to say that being "in the Spirit" makes a vision of God more likely, but what John seems to be saying is that he was permitted to see the heavenly, spiritual realm, that is ordinarily invisible, much like Elisha's servant, Gehazi, *"The Lord opened the servant's eyes, and he looked and saw the hills full of horses and chariots of fire all around Elisha" (2 Kings 6:17)*. He doesn't necessarily imply that it was an "out-of-body-experience." However, in Paul's inexpressible view of Paradise that he alludes to in 2 Corinthians 12, he wasn't sure *"whether it was in the body or out of the body."* We assume he means he wasn't sure whether he was dead or alive, since it probably happened to him following his stoning in Lystra when he was left for dead.

He sees God **on the throne of the universe.** I do not believe John actually saw God, but rather the Shekinah glory of God. He is seen in terms of light, which He is in the essence of His being. The impression is expressed in terms of gem-stone brilliance.

The jasper in John's day was probably a translucent rock crystal, diamond-like, with scintillating brilliant light. The sardian or carnelian (as the NIV translates it) was probably a blood-red stone and the emerald was most likely the green emerald of which we are familiar. The impression was of a blinding, glittering light, brighter than the sun, with dazzling red, filtered through restful green. Paul, in writing to Timothy, spoke of God as *"dwelling in the light unapproachable" (I Tim. 1:16).*

Isaiah's Throne Description

> *"I saw the Lord seated on a throne, high and exalted, and the train of his robe filled the temple" (Isaiah 6:1).*

Ezekiel's Throne Description

> *"Above the expanse over their heads was what looked like a throne of sapphire, and high above on the throne was a figure like that of a man. I saw that from what appeared to be his waist up he looked like glowing metal, as if full of fire, and that from there down he looked like fire; and brilliant light surrounded him. Like the appearance of a rainbow in the clouds on a rainy day, so was the radiance around him. This was the appearance of the likeness of the glory of the Lord. When I saw it, I fell face down" (Ezekiel 1:26-28).*
> *"He wraps himself in light as with a garment" (Psalm 104:2).*
> *"He who is the blessed and only Sovereign, the King of kings and Lord of lords; who alone possesses immortality and dwells in unapproachable light." (I Timothy 6:15-16).*

God's throne is the center of the universe! Everything should relate to that Center of all centers. The Sovereign Lord governs all.

> *"The LORD reigns, let the nations tremble; he sits enthroned between the cherubim, let the earth shake" (Psalm 99:1).*

2
Surrounding The Throne

Twenty-Four Elders

4:4 Surrounding the throne were twenty-four other thrones, and seated on them were twenty-four elders. They were dressed in white and had crowns of gold on their heads.

These "elders" are probably a high-ranking order of angels. Some see in them a representation of the entire church of the old and new dispensation, twelve patriarchs and twelve apostles. This can only be a guess, and probably not a very good one. Do the Old Testament Scriptures give us any clue as to their identity? Yes. What we can say with some degree of certainty is that these Elders, along with the Four Living Creatures, are the Heavenly Worship Team. The earthly counterpart was the 24 different courses of the priesthood that King David set up to serve in the temple (I Chronicles 24:7-19).

> *"Of these, twenty-four thousand are to supervise the work of the temple of the Lord . . . " (I Chronicles 23:4)*

> *". . . they were divided accordingly: sixteen heads of families from Eleazar's descendants and eight heads of families from Ithamar's descendants . . . (I Chronicles 24:4f)*

There were also 24 courses of singers and instrumentalists that ministered by leading in the temple worship. They, too, praised God with harps. (I Chronicles 25:9-31).

Notice that they seem to have a priestly function, offering to God the prayers of the faithful. *"Each one had a harp and they were holding golden bowls full of incense, which are the prayers of the saints" (Rev. 5:8).*

3
From the Throne

Sounds of God's Presence

4:5 From the throne came flashes of lightning, rumblings and peals of thunder.

From the throne there issued those sounds which in the Old Testament have always been associated with God, the flashing of lightning and the rumbling of thunder. These were the audio accompaniment when the law was given to Moses on Mt. Sinai. The next time we experience a thunder and lightning display, let it remind us of the awesomeness of God's power and presence. (See Psalm 29).

> *"The clouds poured down water, the skies resounded with thunder; your arrows flashed back and forth. Your thunder was heard in the whirlwind, your lightning lit up the world; the earth trembled and quaked" (Psalm 77:17-18).*

> *"I looked, and I saw a windstorm coming out of the north—an immense cloud with flashing lightning and surrounded by brilliant light" (Ezekiel 1:4).*

4
Before The Throne

Seven Lamps

Before the throne, seven lamps were blazing. These are the seven spirits of God.

Before the throne was the seven branched lamp stand or Menorah burning. *"These are the seven spirits of God,"* it explains. These probably refer to the sevenfold gifts of the Spirit which rested upon "the Branch" out of Jesse, the Anointed One of God, mentioned in Isaiah 11:l: *"The Spirit of the Lord will rest on him—the Spirit of wisdom and of understanding, the Spirit of counsel and of power, the Spirit of knowledge and of the fear of the Lord."* Also this sevenfold Spirit is described later on as *"seven eyes."* Here we have the heavenly reality of which the Golden Candlestick in the tabernacle was a copy, *"made according to the pattern."*.

We see yet another object in heaven that may well be replicated in the wilderness tabernacle and later in Solomon's temple. John sees also a "sea of glass, clear as crystal" before the throne. The Brazen Laver in the wilderness tabernacle and the "Sea of cast metal (I Kings 7:23) in Solomon's temple correspond to this heavenly "sea." Solomon's "sea" was huge. It held about 230 gallons of water and stood on twelve bulls, three facing in each direction, north, east, south and west. The Laver or Sea was used by the priests for cleansing.

4:6 Also before the throne there was what looked like a sea of glass, clear as crystal.

It seems very likely that the earthly Brazen Laver corresponds to what is here seen in heaven as the "sea of glass". In Solomon's temple, it is called a "sea" of cast metal, a huge circular bowl resting on twelve bulls, and holding a great quantity of water. It was used for the cleansing of the priests. *"He made the Sea of cast metal, circular in shape, . . . The Sea stood on twelve bulls . . . it held two thousand baths" (I Kings 7:23-26).*

5
In The Center Around The Throne

Four Living Creatures

In the center, around the throne, were four living creatures, and they were covered with eyes, in front and in back.

4:7 The first living creature was like a lion, the second was like an ox, the third had a face like a man, the fourth was like a flying eagle.

4:8 Each of the four living creatures had six wings and was covered with eyes all around, even under his wings. Day and night they never stop saying: "Holy, holy, holy is the Lord God Almighty, who was, and is and is to come."

In the center around the throne were four living creatures, covered with eyes, in front and in back. These are most certainly the cherubim, a high ranking order of angel that are guardians of the throne of God. They appear in Ezekiel's vision in chapter 1 and 10, where they are specifically identified as such. The seraphim of Isaiah's vision in chapter 6 are probably the same since they fulfill the same function and sing the same song. Here John sees them each with a different face while Ezekiel's vision seems to indicate that each of them had four faces. The difference may be one of where you are standing. If they stand on all sides of the throne, then John saw only that side which faced him. The other faces may well have been hidden from his view. Barkley suggests that they stand for "everything that is noblest, strongest, wisest, and swiftest in nature, each of them preeminent over his particular sphere." The lion is supreme among the beasts; the ox is supreme among cattle; the eagle is supreme among birds; and man is supreme among them all. (Revelation, Vol. 1, p 200). The Jewish writers tell us that the standards of the lead tribes in the wilderness order of march were Judah with a lion standard, Ephraim with a young ox emblazoned on his, Reuben with a man and Dan with an eagle on their standards. Here may be the earthly counterpart of the heavenly reality.

Ezekiel's Description

"In appearance their form was like that of a man, but each of them had four faces and four wings Their legs were straight; their feet were like those of a calf and gleamed like burnished bronze. Under their wings on their four sides they had the hands of a man. All four of them had faces and wings, and wings touched one another. Each one went straight ahead; they did not turn as they moved. Their faces looked like this: Each of the four had the face of a man, and on the right side each had the face of a lion, and on the left the face of an ox; each also had the face of an eagle. Such were their faces" (Ezekiel 1:5-6, 10-11).

Isaiah's Description

"Above him were seraphs, each with six wings: With two wings they covered their faces, with two they covered their feet, and with two they were flying. And they were calling to one another: 'Holy, holy, holy is the Lord Almighty; the whole earth is full of his glory" (Isaiah 6:2-3).

The earthly representation is the cherubim that covered the mercy seat or "throne" of the Ark of the Covenant.

Ezekiel continues his vision in chapter 10.

"Each of the cherubim had four faces: One face was that of a cherub, the second, the face of a man, the third the face of a lion, and the fourth the face of an eagle. Then the cherubim rose upward. These were the living creatures I had seen by the Kebar River" (Ezekiel 10:14-15).

They are unceasing in their praise. They worship *"the Lord God, the Almighty (the All Powerful One)"*

4:9 Whenever the living creatures give glory, honor and thanks to him who sits on the throne and who lives for ever and ever,

4:10 the twenty-four elders (will) fall down before him who sits on the throne, and worship him who lives forever and ever. They (will) lay their crowns before the throne and say: "You are worthy, our Lord and God, to receive glory and honor and power, for you created all things, and by your will they were created and have their being."

The *"will"* above indicates that this worship will happen when the living creatures give God glory and honor. It happens in chapter 5 when the Lamb takes the scroll and opens the seals. It is significant that their praise centers around the fact that God alone is Creator of all that exists. The earthly service and worship were pale copies of the heavenly.

The crowns speak of reigning authority. But all authority and honor is due to Him who is on the throne, symbolized by casting their crowns before the throne and completely submitting themselves to Him. Their prayer echoes David's prayer in I Chronicles:

"David praised the Lord in the presence of the whole assembly, saying, Praise be to you, O Lord, God of our father Israel, from everlasting to everlasting. Yours, O Lord, is the greatness and the power and the glory and the majesty and the splendor, for everything in heaven and earth is yours. Yours, O Lord is the kingdom; you are exalted as head over all. Wealth and honor come from you; you are the ruler of all things. In your hands are strength and power to exalt and give strength to all. Now, Our God, we give you thanks, and praise your glorious name" (I Chronicles 29:10-13).

6
In The Center Of The Throne

A Lamb

Later in chapter 5, we see a Lamb, looking as if it had been slain, standing in the center of the throne (5:6). John had been weeping because no one could be found to open the sealed book. One of the elders told him to stop weeping, because the Lion of the tribe of Judah, the Root of David was worthy to do so. John turned to see not a Lion but a Lamb. In the Revelation Jesus is called the Lamb no fewer than twenty-nine times. The word for "lamb" is a word which means a lamb brought to slaughter. In heaven, our Lord still bears the marks of suffering and pain. The lamb has seven horns that stand for power and authority and honor. Also it has seven eyes which are the Spirits of the Lord. This speaks of his omniscience—his perfect knowledge. Here we have a marvelous picture of Christ's humiliation in death and the glory of His risen and exalted life.

7
Encircling The Throne

Myriads of Angels

Finally, there are a great host of angels encircling the throne (5:11). There are myriads of them—thousands, and ten thousand times ten thousand. What a tremendous choir!

Here is the greatest chorus of praise the universe can ever hear. It comes in three waves. First, there is the praise of the four living creatures and of the twenty-four elders. *They sing, "You are worthy, our Lord and God, to receive glory and honor and power, for you created all things, and by your will they were created and have their being." (4:11).*

Again they sing a new song. The new song is always a song for the new mercies of God. The new song is a consequence of the new creation. *"You are worthy to take the scroll and to open its seals, because you were slain, and with your blood you purchased men for God from every tribe and language and people and nation. You have made them to be a kingdom and priests to serve our God, and they will reign on the earth."* His death is seen as **emancipating**—we have been purchased and set free! It is seen as **all-embracing**—it was for all men everywhere. And it was **all-availing**—He died to make us kings—to reign with Him, and priests—with the right of direct access to God.

Second, we have the song of the angels. They offer in song a **sevenfold ascription of praise** to the Lamb, *"Worthy is the Lamb, who was slain, to receive power and wealth and wisdom and strength and honor and glory and praise!"* Because of His humiliation he receives exaltation—a name which is above every name! Seven great possessions belong to Him, the Risen, Living Lord. Our Lord makes us worthy in His own worthiness, and all these things ascribed to Him, He imparts to us. (See under verse 11 if chapter 5)

Third, the chorus of praise goes so far that it cannot go any farther, for it reaches throughout the whole of the universe and the whole of creation. All through the world there is one vast song of praise to the Lamb. All nature joins the chorus: *"To him who sits on the throne and to the Lamb be praise and honor and glory and power for ever and ever!"*

And now we can gain a new appreciation of the prayer Jesus taught us to pray.

> Thy name be hallowed . . . .
> Thy kingdom come . . . .
> Thy will be done . . .

ON EARTH AS IT IS IN HEAVEN. The kingdom of God is that realm in which the will of God is perfectly observed and the Word of God is perfectly obeyed. That is what you see here in this heavenly scene. Perfect love, perfect worship, perfect obedience. The climax of the Revelation moves forward to the glorious fulfillment of this prayer. Whisper it now to yourself and to God!

CHAPTER 5

THE SEVEN-SEALED SCROLL

5:1 Then I saw in the right hand of him who sat on the throne a scroll with writing on both sides and sealed with seven seals.

In Revelation 4 and 5 we are allowed to view through the eyes of John the Seer the glories of the heavenly realm. While "in the Spirit" on the Lord's day, he saw a vision of the Sovereign Risen Lord, and here once again "in the Spirit", or in a spiritual state, he finds himself in heaven, and like Isaiah, Daniel and Ezekiel before him he sees there a throne "high and lifted up." There are seven positions around the throne, and seven things associated with the throne. John first sees someone on the throne. Obviously, it is God the Father. But John does not see a distinct form but a vision of flashing gem-like colors, the Shekinah glory of God. He does observe **a seven-sealed scroll** in the right hand of God. Then John saw something in the very center of the throne—next to the Father on the throne. It was a Lamb, *"looking as if it had been slain."* It had seven horns and seven eyes. The Lamb is moving forward to take the scroll out of the Father's hand. Finally, John saw a vast throng of angels encircling the throne, the living creatures and the 24 elders. And they join in a great seven-fold praise of the slain Lamb. So we will briefly look at the significance of the Seven-Sealed Scroll, The Seven Horned Lamb, and the Sevenfold Praise. Central to all is the Worthy Lamb, The Redeemer, The Lamb of God who takes away the sin of the world.

1. The Seven-Sealed Scroll

Here in Revelation 5, we are introduced to a seven-sealed Scroll. Its seals span a week of seven years that will occur at the end of the age according to Daniel's prophecy. In the scroll is recorded the literal unveiling of God's final purposes for the world. It is the great document that determines the climax of human history. **The subject of the sealed scroll is redemption.** Redemption involves the restoration of everything that was lost by sin, including man's soul, his body, and the earth. Redemption has its roots in the past, but its final fulfillment lies in the future. Redemption is linked to both comings—the first as well as the second. When Jesus spoke to His disciples concerning those things which are to precede His Second Coming, He said, *"And when **these things** begin to come to pass, then look up, and lift up your heads; for your **redemption** draws near"* (Luke 21:28). And the apostle Paul speaks of this also in Romans 8:22-23: *"Not only so, but we ourselves, who have the first fruits of the Spirit, groan inwardly as we wait eagerly for our adoption as sons, **the redemption of our bodies.**"* Even creation, according to Paul, experiences redemption, and is renewed at Christ's coming. Redemption here doesn't mean salvation, but the restoration of everything that is lost.

A search is described in verses 2 and 3 to try to determine who qualifies to break the seals and lay claim to the earth? Who has furnished the price of redemption? Who, indeed, is worthy to open the seals?

To aid us in our understanding of what the seven sealed scroll is all about, let me go back to the book of Jeremiah In the Old Testament, if a man lost his land, a near kin could buy it back, that is, redeem it, thereby keeping it in the family estate. The scroll on which the official transaction was recorded was rolled up and sealed, and placed in the court of the Tabernacle or Temple. Jeremiah predicted that Jerusalem would be overthrown by Babylon, and a period of 70 years captivity would ensue. Jeremiah had a cousin named Hanam-e-el who owned a piece of property. Hanameel concluded that the Babylonian invasion and subsequent captivity would render his land useless, so he decided to offer it for sale. God revealed to Jeremiah his plan to sell, and was told to buy the land for the redemption price. He did this and the proper title deed was made and properly sealed. Jeremiah would not enter into possession of it for some time to come. But one day, when the Jews returned, the sealed scroll would be of great value. It would prove that the one who had redeemed the land was entitled to possess it. Jeremiah met the conditions of a kinsman—redeemer, being related to Hanameel, willing to redeem the land, and able to pay the redemption price (Jeremiah 32).

This historical incident gives meaning to the seven-sealed scroll in Rev. 5. The book that John saw in the hand of Him that sat upon the throne is the title deed to the earth, once committed to man to rule for God, but now in the hands of Satan.

When the call went out, "Who is worthy to break the seals and open the scroll?" "**No one was found** worthy to open and to read the book, neither to look thereon" (5:4). And John wept bitter tears, because no one was found in heaven, on earth, or under the earth.

"*I saw*"=the phrase occurs thirty-nine times in Revelation, and indicates that John was there and was an eyewitness to all that he would write about. He saw the scroll, and writing on the outside, so there must have been writing on the inside as well. He saw seven seals as yet unopened. The contents of the scroll would be revealed as the seals were opened. The sealed scroll seems to span the entire week of years, dividing the 70th "seven of Daniel's 70 years into two equal halves of 3 1/2 years or 42 months. There have been many seven sealed scrolls discovered in both the Jewish and Roman worlds.

1. Who Is Worthy?

5:2 And I saw a mighty angel proclaiming in a loud voice, "Who is worthy to break the seals and open the scroll?"

This "mighty angel" is the first of three strong angels mentioned in Revelation (see also 10:1 and 18:21). Michael and Gabriel, in Daniel's prophecy, are two such angels—archangels.

2. No One Is Found!

5:3 But no one in heaven or on earth or under the earth could open the scroll or even look inside it.

The events in Revelation take place in these three realms "heaven, earth, and under the earth." Here a universal quest is made, but no one is found.

5:4 I wept and wept because no one was found who was worthy to open the scroll or look inside.

John was obviously deeply moved that no one could be found to open the seals. Was God's ultimate purpose in redemption and judgment to be defeated after all?

3. Someone Is Found!

5:5 Then one of the elders said to me, "Do not weep! See, the Lion of the tribe of Judah, the Root of David, has triumphed. He is able to open the scroll and its seven seals."

It is interesting that an individual elder comes forward to comfort John in his grief.

The Lion of the Tribe of Judah.

> *"You are a lion's cub, O Judah; you return from the prey, my son. Like a lion he crouches and lies down, like a lioness—who dares to rouse him? The scepter will not depart from Judah, nor the ruler's staff from between his feet, until he comes to whom it belongs and the obedience of the nations is his" (Genesis 49:9-10).*

A lion is the king of the beasts, and so Christ is the king that embodies courage and power as ruler of the nations by divine decree.

It was partially fulfilled when David assumed the throne, but Matthew confirms that Jesus is "the son of David" and rightful successor to David, sovereign of the kingdom God promised to His people.

Root of David

> *"A shoot will come up from the stump of Jesse; from his roots a Branch will bear fruit . . . " (Isaiah 11:1).*

> *"The days are coming," declares the Lord, "when I will raise up to David a righteous Branch, a King who will reign wisely and do what is just and right in the land" (Jeremiah 23:5).*

> *"I am going to bring my servant, the Branch" (Zechariah 3:8). "Here is the man whose name is the Branch, and he will branch out from his place and build the temple of the Lord. It is he who will build the temple of the Lord, and he will be clothed with majesty and will sit and rule on his throne" (Zechariah 6:12).*

The picture is that of a tree that has been felled, leaving only a stump, but from that stump there comes up a healthy shoot and the life of the tree is perpetuated, and eventually restored to its original glory. So the coming of Christ shall be when he sets up His millennial kingdom!

The Lamb

This third title pictures Christ in His sacrificial character, and stresses His redemptive death on behalf of men. With His own blood He paid the redemptive price that sets men free. Because He redeemed the world, He has the right to judge it and to renew it.

5:6 Then I saw a lamb, looking as if it had been slain, standing in the center of the throne, encircled by the four living creatures and the elders. He had seven horns and seven eyes, which are the seven spirits of God sent out into all the earth.

John turns expecting to see a Lion, and instead he sees a Lamb! The "Lamb" appears 28 times in Revelation. "The Lamb is all the glory of Immanuel's land." (Anne Ross Cousin) The Lamb stands "as slain." The picture graphically depicts a lamb with throat cut and blood ebbing out from the open wound. The stress is on the shed blood that constitutes the purchase price for the redemption of the world. This is the primary indicator of His worthiness.

Seven horns represent perfect authority or power; seven eyes symbolize perfect knowledge and absolute sovereignty. He rules over all that He sees.

> *"Seven lights . . . these seven are the eyes of the Lord, which range throughout the earth" (Zechariah 4:10).*

> *"For the eyes of the Lord range throughout the earth to strengthen those whose hearts are fully committed to him" (2 Chronicles 16:9).*

5:7 He came and took the scroll from the right hand of him who sat on the throne.

God extends the scroll that is in His right hand (symbolizing authority), and the Lamb steps forward and takes it.

The New Song of the 24 Elders

5:8 And when he had taken it, the four living creatures and the twenty-four elders fell down before the Lamb. Each one had a harp and they were holding golden bowls full of incense, which are the prayers of the saints.

"Saints" = in both Testaments "saints" refers to the people of God, the people that belong to God. They are "holy" or set apart for His service. In Daniel, the term seems to refer to Israel as the people of God, but even there a qualification is given *"your people—everyone whose name is found written in the book."* In the New Testament, it uniformly refers to believers, either as individuals or as the corporate body. Those who insist the references to "saints" in Revelation must refer to Israel, the Church having already been raptured before chapter 5, fail to see that the references in Revelation are to "blood washed" believers *"who obey God's commandments and hold to the testimony of Jesus"(12:17).* The inference also is that they are those whose names are written in the book of life.

5:9 And they sang a new song: "You are worthy to take the scroll and to open its seals, because you were slain, and with your blood you purchased men for God from every tribe and language and people and nation.

Notice the threefold cause of worthiness:

(1) "you were slaughtered",
(2) "you purchased with your blood", and
(3 "you made them a kingdom and priests."

5:10 You have made them to be a kingdom and priests to serve our God, and they will reign on the earth."

> *"But the saints of the Most High will receive the kingdom and will possess it forever—yes, for ever and ever" (Daniel 7:18).*

> *"Then the sovereignty, power and greatness of the kingdoms under the whole heaven will be handed over to the saints, the people of the Most High. His kingdom will be an everlasting kingdom, and all rulers will worship and obey him" (Daniel 7:28).*

The reign of Christ seems to be a literal reign *"on the earth"* and not a heavenly spiritual reign as suggested by amillennialists.

The Angelic Host
The Sevenfold Song of the Angelic Choir

5:11 Then I looked and heard the voice of many angels, numbering thousands upon thousands, and ten thousand times ten thousand. They encircled the throne and the living creatures and the elders.

> *"Thousands upon thousands attend him; ten thousand times ten thousands stood before him" (Daniel 7:10).*

> *"You have come to Mount Zion, to the heavenly Jerusalem, the city of the living God. You have come to thousands upon thousands of angels in joyful assembly"(Hebrews 12:22).*

5:12 In a loud voice they sang: "Worthy is the Lamb, who was slain, to receive power and wealth and wisdom and strength and honor and glory and praise!"

Now the chorus of praise is taken up by the unnumbered hosts of the angels of heaven. In a great outer circle round the throne and the living creatures and the elders stand the multitude of the angels, and they begin their song.

> *"Worthy is the Lamb that was slain to receive power and riches and wisdom and might and honor and glory and blessing."*

Because of His humiliation he receives exaltation—a name which is above every name' Seven great possessions belong to the Risen, Living Lord.

(1) Power. Frequently the New Testament writers say of our Lord, "He is able" 'He does not plan and never achieve; he does not dream and never realize. To Him belongs the power—all power.

(2) Riches. Paul speaks of *"the unsearchable riches of Christ"* (Eph. 3:8). There is no promise He gives that He does not possess the resources to carry out. There is no claim on Him which He cannot satisfy. He possesses the resources to meet every demand.

(3) Wisdom. Christ is *"the wisdom of God"* (I Cor. 1:24). In Him are hid all the treasures of Wisdom and Knowledge. He knows what makes life work when nothing else is.

(4) Might. He is the strong One who can disarm the powers of evil, and overthrow the Evil One. His strength is adequate, and when manifested through His children, it is more than adequate to cope with anything life dishes out to us.

(5) Honor. The day will come when to Him every knee shall bow, and when every tongue shall confess that He is Lord. He is worthy to be honored of all men.

(6) Glory. Glory belongs to God and to God alone. Jesus is God, and shares the rights and privileges of God. John tells us later on that in heaven, *"the city had no need of the sun, neither of the moon for the glory of God did lighten it, and the Lamb is the light thereof."*

(7) Blessing. There rises to Him from all the redeemed the blessing and the thanksgiving for all that He has done. And that blessing and that thanksgiving are the one gift that we who have nothing can give to Him who possesses all.

The wonderful truth is—Christ makes us worthy in and through His worthiness. All of these things He imparts to us.

(1) Power—"Ye shall receive power . . ."
(2) Riches—" . . . joint-heirs with Christ."
(3) Wisdom—"Christ is made unto us wisdom."
(4) Strength—"to them that have no might He increases strength"
(5) Honor—"if any man serve me, him will my Father honor"
(6) Glory—"the glory which you gave me I have given them"
(7) Blessing—"He has blessed us with all spiritual blessings in Christ Jesus."

The Song of All Creation

5:13 Then I heard every creature in heaven and on earth and under the earth and on the sea, and all that is in them, singing: "To him who sits on the throne and to the Lamb be praise and honor and glory and power, for ever and ever!"

5:14 The four living creatures said, "Amen," and the elders fell down and worshiped.

The climax of praise includes and contains all of creation praising God! All of nature joins in praising Yahweh on His throne. Psalm 148 is a summons to the whole of nature to join in praising God. Listen!

"Praise the Lord. Praise the Lord from the heavens, praise him in the heights above. Praise him, all his angels, praise him, all his

heavenly hosts. Praise him, sun, moon, praise him, all you shining stars. Praise him, you highest heavens and you waters above the skies. Let them praise the name of the Lord, for he commanded and they were created. He set them in place forever and ever; he gave a decree that will never pass away. Praise the Lord from the earth, you great sea creatures and all ocean depths, lightning and hail, snow and clouds, stormy winds that do his bidding, you mountains and all hills, fruit trees and all cedars, wild animals and all cattle, small creatures and flying birds, kings of the earth and all nations, you princes and all rulers on earth, young men and maidens, old men and children. Let them praise the name of the Lord, for his name alone is exalted; his splendor is above the earth and the heavens. He has raised up for his people a horn, the praise of all his saints, of Israel, the people close to his heart. Praise the Lord."

CHAPTER 6

THE SEVEN-SEALED SCROLL

1
The First Seal

A White Horse—Conquest

6:1 I watched as the Lamb opened the first of the seven seals. Then I heard one of the four living creatures say in a voice like thunder, "Come!"

"Come!" A summons by the Living Creature to the horse and its rider to come forward and begin the final sequence of events toward the climax of history, as we know it.

> *"There before me were four chariots coming out from between two mountains—mountains of bronze! The first chariot had red horses, the second black, the third white, and the fourth dappled—all of them powerful" (Zechariah 6:1-4).*

Zechariah calls them the *"four spirits (or winds) of heaven, going out from standing in the presence of the Lord of the whole world"* (6:5). Four mighty winds which God lets loose on the earth!

6:2 I looked, and there before me was a white horse!

*"I saw at night, and behold, a man was riding on a red horse, and
he was standing among the myrtle trees which were in the ravine,
with red, sorrel, and white horses behind him" (Zechariah 1:8).*

**Its rider held a bow, and he was given a crown, and he rode out as a
conqueror bent on conquest.**

Jesus said, *"You will hear of wars and rumors of wars . . . " Matt. 24:6).*

The white horse stands for conquest in war. Since our Lord comes
forth on a white horse in chapter 19, many believe this rider is also Christ.
Daniel, however, predicts that the 70th week will be ushered in by war that
will continue until the end. Jesus also predicted that "wars and rumors of
wars" would set in motion the events leading up to His return. Since the
final Beast will conquer three kingdoms and take control of another seven,
this rider may well represent the campaign of conquest by the Antichrist.
This will be the confederated empire of the last day corresponding to the
ten toes of Nebuchadnezzar's colossus or the ten horns of the fourth beast.

The crown is the victor's crown. The bow stands for war and military
might (See Jeremiah 51:56; Hosea 1:5; Psalm 46:9). The fact that he
"was given" a crown indicates delegated authority. The One who gives the
authority is undoubtedly God Himself.

In Daniel 11 *"the king who does as he pleases"* invades many countries,
and extends his power over many nations. He then invades the Beautiful
Land (Israel). This individual will later be identified as *"the beast out of the
sea"* in Revelation 13.

2
The Second Seal

The Red Horse—Internecine Strife

**6:3 When the Lamb opened the second seal, I heard the second living
creature say, "Come!"**

6:4Then another horse came out, a fiery red one. Its rider was given power to take peace from the earth and to make men slay each other. To him was given a large sword

The function of this horse and rider is to take peace from the earth by setting man against man and nation against nation. Jesus said, *"nation will rise against nation, and kingdom against kingdom" (Matt. 24:7).* The large sword symbolizes the power to savagely put to death the vanquished.

3
The Third Seal

A Black Horse—Famine

6:5 When the Lamb opened the third seal, I heard the third living creature say, "Come!"

I looked, and there before me was a black horse! Its rider was holding a pair of scales in his hand.

6:6 Then I heard what sounded like a voice among the four living creatures, saying, "A quart of wheat for a day's wages, and three quarts of barley for a day's wages, and do not damage the oil and the wine!"

Jesus said, *"There will be famine and earthquakes in various places" (Matt. 24:7).*

Here the horse and rider represent famine. It is a famine which causes great hardship, but not desperate enough to kill. Wheat is obtainable, but at a greatly inflated price; the wine and the oil are not affected. The scale signifies the "eating of bread by weight" which is a sign of great scarcity.

"Son of man, behold, I am going to break the staff of bread in Jerusalem, and they will eat bread by weight and with anxiety, and

drink water by measure and in horror, because bread and water will be scarce; and they will be appalled with one another and waste away in their iniquity: (Ezekiel 4:16-17).

A man's wage (a denarius) would buy only enough grain for himself for a day with nothing left over for other things or for his family.

Notice Zechariah's reference to the horses being *"the four spirits of heaven"* that are sent forth by God.

"With the first chariot were red horses, with the second chariot black horses, with the third chariot white horses, and with the fourth chariot strong dappled horses . . . What are these, my Lord? These are the four spirits of heaven, going forth after standing before the Lord of all the earth" (Zechariah 6:2-5).

4
The Fourth Seal

A Pale Horse—Death And Hades

6:7 When the Lamb opened the fourth seal, I heard the voice of the fourth living creature say, "Come!"

6:8 I looked, and there before me was a pale horse! Its rider was named Death, and Hades was following close behind him. They were given power over a fourth of the earth to kill by sword, famine and plague, and by the wild beasts of the earth.

Here the rider is personified as Death, with Hades following (being the result of death). It is a fourth part of the earth that is affected by death and disaster. The judgments progressively worsen.

"Pale" means livid, ashen (from the word chloros from which we get the word Clorox—to bleach white.)

God said through Ezekiel that even if Noah, Daniel and Job were in the land, they could only save themselves by their righteousness.

"I will send famine and wild beasts against you, and they will leave you childless. Plague and bloodshed will sweep through you, and I will bring the sword against you. I the Lord have spoken" (Ezekiel 17).

"For this is what the Sovereign Lord says: How much worse will it be when I send against Jerusalem my four dreadful judgments—sword and famine and wild beasts and plague"(Ezekiel 14:20-21).

Some have suggested that the correct translation here in verse 8 is "beast" not "wild beast", and the reference is to the two beasts mentioned later, "the beast out of the sea" and "the beast out of the earth." However, this seems to be an allusion to Ezekiel's prophecy quoted above, where the reference is to "wild beasts."

5
The Fifth Seal

Souls Under The Altar

6:9 When he opened the fifth seal, I saw under the altar the souls of those who had been slain because of the word of God and the testimony they had maintained.

6:10 They called out in a loud voice, "How long, Sovereign Lord, holy and true, until you judge the inhabitants of the earth and avenge our blood?"

Jesus said, *"Then you will be handed over to be persecuted and put to death, and you will be hated by all nations because of me"* (Matt. 24:9).

"Rejoice, O nations, with His people; for He will avenge the blood of His servants, and will render vengeance on His adversaries, and will atone for His land and His people" (Deuteronomy 32:43).

6:11 Then each of them was given a white robe, and they were told to wait a little longer, until the number of their fellow servants and brothers who were to be killed as they had been was completed.

The altar here could be the heavenly counterpart to the Altar of Burnt Offering at the bottom of which the blood (the life) of the sacrifice was poured (Lev. 17:11-14). The martyr's life-blood is seen as a sacrifice to God (See Phil. 2:17; 2 Tim. 4:6 where Paul uses such a figure). Another suggestion, equally valid, is that this is the heavenly Altar of Incense that was located in the holy place before the curtain that separated the holy place form the most holy place. The Altar of Incense represented prayer ascending before God, so the souls here are praying, crying out with a loud voice, "How long?" The request suggests that they believe too much time has gone by, and still their persecutors go unpunished. This sentiment occurs many times in the Old Testament, particularly in the Psalms. Obviously, God's judging wrath has not yet begun.

The "souls" here seem to represent those who have recently been martyred (their blood spilled), and are probably the first wave of persecution that erupts when Antichrist breaks his covenant at the mid-point of the seven years, and desecrates the temple. The suffering of God's people intensifies as *"the brothers that will be killed"* are added to their number later in the "week". The great multitude that *"come out of the great tribulation"*, referred to in chapter 7, are probably these brethren. They were killed for precisely the same reason that John was exiled to Patmos *"because of the word of God and the testimony they had maintained."*

Their "white robes" probably are more symbolical than actual dress. It is a metaphor of speech that signifies moral purity. The Lord instructed the Laodicean church to purchase from Him *"white garments"* to clothe themselves, and the Sardian believers were promised that they would *"walk with me, dressed in white"* when the Lord comes. The *"fine linen"* garments of the Bride of the Lamb in chapter 19 are said to stand for the *"righteous acts of the saints."*

6
The Sixth Seal

Celestial Disturbances

6:12 I watched as he opened the sixth seal. There was a great earthquake. The sun turned black like sackcloth made of goat hair, the whole moon turned blood red (became like blood),

Joel says these celestial disturbances will occur *before* the Day of the Lord.

> *"I will show wonders in the heavens and on the earth, blood and fire and billows of smoke. The sun will be turned to darkness and the moon to blood before the coming of the great and dreadful day of the Lord" (2:30-31).*

Luke confirms this. He places the celestial disturbances just before the coming of Christ in the clouds of glory.

> *"There will be signs in the sun, moon and stars. On the earth, nations will be in anguish and perplexity at the roaring and tossing of the sea. Men will faint from terror, apprehensive of what is coming on the world, for the heavenly bodies will be shaken" (Luke 21:25-26)*

"Like"= John frequently employs metaphors and similes. A metaphor says "one thing *is* another thing. A simile says one thing is *like* another. The first is obviously broader than the second. Here John uses a simile to describe the appearance of the sun and moon. They no longer give their light to the earth. An ominous darkness envelops the earth.

6:13 and the stars in the sky fell to earth, as late figs drop from a fig tree when shaken by a strong wind.

> *"Immediately after the distress of those days 'the sun will be darkened, and the moon will not give its light; the stars will fall from the sky, and the heavenly bodies will be shaken" (Matt. 24:29).*

The sun and moon will be darkened, and the stars no longer shine"
(Joel 3:15). This is the probable meaning—the stars will lose
their brightness, just as the sun and moon give off no light.

The quote from Matthew 24 above is from Isaiah 13:10; 34:4,

"The stars of heaven and their constellations will not show their light.
The rising sun will be darkened and the moon will not give its light."
"All the stars of the heavens will be dissolved (rot) and the sky rolled
up like a scroll; all the starry host will fall like withered leaves from
the vine, like shriveled figs from the fig tree."

The specific reference in Isaiah is to the Judgment of the Nations that
in the Revelation occurs at Armageddon following the tribulation. The
heavens will move apart, and those on the earth will view the glorious
descent of the Lamb from heaven.

Peter's description depicts Christ's coming as the Day of the Lord and
is very graphic:

"But the day of the Lord will come like a thief. The heavens will
disappear with a roar; the elements will be destroyed by fire, and
the earth and everything in it will be laid bare. Since everything
will be destroyed in this way, what kind of people ought you to
be? You ought to live holy and godly lives as you look forward to
the day of God and speed its coming (parousia). That day will
bring about the destruction of the heavens by fire, and the elements
will melt in the heat. But in keeping with his promise we are
looking forward to a new heaven and a new earth, the home of
righteousness" (2 Pet. 3:10).

Peter must have had Isaiah 65 and 66 in mind that speak of the
formation of a new heaven and a new earth, a renovated heaven and earth
before the Millennium begins.

"Behold, I will create new heavens and a new earth. The former things
will not be remembered, nor will they come to mind" (Isaiah 65:17).

> *"As the new heavens and the new earth that I make will endure before me," declares the Lord, "so will your name and descendants endure" (66:22).*

6:14 The sky receded like a scroll, rolling up, and every mountain and island was removed from its place.

Every mountain and island are moved out of their original place. It does not say that they cease to exist. See verses 15-16. The wicked cry out in terror to be hidden from the awesome holiness of God's presence.

6:15 Then the kings of the earth, the princes, the generals, the rich, the mighty, and every slave and every free man hid in caves and among the rocks of the mountains.

6:16 They called to the mountains and the rocks, "Fall on us and hide us from the face of him who sits on the throne and from the wrath of the Lamb!

6:17 For the great day of their wrath has come, and who can stand?"

The Greek suggests the sense *"is about to come."* The Day of the Lord and the Return of Christ occur at the same time and are the same thing.

Note the similarity in language with Isaiah 2,

> *"Men will flee to caves in the rocks and to holes in the ground from dread of the Lord and the splendor of his majesty, when he rises to shake the earth . . . they will flee to caverns in the rocks and to the overhanging crags from dread of the Lord and the splendor of his majesty, when he rises to shake the earth" (2:19, 21).*

The Day of the Lord will be a time of great terror. (Isaiah 13:6, 8; Zephaniah. 1:14; Joel 2:1, 11; Malachi 3:1-3; Hosea 10:8; Luke 23:30) It will be a time of universal fear, and the natural consequence of sin is to hide (Genesis 3).

The language here is similar to the language used in chapter 19 when Christ comes to do battle with the nations assembled at Armageddon.

> *"Come, gather together for the great supper of God, so that you may eat the flesh of kings, generals, and mighty men, of horses and their riders, and the flesh of all people, free and slave, small and great."*
> *(19:17-18).*

The sixth trumpet and the sixth bowl also move us to this great battle and the climactic event of the ages, the Second Coming of Christ and the Day of the Lord. The Seventh Seal, Seventh Trumpet and Seventh Bowl all have the same terminus point.

An earthquake. Note the frequency with which this thought occurs in the Old Testament. Amos 8:8; Ezek. 38:19; Joel 2:10; Haggai 2:6 The unshakeable things are shaken.

> *"I looked at the mountains and they were quaking; all the hills were swaying"* (Jeremiah 4:24).

CHAPTER 7

Having covered the entire week leading up to the final seal, John now goes back and gives a more detailed rendering of the last 3 1/2 years of this week of 7 years. In chapter 7, he will describe the two people groups that will be in the Great Tribulation period, the Israeli remnant and the Great Multitude, the Church. The Trumpet Judgments, which are partial and remedial occur during this period, and are God's final warning to the world before His wrath is poured out. They are not a part of The Day of the Lord, but lead up to it, even as the seals did. Chapter 10 reveals the opening of Daniel's sealed scroll which included the time frame reference for the last half of Daniel's 70th week of years (Daniel 12). Chapter 11 cites this time frame for the end of the Times of the Gentiles, and the length of time the dynamic witnesses hold forth. It is also the time allotted to Satan and Antichrist to pursue and persecute the people of God. The Seventh Seal, the Seventh Trumpet, and the Seventh Bowl all terminate at the same time—The Day of the Lord and the Coming of Christ.

144,000 Sealed

7:1 After this I saw four angels standing at the four corners of the earth, holding back the four winds of the earth to prevent any wind from blowing on the land or on the sea or on any tree.

*"The end is coming **on the four corners of the land"** (Ezekiel 7:2).*

*"This is what the Sovereign Lord says: Come **from the four winds**, O breath, and breathe into these slain, that they may live"* (Ezekiel 37:9).

*"He will gather the dispersed of Judah from **the four corners of the earth**"* (Isaiah 11:12).

*"And I will bring upon Elam **the four winds** from the four ends of heaven"* (Jeremiah 49:36).

*"There before me were **four winds of heaven** churning up the great sea"* (Daniel 7:2).

It is interesting that Ezekiel in chapter 37 talks about the revitalization of "dead" Israel, the dry bones coming to life. *"These bones are the whole house of Israel" (37:11) "I will put my Spirit in you and you will live, and I will settle you in your own land" (37:14)*. Here the *"breath"* is supplied by the *"four winds."*

Then, the Lord revealed to Ezekiel that the divided tribes of Israel (Ephraim, representing the northern 10 tribes, and Judah, representing the southern 2 tribes) would come together, and be united as one.

"I will make them one nation in the land, on the mountains of Israel. There will be one king over all of them and they will never again be two nations or be divided into two kingdoms. They will no longer defile themselves with their idols and vile images or with any of their offenses, for I will save them from all their sinful backsliding, and I will cleanse them. They will be my people, and I will be their God" (37:22-23).

Note in Revelation 21, in the description of the New Jerusalem, we have a similar statement, *"Now the dwelling of God is with men, and he will live with them. They will be his people, and **God himself will be with them and be their God"** (v 3)*. In verse 7, it is personalized for the overcomer. *"He who overcomes will inherit all this, **and I will be his God** and he will be my son."*

Here in chapter 11, we note that Dan is dropped from the list of twelve, probably because of his association with idolatry. Here, too, we have a united Israel. Unrecognized in our present day as to tribe, they will be identified in the last days. This will be necessary, for one thing, in order to establish the priestly line that will officiate at the sacred altar in Ezekiel's rebuilt millennial temple.

7:2 Then I saw another angel coming up from the east, having the seal of the living God. He called out in a loud voice to the four angels who had been given power to harm the land and the sea:

This may refer to the sirocco, the hot desert wind that scorches all vegetation. God is often seen in Scripture using the weather patterns to bring either blessing or judgment upon people. Nothing in nature acts on its own, but is seen as a part of God's all-inclusive plan for his universe.

7:3 Do not harm the land or the sea or the trees until we put a seal on the foreheads of the servants of our God."

> *"Go throughout the city of Jerusalem and put **a mark on the foreheads** of those who grieve and lament over all the detestable things that are done in it . . . do not touch anyone who has the mark" (Ezekiel 9:4-6).*

In Ezekiel's day, a remnant refused to acknowledge any other gods save the one true God, and God honors them by providing protection for them, a mark on their forehead. It is interesting that the protective mark in Ezekiel 9 is literally *tav*, the last letter of the Hebrew alphabet which in ancient Hebrew was formed by + or cross, a fact that the early church recognized seeing it as a prophetic symbol of the cross used by Christian to identify themselves.

There will be such a remnant also in the last day that refuse to bow before the image erected by the false prophet of chapter 13, and they are afforded similar protection by God.

7:4 Then I heard the number of those who were sealed; 144,000 from all the tribes of Israel.

Ezekiel's describes the Remnant in the Last Day

> *"They and their children and their children's children will live there (in the land) forever, and David my servant will be their*

*prince forever. I will make **a covenant of peace** with them; it will be an everlasting covenant. I will establish them and increase their numbers, **and I will put my sanctuary among them forever**. My dwelling place will be with them; **I will be their God, and they will be my people**. Then the nations will know that I the Lord make Israel holy, when my sanctuary is among them forever"* (Ezekiel 37:25-28).

Note: A Land forever, a Prince forever, a Covenant forever, and a Sanctuary forever.

Isaiah describes the Remnant of the Last Day.

*"In that day the remnant of Israel, the survivors of the house of Jacob, will no longer rely on him who struck them down but will truly rely on the LORD, the Holy One of Israel. **A remnant will return, a remnant of Jacob will return to the Mighty God**. Though your people, O Israel, be like the sand by the sea, **only a remnant will return**. Destruction has been decreed, overwhelming and righteous.* (Isaiah 10:20-22)

7:5 From the tribe of Judah 12,000 sealed,
from the tribe of Reuben 12,000, from the tribe of Gad 12,000,

7:6 from the tribe of Asher 12,000,
from the tribe of Naphtali 12,000,
from the tribe of Manasseh 12,000,

7:7 from the tribe of Simeon 12,000,
from the tribe of Levi 12,000,
from the tribe of Issachar 12,000,

7:8 from the tribe of Zebulun 12,000,
from the tribe of Joseph 12,000,
from the tribe of Benjamin 12,000.

1. 144,000 are sealed. They are called *"servants of our God."* This probably means that they acknowledge only God as their Lord

and Master, and they resist all attempts by Antichrist to involve them in false worship.

2. They are definitely Jewish (if we do not spiritualize the passage and make them something else). They are sealed as a symbol of possession and protection.

3. The number. It is 12 x 12 x 1,000. (Twelve is the number for Israel in Scripture.) This is a perfect square multiplied by 1,000. It is an all-inclusive number, perfect and complete. It is not meant to be limiting, and is probably used in the same way that Jesus used 70 x 7 to refer to unlimited forgiveness. *Ten* and its multiples seems to symbolize *many*. Zechariah limits the surviving remnant to a third of Israel. *"Two thirds will be struck down and perish; yet one-third will be left in it (Jerusalem)" (13:8).* This group could well be a special vanguard chosen by God to be a witness to Israel of the coming kingdom.

4. A similar numbering occurred in Numbers 1 when the arrangement around the tabernacle was set as well as the order of the march. This also has the feel of an army being put together in preparation for battle.

*"So **twelve thousand men** armed for battle, a thousand from each tribe, were supplied from the clans of Israel" (Numbers 31:5)*

They appear here in chapter 7 as an army marshaled for warfare, and, in Ezekiel 37:10, revived Israel is described in similar language,

*"So I prophesied as he commanded me, and breath entered them; they came to life and stood up on their feet—**a vast army.**"*

The twelve tribes are forever memorialized by their names inscribed on the twelve gates of the New Jerusalem. "On the gates were written the names of the twelve tribes of Israel" (Revelation 21:12) Their names are also inscribed on the gates of Ezekiel's millennial city of Jerusalem, chapter 48 verses 30-35. "And the name of the city from that time on will be: The Lord is there."(v 35).

North Side	Reuben, Judah, Levi
East Side	Joseph, Benjamin, Dan
South Side	Simeon, Issachar, Zebulun
West Side	Gad, Asher, Naphtali

Paul testified before Agrippa, *"This is the promise **our twelve tribes** are hoping to see fulfilled as they earnestly serve God day and night"* (Acts 26:7). Paul is talking about Actual Israel, not Ideal Israel. Ideal Israel, according to some, is the Church.

6. When talking about the remnant in Romans 11, the apostle Paul mentions Elijah's experience in I Kings 19:10, 14 to show that God always has His remnant in every age.

   "God answered him, 'I have reserved for myself seven thousand who have not bowed the knee to Baal. So, too, at the present time there is a remnant chosen by grace . . . the elect" (Romans 11:4-5, 7)

   Then, it was 7,000; here 144,000. Although Paul is talking about the elect Israel, chosen by grace, he does not equate this remnant with the Church. They are faithful Jews who will repent and believe when Christ returns.

7. The order. Manasseh, one of the sons of Joseph, replaces Dan. Dan probably stood for idolatry.

   One (shrine) he set up in Bethel, and the other in Dan. And this thing became a sin . . . " (I Kings 12:29). *"There the Danites set up for themselves idols. (Judges 18:30)*

8. Paul speaks of the salvation of a remnant of the Jews,

   *"Though the number of the Israelites be like the sand by the sea, **only the remnant will be saved"*** (Romans 9:26 quoting from Isaiah 10:22, 23).

> *"Israel has experienced a hardening in part until the full number of the Gentiles has come in. And so **all Israel will be saved**, as it is written: 'The deliverer will come from Zion; he will turn godlessness away from Jacob. And this is my covenant with them when I take away their sins' (Rom. 11:25-27).* This is quoted from Isaiah 59:20-21

> *"The Redeemer will come to Zion, to those in Jacob who repent of their sins," declares the Lord. "As for me, **this is my covenant with them**," says the Lord.*

This remnant is somehow kept from experiencing the plagues associated with the trumpet judgments much in the same way Israel was protected in Goshen when the plagues came upon Egypt. The seal there was the blood of the lamb over the threshold, the "Passover" of the 10th plague.

Chapter 12:13-16 describes how God protects Israel, the woman crowned with twelve stars, in her flight from the dragon for a period of 1,260 days or 3 1/2 years.

It does not say that this remnant is saved at this point, but only that they are marked for protection. Their salvation occurs when the Lord comes back as Zechariah prophesied,

> *"they will look on me, the one they have pierced, and mourn for him as one mourns for an only child . . . someone asks him, 'What are these wounds on your body?' he will answer, 'The wounds I was given at the house of my friends.' (12:10; 13:6)*

Also note Revelation 1:7, *"Look, he is coming with the clouds, and every eye will see him, even those who pierced him . . . "*

Elect Israel will recognize Antichrist for who he really is, and refuse to worship his image. As the Lord warned, when they see, they will flee!

Isaiah's Further Word About the Remnant

> *In that day the Branch of the LORD will be beautiful and glorious, and the fruit of the land will be the pride and glory of the survivors*

in Israel. Those who are left in Zion, who remain in Jerusalem, will be called holy, all who are recorded among the living in Jerusalem. The Lord will wash away the filth of the women of Zion; he will cleanse the bloodstains from Jerusalem by a spirit of judgment and a spirit of fire (Isaiah 4:2-4).

A Shelter and A Shade (Revelation 7:15-16)

Then the LORD will create over all of Mount Zion and over those who assemble there a cloud of smoke by day and a glow of flaming fire by night; over all the glory will be a canopy. It will be a shelter and shade from the heat of the day, and a refuge and hiding place from the storm and rain (Isaiah 4:5,6).

Will the twelve tribes be in the millennium? Yes!

*"I tell you the truth, at the renewal of all things, when the Son of man sits on his glorious throne, you who have followed me will also sit on twelve thrones, judging **the twelve tribes of Israel**"* *(Matthew 19:28).*

Some Additional Thoughts on the Remnant

Almost all the Old Testament prophets speak of a "remnant". And this remnant is always "by grace." Only those who have trusted the promise, and by faith appropriated it are the true Israel of God. The church is born in the same way—"By grace through faith," but the church is not the spiritual successor to Israel. The Church, Paul says, is grafted into the true root and vine, and in the last day, a remnant of Israel will be grafted back in when they "by faith" acknowledge Y'shua as their true Messiah. Zechariah says that at His coming, they will believe. *"On that day"* when the nations gather against Jerusalem, and the Lord comes in His glory, the inhabitants of Jerusalem will look on Him whom they have pierced, and they will mourn for Him. A fountain of cleansing will be opened to the house of David, and a third of Israel will be spared and refined like silver and tested like gold. God will acknowledge them as His own, and they will acknowledge Him as their God (Zechariah 13:9).

What will the 144,000 be doing during the Tribulation Period? They will probably be announcing the good news of the kingdom. Jesus gives us a preview of their witness in Matthew. In chapter 10, he sends out his disciples with instructions to only go *"to the lost sheep of Israel."* As they go, they are to preach this message: *"The kingdom of heaven is near."* The kingdom was near in the sense that the King was present in their midst. Their message constituted a *bona fide* offer of the kingdom. When the Jews rejected their King, saying, *"We will not have this Man rule over us"*, Matthew's gospel becomes a sort of a rehearsal for end times, when the King will come in His glory and sit on David's throne. The criteria for witness, the transfiguration, the judgment of the nations are all previews of this last day witnessing activity. Instruction is given the witnesses as to what they are to do as they enter each town or village. They are warned about the treatment they will receive, and Jesus tells them that when they are persecuted in one place, they are to flee to another. Then He makes this interesting statement: *"I tell you the truth, you will not finish going through the cities of Israel before the Son of Man comes" (Matthew 10:22).* Did he only mean that He would rejoin them before they had completed their mission, or did He have reference to His second coming? I think the latter. The motivation of their witness is loyalty to Him. We see this in chapter 10 and verses 32 and 33, *"Whoever acknowledges me before men. I will also acknowledge him before my Father in heaven. But whoever disowns me before men, I will disown him before my Father in heaven."*

The basis of judgment when Christ judges the nations at His coming mentioned in Matthew 25, is seen here in chapter 10 verse 40 and following:

> *"He who receives you receives me, and he who receives me receives the one who sent me. Anyone who receives a prophet because he is a prophet will receive a prophet's reward, and anyone who receives a righteous man because he is a righteous man will receive a righteous man's reward. And if anyone gives even a cup of cold water to one of these little ones because he is my disciple, I tell you the truth he will certainly not lose his reward."*

So when Jesus addresses the sheep and goat nations (righteous and unrighteous), the basis of His judgment is given, *"I tell you the truth,*

*whatever you did for one of the least of these brothers of mine, you did for me"
(Matthew 25:40)*. And the reverse is true also.

As to who His "brothers" are, He has previously told us in Matthew
12:48-50, *"Who is my mother, and who are my brothers? Pointing to his disciples,
he said, "Here are my mother and my brothers. For whoever does the will of my
Father in heaven is my brother and sister and mother."* That really constitutes
a definition of the "kingdom of heaven" which is being announced. Jesus
describes the kingdom in the prayer He taught to His disciples, *"Thy kingdom
come, thy will be done on earth as it is in heaven."* That is a Hebrew parallelism:
"Thy kingdom come" is the same as *"thy will be done."* Those who believe the
message of the kingdom are obedient to the will of God. And Jesus says in
John's gospel, *"This is the will of him who sent me, that I shall lose none of all
that he has given me, but raise them up at the last day."*

So the message of the Tribulation witnesses will be the same, *"Repent,
for the kingdom of heaven (or God) is near."* And it will take on an even
greater urgency, because the coming of Christ to set up His kingdom is
just a few short months ahead.

Now this is reinforced by a few other references in Matthew. Shortly
after Peter's great confession in chapter 16, Jesus says to His disciples, *"For
the Son of Man is going to come in His Father's glory with His angels, and then
He will reward each person according to what He has done. I tell you the truth,
some who are standing here will not taste death before they see the Son of man
coming in His kingdom" (16:27-28)*. The immediate fulfillment, of course, was
His transfiguration on the mount in chapter 17 that Peter, James and John
witnessed. Moses and Elijah, who are probably the two unidentified witnesses
of Revelation chapter 11, appear and talk with Jesus presumably about His
approaching death, and what will take place just before His return.

In chapter 24, where Jesus outlines for His disciples end-time events,
He uses similar language as that in chapter 10 to describe their witness
during the period just before His return in glory. Note verse 9 and
following, *"Then you will be handed over to be persecuted and put to death,
and you will be hated by all nations because of me . . .* **And this gospel of
the kingdom will be preached in the whole world as a testimony to all
nations,** *and then the end will come" (Matthew 24:9, 14)*. And then He
says, *"When you see . . . flee."* That is, when you see the *"abomination of
desolation"* set up, flee to the mountains.

So these witnesses are loyal Jews who go out with the kingdom message
amidst a growing apostasy: *"Repent, for the kingdom of heaven is near."*

They go primarily to their fellow Israelites to warn them not to receive the mark of the beast, or worship him, but to remain loyal to the true God of Israel whose Anointed One, Christ, will appear soon to set up His kingdom. They go into every town and village in Judea and announce this good news to all. Some will believe it, most will not. That they are Jewish themselves makes their witness more forceful to their own countrymen.

Daniel refers to these as *"those who are wise will shine like the brightness of the heavens, and those who lead many to righteousness, like the stars for ever and ever" (12:3)*. And Isaiah refers to them in these words, *"How beautiful on the mountains are the feet of those who bring good news, who proclaim peace, who bring good tidings, who proclaim salvation, who say to Zion, "Your God reigns!" (52:7)*. And Paul also quotes this in relation to Israel's salvation in the last days (Rom. 10:15).

The Great Multitude

It is asserted by some that this great multitude is the same as the 144,000 mentioned above. They say that John "heard" the number of the Ideal Israel, and here he "sees" them as a great multitude that cannot be numbered. These two groups, according to their view, are two different aspects of the one, universal Church. For me, this view does not do justice to the scores of Old Testament references which speak of a remnant of Israel, a Jewish remnant, "chosen by grace", to be sure, but still ethnically Jewish. The expression "from every nation, tribe, people and language" is a general term that describes basically all people of the world. It is a phrase that simply means "all inhabitants of the earth" (Rev. 13:7-8). But here it seems to draw a distinction between Jews and Gentiles.

7:9 After this I looked and there before me was a great multitude that no one could count, from every nation, tribe, people and language, standing before the throne and in front of the Lamb. They were wearing white robes and were holding palm branches in their hands.

These words are reminiscent of the Feast of Tabernacles (Booths)

"Now on the first day you shall take for yourselves the foliage of beautiful trees, palm branches and boughs of leafy trees and

willows of the brook; and you shall rejoice before the Lord your God for seven days" (Leviticus 23:40).

7:10 And they cried out in a loud voice: "Salvation belongs to our God, who sits on the throne, and to the Lamb."

They are seen in heaven as the victorious multitude in chapter 15, and their song is the same as the great multitude mentioned in chapter 19.

7:11 All the angels were standing around the throne and around the elders and the four living creatures. They fell down on their faces before the throne and worshiped God,

7:12 saying: "Amen! Praise and glory and wisdom and thanks and honor and power and strength be to our God forever and ever. Amen!"

Note again the sevenfold ascription of praise:

1. Praise
2. Glory
3. Wisdom
4. Thanks
5. Honor
6. Power
7. Strength

7:13 Then one of the elders asked me, "These in white robes—who are they, and where did they come from?"

7:14 I answered, "Sir, you know." And he said, "These are they who have come out of the great tribulation; they have washed their robes and made them white in the blood of the Lamb.

This group is distinguished from the 144,000. They come from all tribes and peoples and tongues and are said to come "out of the great tribulation." They have washed their robes in the blood of the Lamb meaning that they have discovered the secret of purity and victory in what Jesus Christ did for them on the cross. These are probably martyred ones, perhaps the ones who would be killed referred to in 6:11. They are those referred to in the "new song" in Revelation 5:9. Surely they are the redeemed Church!

> *"You are worthy to take the scroll and to open its seals, because you were slain, and with your blood you purchased men for God from every tribe and language and people and nation. You have made them to be a kingdom of priests to serve our God, and they will reign on the earth."*

To have come *out of* the great tribulation they must have been *in* the great tribulation. They are most likely identical with the great host of persecuted saints mentioned in chapters 12 and 13, many of whom are killed by the Antichrist and his False Prophet.

7:15 Therefore, they are before the throne of God and serve him day and night in his temple; and he who sits on the throne will spread his tent over them.

Many, however, believe these are the raptured church, thus concluding that the rapture occurs in the middle of the tribulation period of seven years or, as in the pre-wrath view, in the middle of the last 3 1/2 years. But the message to the souls under the altar in connection with the fifth seal is to wait until the rest of your brethren who will be killed is completed. Here the multitude is viewed proleptically, having to face tribulation, but viewed as if they were already delivered and standing before the Lord in heaven.

7:16 Never again will they hunger; never again will they thirst. The sun will not beat upon them, nor any scorching heat.

7:17 For the Lamb at the center of the throne will be their shepherd; he will lead them to springs of living water. And God will wipe away every tear from their eyes."

The two groups are seen again in chapter 12, the Israeli Remnant pursued and protected, and the Beast making war with the saints, and putting many of them to death, because of their refusal to worship his image or receive his mark. Still again, the two groups are seen in chapter

14 at the coming of the Lord. The multitude from heaven is singing the new song of the redeemed in welcoming the newly redeemed 144,000. And later in the chapter the rapture and the resurrection are represented under the figure of the harvest. Just before the seven bowls of wrath are poured out, a great multitude is seen by the sea of glass, victorious over the beast, and praising God with the song of Moses and the Lamb, both songs of deliverance. A great multitude appears again in chapter 19 singing the Hallelujah Chorus, and sitting down with the Lord at His marriage supper, and event that is also synonymous with the rapture (John 14:2-3).

The Bliss of the Blessed

Here is pictured the eternal blessedness of the redeemed. They find their rest in Him. Christ is the end of the world's hunger, thirst, pain and sorrow. The description here has similarities to The Feast of Tabernacles that evidently will be celebrated during the millennial age.

The blessedness is sevenfold:

1. His tabernacle over them
2. Hunger no more
3. Thirst no more
4. No more intense heat
5. Shepherded by the Lamb
6. Guided to living water
7. Eyes wiped of every tear

Something similar is said of Israel when the nation is restored to the land,

> *"They will feed beside the roads and find pasture on every barren hill. They will neither hunger nor thirst, nor will the desert heat or the sun beat upon them. He who has compassion on them will guide them and lead them beside springs of water" (Isaiah 49:9,10)*

Note the interesting figure—the Lamb is their Shepherd! It is equivalent to "The Lord is my Shepherd!" with the added thought of John 10—he laid down His life!

CHAPTER 8

7
The Seventh Seal—Silence

8:1 When he opened the seventh seal, there was silence in heaven for about half an hour.

This is a dramatic pause that heightens the anticipation of what will follow, and allows the prayers of all the saints to be offered. In Tobit 12:15 there are "seven holy angels" that present the prayers of the saints, and which go in and out before the glory of the Holy One. There is also an interesting passage found in Alfred Edersheim's book *The Temple* that throws light on the significance here of the silence, and the offering to follow.

> "As the president gave the word of command, which marked that 'the time of incense had come,' 'the whole multitude of the people without' withdrew from the inner court, and fell down before the Lord, spreading their hands in silent prayer.
>
> It is this most solemn period, when throughout the vast Temple buildings deep silence rested on the worshiping multitude, while within the sanctuary itself the priest laid the incense on the golden altar, and the cloud of 'odors' rose up before the Lord, which serves as the image of heavenly things in this description." (Alfred Edersheim, *The Temple: its Ministry and Services as They Were at the Time of Jesus Christ*, Grand Rapids: William B. Eerdmans, 1980, p. 167).

8:2 And I saw the seven angels who stand before God, and to them were given seven trumpets.

These angels are called the Angels of the Presence. They are probably archangels, of superior rank, who are assigned very important tasks by God. The angel Gabriel who spoke to Joseph and Mary is said to *"stand in the presence of God."* (Luke 1:19). The ancient apocryphal book of Enoch assigns names to each of them:

1. Uriel
2. Raphael
3. Raguel
4. **Michael**
5. Sarakiel
6. **Gabriel**
7. Remiel)

> "These are the names of the angels who watch. Uriel, one of the holy angels, who presides over clamor and terror; Raphael, one of the holy angels, who presides over the spirits of men; Raguel, one of the holy angels, who inflicts punishment on the world and the luminaries; Michael, one of the holy angels, who, presiding over human virtue, commands the nations; Sarakiel, one of the holy angels, who presides over the spirits of the children of men that transgress; Gabriel, one of the holy angels, who presides over Ikesat, over paradise, and over the cherubim." (Enoch 20).

Their names all end with "el" which is short for the name of God.

8:3 Another angel, who had a golden censer, came and stood at the altar. He was given much incense to offer, with the prayers of all the saints, on the golden altar before the throne.

The Altar

> *"Behind the second curtain was a room called the Most Holy Place, which had the golden altar of incense and the gold-covered Ark of the Covenant" (Hebrews 9:3-4).*

> *"Make an altar of acacia wood for burning incense. It is to be square, a cubit long and a cubit wide, and two cubits high (1 1/2 ft. long and wide and about 3 ft. high) . . . Aaron must burn fragrant incense on the altar every morning when he tends the lamps. He must burn incense again when he lights the lamps at twilight so incense will burn regularly before the Lord for the generations to come" (Exodus 30:1-2, 7-8).*

What does this say to us about the need and efficacy of regular times of prayer?

> *"They serve at a sanctuary that is a copy and shadow of what is in heaven. This is why Moses was warned when he was about to build the tabernacle: "See to it that you make everything according to the pattern shown you on the mountain."" (Hebrews 8:5).*

8:4 The smoke of the incense, together with the prayers of the saints, went up before God from the angel's hand.

> *"May my prayer be set before you like incense; may the lifting up of my hands be like the evening sacrifice" (Psalm 141:2).*

There is one prayer yet unanswered that has been prayed by God's people through the centuries of time. It is the prayer our Lord taught us to pray, *"Your kingdom come, your will be done on earth as it is in heaven."* That prayer is about to be answered!

Terminus To Seals

8:5 Then the angel took the censer, filled it with fire from the altar, and hurled it on the earth; and there came peals of thunder, rumblings, flashes of lightning and an earthquake.

This last sentence represents a terminus statement that occurs with slight variation at the end of the trumpet judgments (11:19) and the bowl judgments (16:18).

The Closing Drama at The End of The Age

This type of judgment occurred in Ezekiel's day because of Israel's awful transgression.

> *The Lord said to the man clothed in linen, "Go in among the wheels beneath the cherubim. Fill your hands with burning coals from among the cherubim and scatter them over the city" (Ezekiel 10:2).*

8:6 Then the seven angels who had the seven trumpets prepared to sound them.

Some believe that the trumpet judgments are a part of the Day of the Lord, but that Day is more fittingly represented by the Bowls of Wrath. The Day of the Lord is climactic. It is synonymous with Christ's Coming in glory that is also climactic. The trumpet judgments are partial—a third, and occur during the period of The Great Tribulation or last 3 1/2 years. The "third" may mean that God assigns His limit (three is the number for God) to the judgments in order to affect a remedial purpose. Judgments can frighten, sober, correct, humble, and even reassure. Habakkuk prays, "*In wrath, remember mercy.*" Isaiah 28:21 calls judgment God's *"strange work . . . his alien task."* And Peter reminds us that God does not want anyone to perish, but everyone to come to repentance (2 Peter 3:9). Consider these references from Joel

> *2:13 "Rend your heart and not your garments. Return to the Lord your God, for he is gracious and compassionate, slow to anger and abounding in love, and* **he relents from sending calamity.**" *(A remedial purpose)*

> *2:15 "Blow the trumpet in Zion, declare a holy fast, call a sacred assembly." (Trumpets warn)*

1st Trumpet

8:7 The first angel sounded his trumpet, and there came hail and fire mixed with blood, and it was hurled down upon the earth. A third of the earth was burned up, a third of the trees were burned up, and all the green grass was burned up.

This is very similar to the seventh plague that fell on Egypt during Moses' confrontation of Pharaoh, although minus the element of fire.

2nd Trumpet

8:8 The second angel sounded his trumpet, and something like a huge mountain, all ablaze, was thrown into the sea. A third of the sea turned into blood, a third of the living creatures in the sea died, and a third of the ships were destroyed.

This could be a volcanic eruption or a huge meteor falling out of space into the ocean. The sea becomes blood red. There is no reason that this couldn't be actual blood, perhaps the blood of the sea creatures killed by the falling object.

3rd Trumpet

8:10 The third angel sounded his trumpet, and a great star, blazing like a torch, fell from the sky on a third of the rivers and on the springs of water—

8:11 the name of the star is Wormwood. A third of the waters turned bitter, and many people died from the waters that had become bitter.

This may be a comet that poisons the waters by emitting some sort of radiation. A fore= gleam of this might have been the atomic accident at Chernobyl.

> "Therefore, this is what the Lord Almighty, the God of Israel, says: 'See, I will make this people eat bitter food and drink poisoned water'" (Jeremiah 9:15; 23:15).

4th Trumpet

8:12 The fourth angel sounded his trumpet, and a third of the sun was struck, a third of the moon, and a third of the stars, so that a third of them turned dark. A third of the day was without light, and also a third of the night.

> *"Then the Lord said to Moses, 'Stretch out your hand toward the sky so that darkness will spread over Egypt—darkness that can be felt'" (Exodus 10:21).*

> The Lord said, *"There will be signs in the sun, moon and stars. On the earth, nations will be in anguish and perplexity at the roaring and tossing of the sea. Men will faint from terror, apprehensive of what is coming on the world, for the heavenly bodies will be shaken" (Luke 21:25-26).*

8:13 As I watched, I heard an eagle that was flying in midair call out in a loud voice: "Woe! Woe! Woe to the inhabitants of the earth, because of the trumpet blasts about to be sounded by the other three angels!"

Perhaps you have noticed that each of the judgment series is divided 4 + 3. The first four relate, in each case, to the physical and the latter 3 to the spiritual. The series of three judgments could be referred to as "bad," "worse," and "worst." They end in a crescendo.

CHAPTER 9

5th Trumpet

First Woe

9:1 The fifth angel sounded his trumpet, and I saw a star that had fallen from the sky to the earth. The star was given the key to the shaft of the Abyss (the bottomless pit).

This star appears to be an angel. Angels are sometimes referred to as stars. That the angel is described as "fallen" need only refer to the metaphor of a falling star, and not to his status as a "fallen" angel. He is another of God's angelic messengers bent on a mission. He has the key to the "shaft" that prevents these supernatural beings from escaping.

9:2 When he opened the Abyss, smoke rose from it like the smoke from a gigantic furnace. The sun and sky were darkened by the smoke from the Abyss.

> *"And the angels who did not keep their positions of authority but abandoned their own home—these he has kept in darkness, bound with everlasting chains for judgment on the great Day" (Jude 6).*

The Abyss, or bottomless pit, which is mentioned nine times in the New Testament, is a prison for supernatural beings. Demonic beings are consigned there, and will be tormented there (Mark 8:29). The beast of

Revelation 11:7, 8 will ascend from there, and Satan will be chained and imprisoned there during the millennial age.

The Demonic Locusts

9:3 And out of the smoke locusts came down upon the earth.

9:4 They were told not to harm the grass of the earth or any plant or tree, but only those people who did not have the seal of God on their foreheads.

Again God's people are protected from this plague much as Israel was during the plagues on Egypt. This was one of the reasons for the sealing of the 144,000 in chapter 7. The sealing was for protection. It does not mean that they were believers at this time.

9:5 They were not given power to kill them, but only to torture them for five months. And the agony they suffered was like that of the sting of a scorpion when it strikes a man.

This appears to be demonic oppression of the very worst kind. They are given scorpion like "authority," or stinging power to torment their victims. Many scholars feel that the "five months" should not be taken literally, but there is no good reason why the period should not be viewed as literal. The time period underscores the severity of the torment.

9:6 During those days men will seek death, but will not find it; they will long to die, but death will elude them.

Their Appearance

9:7 The locusts looked like horses prepared for battle. On their heads they wore something like crowns of gold, and their faces resembled human faces.

9:8 Their hair was like woman's hair, and their teeth were like lions' teeth.

9:9 They had breastplates like breastplates of iron, and the sound of their wings was like the thundering of many horses and chariots rushing into battle.

9:10 They had tails and stings like scorpions, and in their tails they had power to torment people for five months.

9:11 They had as king over them the angel of the Abyss, whose name in Hebrew is Abaddon, and in Greek, Apollyon.

The Destroyer. One of Satan's highest and most powerful devils. Since the Antichrist is said to come up out of the Abyss, some have suggested that this sinister demonic king of demons, Apollyon, is the Satanic controlled Man of Lawlessness mentioned by Paul in 2 Thessalonians 2:3 since Paul refers to him as "the son of destruction (abaddon)." It is interesting that Jesus referred to Judas, the betrayer, as "the son of perdition (abaddon).

9:12 The first woe is past; two other woes are yet to come.

6th Trumpet

Second Woe

9:13 The sixth angel blew his trumpet, and I heard a voice coming from the horns of the golden altar that is before God.

9:14 It said to the sixth angel who had the trumpet, 'Release the four angels who are bound at the great river Euphrates.'

9:15 And the four angels who had been kept ready for this very hour and day and month and year were released to kill a third of mankind.

"Hour, day, month and year"=indicates that God has a predetermined plan for end time events. These four angels will *"kill a third of mankind"*

which probably means that they will lead this vast army to destroy a third of mankind (see v 19).

The Horses And Riders

9:16 The number of the mounted troops was two hundred million. I heard their number.

This number staggers the imagination. All the existing armies of the earth put together do not number 200 million. We need not assume that this vast army all comes from the East. That the angels are four probably stands for the number of worldwide human government. Here is a coalition of armies from north, east, south and west linking in the plain of Megiddo or Armageddon where they will be finally judged at the coming of Christ.

9:17 The horses and riders I saw in my vision looked like this: Their breastplates were fiery red, dark blue, and yellow as sulfur. The heads of the horses resembled the heads of lions, and out of their mouths came fire, smoke and sulfur.

We may have modern warfare here described in military terms of John's day. Acquainted with modern warfare, one can almost see the tanks, cannon fire, helicopters with machine-guns and missile launchers.

This vast army on horseback seems to be different than the locusts of the fifth trumpet. The locusts torment while these kill.

9:18 A third of mankind was killed by the three plagues of fire, smoke and sulfur that came out of their mouths.

9:19 The power of the horses was in their mouths and in their tails; for their tails were like snakes, having heads with which they inflict injury.

The Effect

9:20 The rest of mankind that were not killed by these plagues still did not repent of the work of their hands; they did not stop

worshiping demons, and idols of gold, silver, bronze, stone and wood—idols that cannot see or hear or walk.

9:21 Nor did they repent of their murders, their magic arts, their sexual immorality or their thefts.

Seven sins are mentioned closely paralleling the 10 commandments in Exodus 20. These verses seem to underscore the point that God's judgments were meant to be remedial, but on most the effect was the opposite even as it was with Pharaoh of old. The sun softens the wax but hardens the clay.

CHAPTER 10

1
The Mighty Angel

10:1 Then I saw another mighty angel coming down from heaven. He was robed in a cloud, with a rainbow above his head; his face was like the sun, and his legs were like fiery pillars.

Some identify this angel with Christ, but it is probably another of the archangels. Another "mighty angel" is mentioned in chapter 5:2, in connection with the seven-sealed scroll. He proclaims in a loud voice, *"Who is worthy to break the seals and open the scroll?"* This may well be the same angel.

The other archangel mentioned in Daniel, along with Michael, is Gabriel. He appears several times to Daniel, and was awesome to behold.

> *"I looked up and there before me was a man dressed in linen, with a belt of finest gold around his waist. His body was like chrysolite, his face like lightning, his eyes like flaming torches, his arms and legs like the gleam of burnished bronze, and his voice like the sound of a multitude" (Daniel 10:4-6).*

Daniel was left virtually helpless, and needed to be strengthened in order to hear the message of the angel.

2
The Little Scroll

10:2 He was holding a little scroll, which lay open in his hand. He planted his right foot on the sea and his left foot on the land,

The sealed scroll probably refers to the sealed scroll in Daniel 12, *". . . close up and seal the words of the scroll until the time of the end." (v.4)*. The "time of the end" is now very close. The question is asked of the man (angel) clothed in linen, who was above the waters of the river, *"How long will it be before these astonishing things are fulfilled?"* The reply was, *"It will be for a time, times and a half time."* This is the same time frame that is repeated in Revelation 11, 12 and 13. So the angel here in chapter 10 is now revealing what was sealed. The redemption of Israel is now drawing near. Antichrist will be defeated in 1290 days, three and one half years plus 30 days. Israel will be refined and then the remnant will be revived and redeemed.

> *"Come, let us return to the Lord. He has torn us to pieces but he will heal us; he has injured us but he will bind up our wounds. After two days he will revive us; on the third day he will restore us that we may live in his presence. Let us acknowledge the Lord; let us press on to acknowledge him. As surely as the sun rises, he will appear; he will come to us like the winter rains, like the spring rains that water the earth" (Hosea 6:1-3)*

10:3 and he gave a loud shout like the roar of a lion. When he shouted the voices of the seven thunders spoke.

> *"They will follow the Lord; he will roar like a lion. When he roars, his children will come trembling from the west. They will come trembling like birds from Egypt, like doves from Assyria. I will settle them in their homes," declares the Lord" (Hosea 11:10-11).*

3
The Seven Thunders

10:4 And when the seven thunders spoke, I was about to write; but I heard a voice from heaven say, "Seal up what the seven thunders have said and do not write it down."

We obviously do not know what the seven thunders spoke, but they may be another series of judgments which God had prepared, but cancels when the response of the remedial trumpet judgments met with unrepentant hearts (9:21). Now without delay, events will move to their appointed climax.

10:5 Then the angel I had seen standing on the sea and on the land raised his right hand to heaven.

Gabriel, who interprets Daniel's vision (8:15), may also be the angel *"above the waters of the river"* in Daniel 12:7 who lifts both hands toward heaven and swears by him who lives forever, saying *"It will be for a time, times and half a time."*

> *"The man clothed in linen, who was above the waters of the river, lifted his right hand and his left hand toward heaven, and I heard him swear by him who lives forever, saying, "It will be **for a time, times and half a time**. When the power of the holy people has been finally broken, all these things will be completed."*

Notice the similarity of wording in the next verse. The message is that all delay is over, and the period of the end is irrevocably set in motion. The Gentiles will occupy the city for 3 1/2 years. The two witnesses will testify for the same period of time. The dragon will persecute the people of God and they will be protected for the same period of time, and the Lawless One will persecute the saints for the same period of time. Then the seventh trumpet will be blown, Christ will come in His glory, and the bowls of wrath will be poured out in quick succession on the earth.

4
The Solemn Oath

10:6 And he swore by him who lives for ever and ever, who created the heavens and all that is in them, the earth and all that is in it, and the sea and all that is in it, and said, "There will be no more delay!

Chapter 10 is a timeframe marker. It announces the suspension of God's "delay" and indicates that the events of the last 3 1/2 years will now move toward the climax of the ages.

5
The Mystery of God

10:7 But in the days when the seventh angel is about to sound his trumpet, the mystery of God will be accomplished, just as he announced to his servants the prophets."

The "mystery of God" probably refers to the salvation of Israel. Paul wrote,

> *"I do not want you to be ignorant of **this mystery**, brothers, so that you may not be conceited: Israel has experienced a hardening in part until the full number of the Gentiles has come in. And so all Israel will be saved, as it is written: 'The deliverer will come from Zion; he will turn godlessness away from Jacob. And this is my covenant with them when I take away their sins." (Romans 11:25-27)*

The unveiling (apocalypse) will now take place. Christ will return, the kingdom established, and God's enemies destroyed. Is it possible to construct an itinerary of the Lord's coming? Let me suggest one:

1. He will go first to Edom, where the remnant of Israel has sheltered, then to Jerusalem and Mount Zion.

   > *"Who is this coming from Edom, from Bozrah, with his garments stained crimson? Who is this, robed in splendor, striding forward*

in the greatness of his strength 'It is I, speaking in righteousness, mighty to save.' I have trodden the winepress alone; from the nations no one was with me. I trampled them in my anger and trod them down in my wrath; their blood spattered my garments, and I stained all my clothing. For the day of vengeance was in my heart, and the year of my redemption has come." (Isaiah 63:1-4).

The prophet Micah speaks to this event:

"I will surely gather all of you, O Jacob; I will surely bring together the remnant of Israel. I will bring them together like sheep in a pen, like a flock in its pasture; the place will throng with people. One who breaks open the way will go up before them; they will break through the gate and go out. Their king will pass through before them, the Lord at their head" (Micah 2:12-13).

Habakkuk also speaks of this coming from Edom:

"God came from Teman (an Edomite village), the Holy One from Mount Paran (borders Edom and Sinai). His glory covered the heavens and his praise filled the earth. His splendor was like the sunrise; rays flashed from his hand, where his power was hidden" (Habakkuk 3:3-4).

2. The Mystery of God Completed

The end of Daniel's seventieth week marks the end of Gentile domination, and Israel's penalty as a nation for unbelief. A few days after the Seventieth Week ends, *"all Israel will be saved . . . "* Israel is saved just before the seventh trumpet sounds. *"He will revive us after two days; He will raise us up on the third day" (Hosea 6:2).* It was on the third day that God established the Old Covenant with Israel on Sinai (Exodus19:5, 8, 10, 11, 16, 17) The New Covenant parallels the Old Covenant. Three days after Israel atones for her sins, saying *"Come, let us return to the Lord" (Hosea 6:1),* the New Covenant will be established with Israel. Then *"He will raise us up on the third day that we may live before Him" (v 2).*

217

3. The Two Witnesses are Brought Back to Life

"But after three and a half days a breath of life from God entered them, and they stood on their feet." (Rev. 11:11). A great earthquake occurs.

4. The Seventh Trumpet Sounds

"And the kingdom of the world becomes the kingdom of our Lord and of his Christ, and he will reign forever and ever" (Rev. 11:15).

5. Christ On Mount Zion

The Mount of Olives splits forming a valley through which the remnant of Israel might flee to escape the utter devastation about to fall on Jerusalem.

"On that day his feet will stand on the Mount of Olives, east of Jerusalem, and the Mount of Olives will be split in two from east to west, forming a great valley, with half of the mountain moving north and half moving south. You will flee by my mountain valley, for it will extend to Azel. You will flee as you fled from the earthquake in the days of Uzziah king of Judah. Then the Lord God will come, and all the holy ones with him." (Zechariah 14:4-5).

6. The Harvest of the Earth—The Rapture takes place

The Bema Seat of Christ—Christ returns to heaven, right after the seventh trumpet sounds. *". . . the time came for the dead to be judged . . . to give their reward to Thy bond-servants the prophets and to the saints and to those who fear Thy name . . . " (Rev. 11:18).*

". . . his work will be shown for what it is, because that Day will bring it to light. It will be revealed with fire, and the fire will test the quality of each man's work" (I Corinthians 3:13).

> *"For we must all appear before the judgment seat of Christ, that each one may receive what is due him for the things done while in the body, whether good or bad" (II Corinthians 5:10).*

Men should have been amply warned by the message of the prophets that God would judge iniquity.

> *He said to them, "How foolish you are, and how slow of heart to believe all that the prophets have spoken! Did not the Christ have to suffer these things and then enter his glory? And beginning with Moses and all the Prophets, he explained to them what was said in all the Scriptures concerning himself" (Luke 24:25-27).*

> *"He said to him, 'If they do not listen to Moses and the Prophets, they will not be convinced even is someone rises from the dead'" (Luke 16:31).*

10:8 Then the voice that I had heard from heaven spoke to me once more: "Go, take the scroll that lies open in the hand of the angel who is standing on the sea and on the land."

6
Eating the Scroll

10:9 So I went to the angel and asked him to give me the little scroll. He said to me, "Take it and eat it. It will turn your stomach sour, but in your mouth it will be as sweet as honey."

10:10 I took the little scroll from the angel's hand and ate it. It tasted as sweet as honey in my mouth, but when I had eaten it, my stomach turned sour.

> *"Then I looked, and I saw a hand stretched out to me. In it was a scroll, which he unrolled before me. On both sides of it were written words of lament and mourning and woe. And he said to me, "Son of man, eat what is before you, eat this scroll; then go and speak to the house of Israel." So I opened my mouth, and he gave*

me the scroll to eat. Then he said to me, "Son of man, eat this scroll
I am giving you and fill your stomach with it." So I ate it, and it
tasted as sweet as honey in my mouth" (Ezekiel 2:9-3:3).

On both sides of this scroll were written words of lament and mourning and woe. That is probably the case here also, for when John digests the message, it makes him ill.

10:11 Then I was told, "You must prophesy again about many peoples, nations, languages and kings."

7
The Command To Prophesy

This expression is common in Revelation referring to people worldwide who must hear the message.

"And whether they listen or fail to listen—for they are a rebellious
house—they will know that a prophet has been among them. You
must speak my words to them, whether they listen or fail to listen,
for they are rebellious. But you, son of man, listen to what I say to
you. Do not rebel like that rebellious house; open your mouth and
eat what I give you" (Ezekiel 2:5).

CHAPTER 11

THE TWO WITNESSES

11:1 I was given a reed like a measuring rod and was told, "Go and measure the temple of God and the altar, and count the worshipers there.

Great differences exist in interpreting this chapter. The differences come in whether the chapter is viewed in a literal manner, or considered highly symbolic. I have chosen the former approach since the latter opens up a whole range of hypothetical views regarding what the symbols are supposed to convey. I believe that the temple is an actual temple reconstructed in the last day, the two witnesses are actual persons, either Moses and Elijah themselves, or two who are modeled after Moses and Elijah, and come with the power or authority of both. The temple had been destroyed almost 20 years before this was written. This presupposes the rebuilding of the temple in Jerusalem.

Both Joshua and Zerubbabel were associated with the ancient temple, Joshua as its priest and Zerubabbel as its rebuilder.

Measuring the temple (the inner sanctuary) may be a call by God for his people to repent, and turn to Him without reservation. Measuring was a means to distinguish or divide between the holy and the profane. Some believe that it was actually and act signifying preservation, and has as its background Ezekiel 40-42 where every part of the prophesied restoration of the temple is carefully measured. Why would this signify preservation? Daniel tells us that *"the ruler that will come"* will desecrate the temple at the midpoint of the seven-year period, and break his covenant. The sanctuary is to be trodden under foot by "the little horn" and his pagan followers ushering in a great persecution of the people of God.

Ezekiel goes on to describes the measuring of the temple as a call to repentance.

> *"I will live among them forever. Son of man, describe the temple to the people of Israel, that they may be ashamed of their sins. Let them consider the plan, and if they are ashamed of all they have done, make known to them the design of the temple—its arrangement, its exits and entrance—its whole design and all its regulations and laws. Write these down before them so that they may be faithful to its design and follow its regulations" (Ezekiel 43:10-11).*

11:2 But exclude the outer court; do not measure it, because it has been given to the Gentiles. They will trample on the holy city for 42 months.

> *"When you see Jerusalem surrounded by armies, you will know that its desolation is near. Then let those who are in Judea flee to the mountains, let those in the city get out, and let those in the country not enter the city. For this is the time of punishment in fulfillment of all that has been written. (Luke 21:20)*

This is part of why John was commanded to *"prophecy again about many peoples, nations, languages, and kings" (10:11).* The time period is 3 1/2 years, and the occupying force is probably those 10 confederated nations over which Antichrist rules. This specific time designation is borrowed from Daniel's prophecy, and denotes a period of great suffering under the despotic rule of "the little horn."

This time period suggests that the time of Gentile domination, the duration of the testimony borne by the two witnesses, the pursuit and persecution by the Dragon of the Woman, and the conquering of the Saints by The Beast out of the Sea are simultaneous. This surely refers to the last half of the 7 year period known as The Great Tribulation, and to the Times of the Gentiles that will cease at the coming of the Lord in glory to inaugurate his reign of righteousness. Daniel's colossus will soon come tumbling down!

Luke confirms this,

> *"For this is the time of punishment in fulfillment of all that has been written. How dreadful it will be in those days for pregnant*

*women and nursing mothers! There will be great distress in the land and wrath against this people. They will fall by the sword and will be taken as prisoners to all the nations. **Jerusalem will be trampled on by the Gentiles until the times of the Gentiles are fulfilled"** (Luke 21:22-24).*

So the time frame is 42 months, and immediately after this, in Luke's account, the celestial signs appear in heaven marking the conclusion of The Great Tribulation, and ushering in the Day of the Lord and Christ's return. The Times of the Gentiles concludes when the Lord returns to judge the nations and inaugurate His kingdom.

Preterists believe that this refers to the destruction of Jerusalem under Titus in 70 A.D, and marks the transition from the Old Covenant to the New. It is true that the siege of Jerusalem under Vespasian and Titus did last a literal three and a half years, from 67 to 70, but Daniel reveals that "the times of the Gentiles" will not end until the "toes" of the colossus and the "horns" of the fourth beast appear—a confederation of 10 kingdoms in the last day under the dominion of the world's last great dictator. The Fall of Jerusalem did not include the Second Coming of Christ, the end of the world, and the final rapture and revelation of God's people. This must still be future.

11:3 And I will give power (grant authority) to my two witnesses, and they will prophesy for 1,260 days, clothed in sackcloth.

Again the time period is 3 1/2 years during which time the two witnesses prophesy. The sackcloth is a sign of mourning and repentance.

11:4 These are the two olive trees and the two lampstands that stand before the Lord of the earth.

> *"I see a solid gold lampstand with a bowl at the top and seven lights on it, with seven channels to the lights. Also there are two olive trees by it, one on the right of the bowl and the other on its left." Then I asked him, "What are these two olive branches beside the two gold pipes that pour out golden oil?" He replied, "These are the two who are anointed to serve the Lord of all the earth . . . **Not by might nor by power, but by my Spirit, says the Lord Almighty** (Zechariah 4:2-3, 5, 12-14).*

In this instance, they are Joshua the high priest and Zerubbabel. These are God's "former day" witnesses. Moses and Elijah are His "latter day" witnesses. As prophetic witnesses they fulfill the role of kings (like Zerubbabel) and priests (like Joshua). The emphasis is upon their empowerment by the Holy Spirit for their prophetic ministry.

11:5 If anyone tries to harm them, fire comes from their mouths and devours their enemies. This is how anyone who wants to harm them must die.

> *"I will make my words in your mouth a fire and these people the wood it consumes." (Jeremiah 5:14).*

> *"Is not my word like fire?" declares the Lord. (Jeremiah 23:29)*

> *Elijah answered the captain, "If I am a man of God, may fire come down from heaven and consume you and your fifty men!" Then fire fell from heaven and consumed the captain and his men. (2 Kings 1:10).*

11:6 These men have power to shut up the sky so that it will not rain during the time they are prophesying;

God has given these two the choice of what plagues to use and how often they strike.

> *"Elijah was a man just like us. He prayed earnestly that it would not rain, and it did not rain on the land for three and a half years" (James 5:17).*

> *"Remember the law of my servant **Moses,** the decrees and laws I gave him at Horeb for all Israel. See, I will send you the prophet **Elijah** before that great and dreadful day of the Lord comes. He will turn the hearts of the fathers to their children, and the hearts of the children to their fathers; or else I will come and strike the land with a curse" (Malachi 4:4-6).*

The priests and Levites were well aware that Elijah was to come and prepare the way for Messiah. When they came to John, the first thing they asked him was, *"Are you Elijah? Are you the Prophet (Moses)?* John replied, *"Neither."* *"I am the voice of one calling in the desert, 'Make straight the way of the Lord.'" (John 1:19-23)* Even modern Jews, in observing the Sedar or Passover meal, leave an empty chair in anticipation of Elijah's coming. He was to be a minister of reconciliation and restoration to Israel. It seems natural that God would send these two, Moses and Elijah, before the Second Advent to prepare His way.

Why is it necessary to say these two are symbols of something else, and not real people fulfilling a specific role as forerunners of the coming Christ?

> *"Why then do the teachers of the law say that Elijah must come first?" Jesus replied, "To be sure, Elijah comes and will restore all things."(Matthew 17:10-11).*

Here in this reference Jesus says that John the Baptist, in a sense, was Elijah, coming in the spirit and power of Elijah, and doing essentially what Elijah would do when he comes to be the forerunner of Christ's second coming.

. . . and they have power to turn the waters into blood and to strike the earth with every kind of plague as often as they want.

> *"Moses . . . raised his staff in the presence of Pharaoh and his officials and struck the water of the Nile, and all the water was changed into blood" (Exodus 7:20).*

It was Moses and Elijah who *actually* appeared with Jesus on the Mount of Transfiguration.

> *"And behold, two men were talking with Him; and they were Moses and Elijah, who, appearing in glory, were speaking of His departure which He was about to accomplish at Jerusalem" (Luke 9:30, 31).*

Jesus said this was a glimpse of the kingdom of God. *"I tell you the truth, some who are standing here will not taste death before they see the kingdom of God" (v 27).*

Moses and Elijah, then, are the best choices to identity these two. They represent both the Law and the Prophets, and will powerfully convince from the Scriptures, those who have a heart for God, that Jesus is their true Messiah.

Note, too, that this is how Jesus taught his disciples and the people—from Moses and the Prophet—that He was the long promised One.

> *"They have **Moses and the Prophets**; let them listen to them . . . . "*
> *If they do not listen to Moses and the Prophets, they will not be convinced even if someone rises from the dead" (Luke 16:29, 31).*

> *He said to them, "How foolish you are, and how slow of heart to believe all that the prophets have spoken! And beginning with **Moses and all the Prophets**, he explained to them what was said in all the Scriptures concerning himself" (Luke 24:25-26).*

> *"This is what I told you while I was still with you: Everything must be fulfilled that is written about me in the Law **of Moses, the Prophets and the Psalms**" (Luke 24:44).*

> *"I am saying nothing beyond what **the prophets and Moses** said would happen—that the Christ would suffer and, as the first to rise form the dead, would proclaim light to his own people and to the Gentiles" (Acts 26:22-23).*

Witnesses Killed

11:7 Now when they have finished their testimony, the beast that comes up from the Abyss will attack them, and overpower and kill them.

For 3 1/2 years these witnesses faithfully testify to the salvation in Christ and the impending judgment of God on a wicked world. They are protected until their witness is completed. That God sent them is another indication that he is giving mankind one more chance before His terrible wrath is outpoured.

The "beast" is said to come out of the Abyss, which underscores his demonic origin and character. He is later pictured as coming up out of the sea. The sea represents the nations of the world (17:15). His bestial nature shows him to be both brutal and dangerous.

11:8 Their bodies will lie in the street of the great city, which is figuratively called Sodom and Egypt, where also their Lord was crucified.

Some see the "great city" here as referring to Rome, but the final phrase would lend support for it being Jerusalem. Sodom and Egypt, figuratively, represent God's visitation in judgment on the nation Israel for their refusal to believe. Sodom refers to a city and Egypt to a country, and Jerusalem and Israel will likewise fall under judgment.

> *"And among the prophets of Jerusalem I have seen something horrible: They commit adultery and live a lie. They strengthen the hands of evildoers, so that no one turns from his wickedness. They are all like Sodom to me; the people of Jerusalem are like Gomorrah" (Jeremiah 23:14).*

> *"Unless the Lord Almighty had left us some survivors, we would have become like Sodom, we would have been like Gomorrah" (Isaiah 1:9).*

11:9 For three and half days men from every people, tribe, language and nation will gaze on their bodies and refuse them burial.

Notice the response of the peoples of the whole world to the prophetic message. Here again is a reason for John's continuing prophecy against the nations. We have no problem today understanding how the peoples of the earth could simultaneously view this scene. Their collective hatred and anger is evident.

11:10 The inhabitants of the earth will gloat over them and will celebrate by sending each other gifts, because these two prophets had tormented those who live on the earth.

The "inhabitants of the earth" celebrate the death of the witnesses. The rejoicing seems to be a perverse version of the Feast of Purim—*"a day for gladness and feasting . . . a day on which they send choice portions to one another . . . and gifts to the poor"* (Esther 9:19, 22). Jesus had warned his disciples that the period between His crucifixion and resurrection would be a time of weeping and lamenting for the disciples, but *"the world will rejoice" (John 16:20).* Note that they are now called "prophets" since their prophetic message has been delivered.

Witnesses Brought Back to Life

11:11 But after the three and a half days a breath of life from God entered them, and they stood on their feet, and terror struck those who saw them.

This will also occur for the nation Israel in the last day according to Ezekiel 37.

> *"Come, from the four winds, O breath, and breathe into these slain, that they may live" (v 9).*

Some see this whole chapter as depicting the restoration of the Jewish remnant and their salvation which will be accomplished by a miracle of resurrection. There could be a double reference indicated, since the witnesses conclude their task at the end of 42 months, and Christ's appearing to the Israeli Remnant is at hand. According to Zechariah, the remnant will believe, Christ will enter into the New Covenant relationship with the redeemed nation, and they will be preserved alive to enter the kingdom.

11:12 Then they heard a loud voice from heaven saying to them, "Come up here." And they went up to heaven in a cloud, while their enemies looked on.

Perhaps this is the same voice that beckoned John to come up to heaven in chapter 4 and verse 1. Their mode of transportation is a cloud, even as we who believe will be caught up to meet the Lord in the clouds of heaven at the resurrection when our Lord returns.

A Severe Earthquake
7,000 killed
Glory Given to God

11:13 At that very hour there was a severe earthquake and a tenth of the city collapsed. Seven thousand people were killed in the earthquake, and the survivors were terrified and gave glory to the God of heaven.

This is God's immediate response in judgment on those in the immediate vicinity of Jerusalem. A great number are buried in the rubble. Ezekiel 38:19-20 predicts a great earthquake which will take place when Gog attacks Israel.

> *"In my zeal and fiery wrath I declare that at that time there shall be a great earthquake in the land of Israel. The fish of the sea, the birds of the air, the beasts of the field, every creature that moves along the ground, and all the people on the face of the earth will tremble at my presence. The mountains will be overturned, the cliffs will crumble and every wall will fall to the ground."*

Their response indicates that God is recognized as the author of the judgment. The language is not necessarily the language of conversion. There is no indication that it produced any remedial effect or repentance.

11:14 The second woe has passed; the third woe is coming soon.

This furnishes us with a time-frame clue. The second woe or sixth trumpet ends as the two witnesses finish their work (after 42 months). So the sixth trumpet isn't finished until the very end of the Tribulation period. This shows that it parallels the sixth seal (6:15-17), and the seventh trumpet, which is now to be blown, will reach its climax in the Day of the Lord (the bowls of wrath) and the coming of Christ.

7th Trumpet

Third Woe

"Thy Kingdom Come"

This is the Time!

11:15 The seventh angel sounded his trumpet, and there were loud voices in heaven, which said: "The kingdom of the world has become the kingdom of our Lord and of his Christ, and he will reign for ever and ever."

This is now the consummation of the long repeated prayer, *"Thy kingdom come."* The Kingdom of Heaven becomes The Kingdom on Earth with Christ reigning.

Some see this trumpet, the seventh, corresponding to Rosh Hashanah, The Day of Trumpets celebrated each year on Tishri 1, the first day of the seventh month in the liturgical year, and the first month in the civil year. It seemed to signal new beginnings, and consequently was believed to be the first day of creation (world's beginning and, here, a new beginning for a renewed earth), and Noah's birthday (new beginning for the earth after the flood). Each of the Jewish months was introduced by the blowing of trumpets (Numbers 10:10). The festival year (seven feasts) of seven months ended with Tishri, and the blowing of the trumpets, thus called 'the Day of trumpets.' This was the last trumpet sounded in a series of seven. It is also of interest that the ancient kings and rulers of Judah recognized Tishri 1 as their day of inauguration to rule (I Kings 1:34; 2 Kings 11:14). Thus The Day of Trumpets signals the beginning of the New World, the New Creation, and the coronation day for the King of kings and Lord of lords.

11:16 And the twenty-four elders, who were seated on their thrones before God, fell on their faces and worshiped God,

The twenty-four elders once again fall on their faces and offer worship to God that His purpose will now be realized. In great power and glory, Christ will enter upon his eternal reign.

11:17 saying: "We give thanks to you, Lord God Almighty, who is and who was, because you have taken your great power and have begun to reign.

In the 4th verse of chapter 1, God is the one *"who is, who was, and who is to come."* In this verse and in 16:5, the third phrase is omitted because His coming has arrived, and is no longer in the future. God through Christ now reasserts His rightful authority over the nations.

This section constitutes a preview of that which is to come.

What Happens at the Seventh Trumpet?

1. The Time For God's Wrath Has Come

11:18 The nations were angry; and your wrath has come.

Psalm 2 is the best commentary here:

> *"Why do **the nations rage** and the peoples plot in vain? The kings of the earth take their stand and the rulers gather together against the Lord and against his Anointed One. Let us break their chains,"* they say, *"and throw off their fetters." The One enthroned in heaven laughs; the Lord scoffs at them. **Then he rebukes them in his anger and terrifies them in his wrath**, saying, "I have installed my King on Zion, my holy hill." I will proclaim the decree of the Lord: He said to me, "You are my Son; today I have become your Father. Ask of me, and I will make the nations your inheritance, the ends of the earth your possessions. You will rule them with an iron scepter; you will dash them to pieces like pottery." Therefore, you kings, be wise; be warned, you rulers of the earth. Serve the Lord with trembling. Kiss the Son, **lest he be angry and you be destroyed in your way, for his wrath can flare up in a moment**. Blessed are all who take refuge in him."*

God here tailors the punishment to fit the crime. The nations are angry and scornful; they will experience the anger and scorn of Almighty God.

2. The Time for Judging the Dead Has Come

Questions have been raised about the appropriateness of a judgment of the wicked at this time. But this language is similar to Paul's reference to Christ's coming in 2 Thessalonians Both judgment for the wicked and rewards for the righteous are in view.

> *"God is just: He will pay back trouble to those who trouble you, and give relief to you who are troubled, and to us as well. This will happen when the Lord Jesus is revealed from heaven in blazing fire with his powerful angels. He will punish those who do not know God and do not obey the gospel of our Lord Jesus. They will be punished with everlasting destruction and shut out from the presence of the Lord and from the majesty of his power **on the day he comes to be glorified in his holy people and to be marveled at among all those who have believe"** (2 Thessalonians 6-9).*

The Bema Seat of Christ occurs at His coming. We can't be sure in what order, although the parallel passage in Revelation 19 gives the order as the Marriage Supper, defeat of the nations, judgment of the Satanic triumvirate, and judgment thrones (which may include both the Bema and the Sheep and Goat nations.)

> *"For **we must all appear before the judgment seat of Christ**, that each one may receive what is due him for the things done while in the body, whether good or bad" (2 Corinthians 5:10).*

> *"You, then, why do you judge your brother? Or why do you look down on your brother? **For we will all stand before God's judgment seat**. It is written: 'As surely as I live,' says the Lord, 'Every knee will bow before me; every tongue will confess to God.' So then, each of us will give an account of himself to God" (Romans 14:10-12).*

> *"For no one can lay any foundation other than the one already laid, which is Jesus Christ. If any man builds on this foundation using gold, silver, costly stones, wood, hay or straw, his work will be shown for what it is, because **the Day will bring it to light**. It will be*

revealed with fire, *and the fire will test the quality of each man's work. If what he has built survives, he will receive his reward. If it is burned up, he will suffer loss; he himself will be saved, but only as one escaping through the flames" (I Corinthians 3:11-15).*

*"Therefore do not go on passing judgment before the time, but **wait until the Lord comes** who will both bring to light the things hidden in the darkness and disclose the motives of men's hearts; and then each man's praise will come to him from God" (I Corinthians 4:5)*

3.   The Time for Rewarding Faithfulness Has Come

and for rewarding your servants the prophets and your saints and those who reverence your name, both small and great—

*"Behold, the Lord God will come with might, with His arm ruling for Him. Behold, **His reward is with Him, and His recompense before Him**. Like a shepherd He will tend His flock, in His arm He will gather the lambs, and carry them in His bosom; He will gently lead the nursing ewes" (Isaiah 40:10—11).*

*"For the Son of Man is going to come in his Father's glory with his angels, and **then he will reward each person according to what he has done**" (Matthew 16:27).*

*"Rejoice in that day and leap for joy, because **great is your reward** in heaven. For that is how their fathers treated the prophets" (Luke 6:23).*

*"I have fought the good fight, I have finished the course, I have kept the faith; in the future there is laid up for me **the crown of righteousness**, which the Lord, the righteous Judge, **will award to me on that Day**; and not only to me, but also to all who have loved His appearing" (2 Timothy 4:7-8).*

4. The Time for Destroying the Destroyers Has Come

and for destroying those who destroy the earth."

Those who destroy will be destroyed.

> *"The day is near, the day of the Lord is near—a day of clouds, a time of doom for the nations" (Ezekiel 30:3).*

> *"Alas for that day! For the day of the Lord is near; it will come like destruction from the Almighty" (Joel 2:1).*

> *"The day of the Lord is near for all nations. As you have done, it will be done to you; your deeds will return upon your own head" (Obadiah 15).*

Notice, God repays in kind, *"as you have done, it will be done to you."*

> *"By the same word the present heavens and earth are reserved for fire, being kept for the Day of Judgment and destruction of ungodly men" (2 Peter 3:7).*

11:19 Then God's temple in heaven was opened, and within his temple was seen the Ark of the Covenant.

Now is the glory (Shekinah) of God to be revealed in all its blinding brilliance. The covenant he has made with His people will surely be kept. This is the heavenly Ark. The Ark of the Covenant on earth was the symbol to His people of His abiding presence in their midst.

Terminus To Trumpets

And there came flashes of lightning, rumblings, peals of thunder, an earthquake and a great hailstorm.

Although John has further details to unfold regarding the events leading up to this climactic moment, this last trumpet parallels the last bowl, and the coming of our Lord in chapter 19. It is my view that the three terminus statements at the end of the Seals, Trumpets and Bowls indicate that everything reaches a climax at the same time with the coming of the Lord on the clouds. Although the Seals, Trumpets and Bowls do not run parallel, they are *progressively* parallel in the sense that they reach a climax at the same time with the Lord's coming.

In connection with the bowls, the indication is that Christ comes and the rapture occurs just before the bowls of wrath are poured out or as they are poured out. As Christ comes, the bowls are poured out in quick succession on the earth.

Now John will give a fuller description of what happens to the two people groups of chapter 7, the 144,000 and the Great Multitude, during the Great Tribulation. This series of seven persons reaches its climax with the coming of Christ to Mount Zion that brings to an end this great period of suffering at the hands the Satanic triumvirate.

CHAPTER 12

SEVEN PERSONS IN THE FINAL DRAMA AT THE CLIMAX OF THE AGE

Since this book is a book of consummations, the signs which now appear refer to the times and scenes in which everything runs to its climax or final end. There are seven persons that come on the final stage of history that depict the characters which have in some way figured in the spiritual drama of redemption from the very beginning of time, but are now to be seen in their final manifestation. They will run their course and reach their climax at the end of the 3 1/2 year period of great tribulation.

It is the author's view that the Lamb is the seventh person in the sequence. This underscores again the climactic nature of His coming.

- ➤ The Radiant Woman
- ➤ The Male Child
- ➤ The Dragon
- ➤ Michael the Archangel
- ➤ Beast Out of the Sea
- ➤ Beast Out of the Earth
- ➤ The Lamb

This section explains in greater detail what happens to the two people groups mentioned in chapter 7, the Israeli Remnant and the Great Multitude, the Church, *"the rest of her offspring."* After being cast out and down from heaven, Satan now vents his anger on God's people knowing that his time is short. Severe tribulation will now be unleashed on Israel (although a remnant will be preserved and protected by God), and the Church. It is true that the people of God are one throughout all redemptive history, children of the promise, but the remnant of Israel here have not yet reached their day of repentance and redemption with the New Covenant confirmed to them by Messiah Jesus when he appears to them at His coming.

1
The Woman

12:1 A great and wondrous sign appeared in heaven: a woman clothed with the sun, with the moon under her feet and a crown of twelve stars on her head.

This Woman here, as some believe, does not stand in contrast to the Scarlet Woman of chapter 17. The Prostitute there is contrasted with the Pure Bride of Christ.

The "great sign" harks back to Isaiah's prophecy,

> *"Therefore **the Lord himself will give you a sign**: The virgin will be with child and will give birth to a son, and will call him Immanuel" (7:14)*

This Woman stands for the nation Israel specifically, but more generally, she is the "woman" mentioned in Genesis 3:15,

> *"And I will put enmity between you and **the woman**, and between your offspring and hers; he will crush your head, and you will strike his heel."*

Two "seeds" or offspring are in view here: the seed of the serpent and the seed of the woman. A glance at verse 9 reveals that the "dragon" here is the "super-serpent" of Genesis 3, *"The great dragon—.that ancient serpent called the devil or Satan, who leads the whole world astray."*

The history outlined in the Old Testament shows that God carefully preserved and protected the "seed" of the woman—the Messianic line. The Redeemer was promised to Abraham through the child of promise, Isaac, then to Isaac himself, and to Jacob, then through the patriarchs, the twelve sons of Jacob. Specifically Messiah would come through the kingly line of Judah, from which lineage Jesus the Messiah was born, the Son of David.

Two verses offer sufficient proof that the primary meaning of this woman is the "woman" of Genesis 3:15, eventually to be embodied in the nation Israel which God ordained as a channel through which the Messiah would come. Consider first Joseph's dream recorded in chapter 37 and verse 9,

> *"Listen, I had another dream, and this time the sun and the moon and eleven stars were bowing down to me."*

The fulfillment of that dream, of course, was when Joseph's whole family came into Egypt and bowed before him as the second ruler of the land. Joseph's star would make the twelfth star of the woman's 12-starred crown. The twelve sons of Jacob or Israel, then, are the twelve stars Paul in Romans 9:5 gives us the second verse.

> *"Theirs are the patriarchs, and from them is traced the human ancestry of Christ, who is God over all, forever praised! Amen."*

12:2 She was pregnant and cried out in pain as she was about to give birth.

> *"Before she goes into labor, she gives birth; before the pains come upon her, she delivers a son"* (Isaiah 66:7).

Only Israel is said to give birth to the Messiah. It is why God raised Israel up as a nation to be a channel for the coming Christ.

This imagery of birth is also taken from Isaiah 26:17,

> *"As a woman with child and about to give birth writhes and cries out in her pain . . . "*

It should go without saying that John's model here is Israel and the twelve tribes, not, as some have supposed, the constellation Virgo, which has a "crown" of twelve stars, and that the twelve stars represent the twelve signs of the Zodiac. It is true that in ancient times these twelve signs were often regarded as symbols of the twelve tribes of Israel, but it seems highly unlikely that this is John's reference here.

2
The Dragon

12:3 Then another sign appeared in heaven: an enormous red dragon with seven heads and ten horns and seven crowns on his heads.

The dragon is identified as the ancient serpent, Satan, in verse 9. Satan is seen as that malignant power behind the imperial powers of the ancient world, and behind a confederated group of 10 nations and 10 kings at the end of the age. He is Satan, The Deceiver and Destroyer. Later, he incarnates himself in the Man of Sin, the Antichrist, the Beast out of the Sea. He is the avowed enemy of God. A description of the Beast closely parallels what is said of Satan (17:7-11).

> *"The seven heads are seven hills on which the woman sits. They are also seven kings. Five have fallen, one is, the other has not yet come; but when he does come, he must remain for a little while. The beast who once was, and now is not, is an eighth king. He belongs to the seven and is going to his destruction. The ten horns you saw are ten kings who have not yet received a kingdom, but who for one hour will receive authority as kings along with the beast. They have one purpose and will give their power and authority to the beast."*

Our Lord is described in 19:12, 16 as having *"many diadems."* Satan arrogates to himself power in opposition to the King of Kings and Lord of Lords.

The description of the Beast is slightly different. The crowns are on the ten horns rather than the seven heads. These ten will come into power later, and are then crowned. The seven crowned heads of the dragon are seven nations, two of which preceded Babylon, namely, Egypt and Assyria. Six great world empires have figured into Israel's history. The seventh will come in the form of a ten-nation confederation in the last day. (See notes under 17:9-13) Satan is seen to be the malevolent power behind these nations as each, in turn, has sought to destroy the people of God.

12:4 His tail swept a third of the stars out of the sky and flung them to the earth. The dragon stood in front of the woman who was about to give birth, so that he might devour her child the moment it was born.

Note Daniel's vision of "The Little Horn that Grows":

> *"It grew until it reached the host of the heavens, and it threw some of the starry host down to the earth and trampled on them"* *(Daniel 8:10).*

This is a figurative way of expressing the great power and authority exercised by this one. It may indicate that Satan, in his original rebellion in heaven against God, was able to influence a third of the angels to rebel with him. Jude refers to these as *"wandering stars, for whom blackest darkness has been reserved forever,"* and *"those who abandoned their own home—these he has kept in darkness, bound with everlasting chains for judgment on the great Day"* *(Jude 6, 13).*

3
The Male Child

12:5 She gave birth to a son, a male child, who will rule all the nations with an iron scepter. And her child was snatched up to God and to his throne.

The act of ruling with "an iron scepter" is language taken from the great Messianic psalm, Psalm 2 verse 9 quoted above. The rod may refer to the shepherd's rod by which he engages the enemies of His flock (See 7:17). The child is obviously the Christ-Child. In Revelation 2:27 we read concerning the overcoming ones who do His will to the end.

> *"I will give authority over the nations—'He will rule them with an iron scepter; he will dash them to pieces like pottery'—just as I have received authority from my Father."*

The description here moves from the incarnation to the ascension, the purpose being to show the enmity between the serpent and the woman that has been true from the very beginning. John's purpose is best suited by brevity. It makes for a fascinating study to trace from the very beginning how the dragon, Satan, lay in wait to destroy the "seed of the woman," but God repeatedly "snatched" the "seed" out of his hands, and preserved the line of the Christ. This age old battle will now reach its consummation in the world's last great conflict.

12:6 The woman fled into the desert to a place prepared for her by God, where she might be taken care of for 1,260 days.

> *Jesus said, "When you see Jerusalem surrounded by armies, you will know that its desolation is near. Then let those who are in Judea flee to the mountains, let those in the city get out, and let those in the country not enter the city. For this is the time of punishment in fulfillment of all that has been written. How dreadful it will be in those days . . . " (Luke 21:20-23).*

God's people, Israel, flee from the terrors of the satanic trinity into the wilderness, perhaps to Petra where they had fled during the siege of Jerusalem in 70 A.D. when the Romans destroyed Jerusalem. This probably occurs when the "abomination of desolation" spoken of by Daniel, takes place at the midpoint of the 7 year period. It isn't the whole nation of Israel, however, that is sealed and protected by God from Satan's wrath for 3 1/2 years. It is the "sealed" ones of chapter 7, the 144,000, plus those who respond to their witness. The time designation is The Great Tribulation or the last 3 1/2 years of Daniel's 70th week.

> *"So when you see standing in the holy place the abomination that causes desolation, spoken of through the prophet Daniel—let the reader understand—then let those who are in Judea flee to the mountains" (Matthew 24:15-16).*

> *"Therefore I am now going to allure her; I will lead her into the desert (wilderness) and speak tenderly to her" (Hosea 2:14).*

To the Jews, the wilderness would always be associated with God's provision and protection from the Egyptian Dragon when they wondered there for 40 years.

4
Michael

12:7And there was war in heaven. Michael and his angels fought against the dragon, and the dragon and his angels fought back.

Michael (which means Who is like God?) *"is the great prince who stands for your people Israel."* The archangel has a special guardian relationship to Israel. He has fought on her behalf in the past when He assisted Gabriel, another of the archangels. It is a stretch to say, as some do, that Michael here is a symbolical representation of Christ, and that the "angels" who accompany Him are His apostles.

> *"Then Michael, one of the chief princes, came to help me, because I was detained there with the king of Persia" (Dan. 10:13).*

> *"No one supports me against them except Michael, your prince" (10:21).*

> *"But even the archangel Michael, when he was disputing about the body of Moses, did not dare to bring a slanderous accusation against him (Satan), but said, "The Lord rebuke you!" (Jude 9).*

This is the great cosmic prelude to the final climax. It shows why the people of God are pursued and persecuted by the outraged Dragon. He recognizes that his time is short. He is rapidly losing ground, and must renew his efforts to destroy the people of God.

12:8 But he was not strong enough, and they lost their place in heaven.

The book of Job seems to indicate that Satan, though cast down from his exalted position as Lucifer, Son of the Morning, still has access to the presence of God. Satan means Adversary. He is the adversary of

God and the people of God, and continually accuses. The Devil means Slanderer or Divider. He is the Great Liar, the Deceiver. *"He deceived Eve by his cunning"* (2 Corinthians 11:3) He will be released at the end of the millennial age, and deceive the nations. Now Satan is to be cast out where he can no longer accuse the brethren.

Note Isaiah's description of Satan's fall from heaven.

> *"How you have fallen from heaven, O morning star, son of the dawn! You have been cast down to the earth, you who once laid low the nations! You said in your heart, "I will ascend to heaven; I will raise my throne above the stars of God; I will sit enthroned on the mount of assembly, on the utmost heights of the sacred mountain. I will ascend above the tops of the clouds; I will make myself like the Most High." But you are brought down to the grave, to the depths of the pit. Those who see you stare at you, they ponder your fate: "Is this the man who shook the earth and made kingdoms tremble" (Isaiah 14:12-16).*

The book of Zechariah also pictures Satan accusing the saints of God.

> *"Then he showed me Joshua the high priest standing before the angel of the Lord, and Satan standing at his right side to accuse him. The Lord said to Satan, 'The Lord rebuke you, Satan!" (3:1-2).*

Or consider Ezekiel's lament concerning the King of Tyre (Satan being the power behind the king, energizing him and working through him):

> *"You were the model of perfection, full of wisdom and perfect in beauty. You were in Eden, the garden of God; every precious stone adorned you: ruby, topaz and emerald, chrysolite, onyx and jasper, sapphire, turquoise and beryl. Your settings and mountings were made of gold; on the day you were created they were prepared. You were anointed as a guardian cherub, for so I ordained you. You were on the holy mount of God; you walked among the fiery stones. You were blameless in your ways from the day you were created till wickedness was found in you. Through your widespread trade you were filled with violence, and you sinned. So I drove you in disgrace from the mount of God, and I expelled you, O guardian cherub, from among the fiery stones. Your heart became proud on*

*account of your beauty, and you corrupted your wisdom because of your splendor. **So I threw you to the earth**; I made a spectacle of you before kings. By your many sins and dishonest trade you have desecrated your sanctuaries. So I made a fire come out from you, and it consumed you, and I reduced you to ashes on the ground in the sight of all who were watching. All the nations who knew you are appalled at you; **you have come to a horrible end and will be no more**" Ezekiel 28:12-19).*

Note also the interesting statement of our Lord upon the return of the 72 witnesses in Luke 10. *"I saw Satan fall like lightning from heaven" (v 18).* Satan and his demonic emissaries were being overthrown by the effective witness of those Jesus sent out.

12:9 The great dragon was hurled down—that ancient serpent called the devil or Satan, who leads the whole world astray. He was hurled to the earth, and his angels with him.

The Deceiver of the world and the Accuser of the brethren is now cast out of heaven! As his end draws near, his hatred and hostility become more intense.

The Voice From Heaven
The Battle is About To Be Joined

12:10 Then I heard a loud voice in heaven say:

"Now has come the salvation and the power and the kingdom of our God, and the authority of his Christ. For the accuser of our brothers, who accuses them before our God day and night, has been hurled down.

We are not told who is responsible for this sudden outburst of praise. It serves to show that the end is now drawing near, and Satan's hostility is due to his awareness that he doesn't have very much time left to achieve his diabolical ends.

The Overcomers

12:11 They overcame him by the blood of the Lamb and by the word of their testimony; they did not love their lives so much as to shrink from death.

This reference continues the theme of overcomers began in Christ's message to the seven churches, and indicates that those in the church are the ones challenged to be overcomers by refusing the mark, and testifying to their love and loyalty to Christ even though it might cost them their lives. These are probably those who *"came out of the Great Tribulation"* and had washed their robes in the blood of the Lamb. So Satan suffers a double defeat, by Michael and his angels, and by the conquering saints of heaven who overcome by the blood that establishes the basis for their victory. What is said here reminds us of king Nebuchadnezzar's words to the three Hebrew friends of Daniel after they survived the blazing furnace *"They were willing to give up their lives rather than serve or worship any god except their own God"(Daniel 3:28).*

The Devil's Time is Short

12:12 Therefore rejoice, you heavens and you who dwell in them! But woe to the earth and the sea, because the devil has gone down to you! He is filled with fury, because he knows that his time is short."

A contrast is here presented between those who are in heaven and those who are on earth. Those in heaven are rejoicing, because their accuser has been cast out, and because all accusations have been answered by reference to the shed blood of the Lamb which gives them their access to the heavenly realm, and by their faithful witness even to the point of death which they rendered to their Lord on earth. No accusation of the Devil can avail against believers who have put their trust in the Redeemer.

> *"Who will bring any charge against those whom God has chosen? It is God who justifies. Who is he that condemns? Christ Jesus, who died—more than that, who was raised to life—is at the right hand of God and is also interceding for us" (Romans 8:33-34).*

245

> *"But if anybody does sin, we have one who speaks to the Father in our defense—Jesus Christ, the Righteous One. He is the atoning sacrifice for our sins, and not only for ours but also for the sins of the whole world" (I John 2:1-2).*

Those on earth are to experience now the fury of the devil because he knows his time is running out. Now occurs what Daniel calls *"a time of distress such has not happened from the beginning of nations until then" (12:1).*

In 2 Thessalonians 2:7-8 we read

> *"For the secret power of lawlessness is already at work; but the one who now holds it back will continue to do so till he is taken out of the way (he who now hinders will continue to hinder until he is taken out of the way). And then the lawless one will be revealed, whom the Lord Jesus will overthrow with the breath of his mouth and destroy by the splendor of his coming."*

Michael, The Restrainer?

Paul speaks of the one hindering being taken out of the way (v. 7). The word "hinders" means to hold down, and the phrase "taken out of the way" means to step aside. (Young's Concordance = "To stand, stand still or fast" Strong's Concordance = "cease" or "stand still") The one who had the job of hindering the Antichrist will step aside; that is, will no longer be a restraint between the Antichrist, and those the Antichrist is persecuting. We believe Michael, the Archangel, is the personage who will step aside. Daniel 12:1 says,

> *"And at that time shall Michael stand up (stand aside), the great prince who stands for the children of your people, and there shall be a time of trouble, such as never was since there was a nation even to that same time."*

"That time" refers to "the time of trouble" or the Great Tribulation. As we have seen, the word "stand up" literally means to "stand still." Michael would "stand still" or "stand aside" or "be inactive."

The Midrash, commenting on this verse, says, "The Holy One, Blessed be He, said to Michael, 'You are silent? You do not defend my children.'" God sends a strong delusion to Israel that is both a punishment for sin and a moral consequence of their rejection of the truth (2 Thessalonians 2:10-12).

This war in heaven occurs at the midpoint of Daniel's 70th week. The Antichrist and False Prophet introduce their image and forcefully demand the worship of the world. They have authority to do this for 42 months.

War on Earth—The Woman Pursued

12:13 When the dragon saw that he had been hurled to the earth, he pursued the woman who had given birth to the male child.

The remnant of Israel are now aware of the true character of the Antichrist, and flee to escape the wave of persecution that he is about to introduce. Note how Daniel 12 continues.

> *"But at that time your people—everyone whose name is found written in the book—will be delivered. Multitudes who sleep in the dust of the earth will awake: some to everlasting life, others to shame and everlasting contempt. Those who are wise will shine like the brightness of the heavens, and those who lead many to righteousness, like the stars for ever and ever" (Daniel 12:1-3).*

This, coupled with Isaiah 52:7, may indicate that the 144,000 will have a witnessing role during this period of time . . . . *"those who lead many to righteousness"* and *"those who bring good news, who proclaim peace, who bring good tidings, who proclaim salvation . . . "* It may not be a gospel witness—that is a witness to Christ's redeeming work, but a call to be faithful to God, and not be guilty of worshiping the beast or his image. It would be a kingdom witness.

> *"Therefore my people will know my name; therefore in that day they will know that it is I who foretold it. Yes, it is I. How beautiful on the mountains are the feet of those who bring good news, who proclaim peace, who bring good tidings, who proclaim salvation, who say to Zion, **"Your God reigns!"** (Isaiah 52:6-7).*

These, then, are the remnant, the sealed ones of Chapter 7, the 144,000, whose final deliverance is pictured in chapter 14. This occurs at the coming of Christ in the clouds.

12:14 The woman was given the two wings of a great eagle, so that she might fly to the place prepared for her in the desert, where she would be taken care of for a time, times and half a time out of the serpent's reach.

There are certainly allusions here to the Exodus, and how God cared for His people in the wilderness.

> *"You yourself have seen what I did in Egypt, and how I carried you on eagles' wings and brought you to myself" (Exodus 19:4).*

The wings are symbolic of the supporting arms of God. They speak of deliverance and enablement.

Moses in speaking to Israel at the end of his life alludes to how God saved them in the wilderness.

> *"In a desert land he found him, in a barren and howling waste. He shielded him and cared for him; he guarded him as the apple of his eye, like an eagle that stirs up its nest and hovers over its young, that spreads its wings to catch them and carries them on its pinions" (Deuteronomy 32:10-11)*

Here also we see the time indicator given again—time, times, and half a time or 42 months. Does this refer to the 42 months of Jewish oppression under the Syrian tyrant Antiochus Epiphanes, as many believe, or to the "Little Horn" that will come in the last day? The latter seems to be in view, since it is leading up to the Great Unvailing of the Coming King.

12:15 Then from his mouth the serpent spewed water like a river, to overtake the woman and sweep her away with the torrent.

"Surely when the mighty waters rise, they will not reach him" (*Psalm 32:6*).

12:16 But the earth helped the woman by opening its mouth and swallowing the river that the dragon had spewed out of his mouth.

"Had it not been the Lord who was on our side," Let Israel now say, Had it not been the Lord who was on our side, when men rose up against us; then they would have swallowed us alive, when their anger was kindled against us; then the waters would have engulfed us, the stream would have swept over our soul; then the raging waters would have swept over our soul." (Psalm 124:1-5).

The Rest of Her Offspring

12:17 Then the dragon was enraged at the woman and went off to make war against the rest of her offspring—those who obey God's commandments and hold to the testimony of Jesus.

"If you belong to Christ, then you are Abraham's seed, and heirs according to the promise" (Gal. 3:29).

Paul says that Hagar and Sarah represent two covenants—Mt. Sinai or the present Jerusalem and the *"Jerusalem that is above"* which is free, and *"she is our mother"* (Gal. 4:25-26). Again the emphasis is upon the children of promise—those who are the spiritual seed of Abraham through faith.

These are the "overcomers" (12:11), the believing saints, the Church on earth who *"do not love their lives to shrink from death."* The Antichrist makes *"war against the saints and to conquer them."* Many are killed by the sword, and are called upon to *"patiently endure and continue faithful"* (see verses 7 and 10 of Chapter 13). I believe these to be the Great Multitude mentioned in chapter 7 who *"come out of the great tribulation"* many by martyrdom. Are all killed? No, but a great number will be. They, along with the rest of the saints, await the rapture and resurrection soon to take place at Christ's coming. In chapter 15, they are seen *"victorious over the beast and his image,"* and sing the song of deliverance.

CHAPTER 13

5
The Beast Out of The Sea

13:1 And I saw a beast coming out of the sea. He had ten horns and seven heads, with ten crowns on his horns, and on each head a blasphemous name.

Here are introduced the two agents Satan will use to carry out his devilish purposes. From an apocalyptic perspective, they are beasts—beastly.

"Coming out of the sea" The sea was associated with evil in that day, and it is fitting that the last great enemy of God and God's people would arise from "the sea." He is also pictured as coming up out of the abyss. Both references stress the source of evil. The scene is probably suggested by Daniels vision of the four beasts that came up from the sea. Note Isaiah's words (57:20), *"But the wicked are like the tossing sea, which cannot rest, whose waves cast up mire and mud. There is no peace", says my God, "for the wicked."*

In the last days, a powerful, charismatic leader will arise, demonically inspired (from the Abyss) and Satanically controlled. He will conquer three kingdoms, and assume control over 7 other kingdoms that will come into being in the last day. The ten horns represent the seventh head or seventh kingdom. The beast himself is an eighth king, but is also the head of the seventh kingdom confederacy. The last kingdom will follow a procession of six kingdoms, including the two that preceded Daniel's four. The Beast will evidently gain empire status, controlling the minds and hearts of vast numbers of people on the earth.

"I also wanted to know about the ten horns on its head and about the other horn that came up, before which three of them fell—the horn that looked more imposing than the others and that had eyes and a mouth that spoke boastfully" (Daniel 7:20).

13:2 The beast I saw resembled a leopard, but had feet like those of a bear and a mouth like that of a lion. The dragon gave the beast his power and his throne and great authority.

Hosea mentions these three beasts:

"So I will come like a lion, like a leopard I will lurk by the path. Like a bear robbed of her cubs, I will attack them" (Hosea 13:7-8).

Daniel, of course, does also. This beast is so terrible that it seems to include all the terrors of the evil empires that had gone before. John sets him forth as the climax of bestial opposition to the seed of the woman.

1. Babylon—lion
2. Medo-Persia—bear
3. Greece—leopard
4. Rome—nondescript

The beast has ten horns and seven heads. The ten horns, like that of the dragon, picture his power over ten confederated kingdoms that will arise out of the old Roman empire. His power is delegated authority from Satan, although God is directing all (17:17).

13:3 One of the heads of the beast seemed to have had a fatal wound, but the fatal wound had been healed. The whole world was astonished and followed the beast.

There are some who see in this "beast" a description of Emperor Nero himself. He certainly was bestial, a degenerate in every way, but John's vision seems to be of a world ruler that surfaces just before the return of Christ in glory.

Some suggest this is a reference to the legend of Nero's resurrection. I do not think so. It probably is an attempt by Antichrist to duplicate the resurrection of Christ. The Antichrist is the supreme counterfeit.

Note the description of Daniel's "little horn."

> *"As I watched, this horn was waging war against the saints and defeating them, until the Ancient of Days came and pronounced judgment in favor of the saints of the Most High, and the time came when they possessed the kingdom. He will speak against the Most High and oppress his saints and try to change the set times and the laws. The saints will be handed over to him for a time, times and half a time. But the court will sit, and his power will be taken away and completely destroyed forever. Then the sovereignty, power and greatness of the kingdoms under the whole heaven will be handed over to the saints, the people of the Most High. His kingdom, will be an everlasting kingdom, and all rulers will worship and obey him." (Daniel 7:21-22, 25-27).*

This gives us a thumbnail sketch of the final demise of this powerful world figure that opposes so vehemently the people of God. Jesus enlarges on this terrible time of persecution in Matthew 24, and the parallel passages in Mark and Luke.

13:4 Men worshiped the dragon because he had given authority to the beast, and they also worshiped the beast and asked, "Who is like the beast? Who can make war against him?"

Men will be faced with a decisive choice in the last day between love for Christ, and loyalty to the ruling authority that sets himself up as God. Of course, emperor worship was nothing new.

13:5 The beast was given a mouth to utter proud words and blasphemies and to exercise his authority for forty-two months.

Some try to make this time-frame reference purely symbolic, signifying a time of trouble, when the enemies of God are in power, or when judgment is being poured out. Daniel's perspective is that the 3 1/2 years are the second part of a week of years, his Seventieth Week, and thus it refers to an actual period of time.

> *"The saints will be handed over to him for a time, times and half a time . . . "(Daniel 7:25).* This is 42 months.

> *"The man clothed in linen, who was above the waters of the river, lifted his right hand and his left hand toward heaven, and I heard him swear by him who lives forever, saying, 'It will be for a time, times and half a time (42 months). When the power of the holy people has been finally broken, all these things will be completed"* *(Daniel 12:7).*

Note, too, the additional time period.

> *"From the time that the daily sacrifice is abolished and the abomination that causes desolation is set up, there will be 1,290 days. Blessed is the one who waits for and reaches the end of the 1,335 days" (Daniel 12:11).*

These time frame references point to events that will occur following the Seventieth Week. Thirty days corresponds to a time of mourning for Israel, and also marks the overthrow of The Satanic Triumvirate. The additional 45 days may refer to the celebration of Hanukkah, and the cleansing of the defiled temple in the days of Antiochus Epiphanes. In this case, it may refer to the cleansing of the temple that Antichrist desecrates. The present day Hanukkah occurs 70 days following the great Day of Atonement. Many believe that Christ will return and present Himself to Israel on that great day, followed by a time of mourning associated with it.

13:6 He opened his mouth to blaspheme God, and to slander his name and his dwelling place and those who live in heaven.

Notice Paul's description of this "man of lawlessness" in 2 Thessalonians 2.

> *"Don't let anyone deceive you in any way, for that day (the day of the Lord) will not come until the rebellion occurs and the man*

of lawlessness is revealed, the man doomed to destruction. **He opposes and exalts himself over everything that is called God or is worshiped, and even sets himself up in God's temple, proclaiming himself to be God.** *Don't you remember that when I was with you I used to tell you these things? And now you know what is holding him back, so that he may be revealed at the proper time. For the secret power of lawlessness is already at work; but the one who now holds it back will continue to do so till he is taken out of the way. And then the lawless one will be revealed, whom the Lord Jesus will overthrow with the breath of his mouth and destroy by the splendor of his coming. The coming of the lawless one will be in accordance with the work of Satan displayed in all kinds of counterfeit miracles, signs and wonders, and every sort of evil that deceives those who are perishing. They perish because they refused to love the truth and so be saved. For this reason God sends them a powerful delusion so that they will believe the lie and so that all will be condemned who have not believed the truth but have delighted in wickedness"* (2 Thessalonians 2:3-12).

13:7 He was given power to make war against the saints and to conquer them. And he was given authority over every tribe, people, language and nation.

"was given"—indicates his subordinate role; subordinate to the dragon, but also acting by divine permission. Daniel's prophecy indicates that the saints, *"will be handed over to him for a time, times and a half time"* (Daniel 7:25).

The phrase *"every tribe, people, language and nation"*, frequently employed in both Daniel and the Revelation, indicates his control over vast numbers of people who inhabit the earth. See the next phrase *"all the inhabitants of the earth will worship the beast."*

13:8 All inhabitants of the earth will worship the beast—all whose names have not been written in the book of life belonging to the Lamb that was slain from the creation of the world.

The Book of Life is a register of the names of those who belong to God. 17:8 reads similarly, *"The inhabitants of the earth whose names have not been written in the book of life from the creation of the world will be astonished when they see the beast . . . "*

I Peter 1:19,20 speaks of the Lamb slain from the foundation of the world. God knows his own from everlasting to everlasting, and no earthly danger can remove than from His hand. The death of Christ was a redemptive sacrifice decreed in the counsels of eternity past.

The King Who Exalts Himself

> *"The king will do as he pleases. He will exalt and magnify himself above every god and will say unheard of things against the God of gods. He will be successful until the time of wrath is completed, for what has been determined must take place. He will show no regard for the gods of his fathers or for the one desired by women, nor will he regard any god, but will exalt himself above them all. Instead of them, he will honor a god of fortresses; a god unknown to his fathers he will honor with gold and silver, with precious stones and costly gifts. He will attack the mightiest fortresses with the help of a foreign god and will greatly honor those who acknowledge him. He will make them rulers over many people and will distribute the land at a price" (Daniel 11:36-39).*

The narrative in Daniel moves to the future here, and refers to one who will come in the last day, and replicate the actions of Antiochus Epiphanes in a former day, even moving well beyond him in his desire for world conquest and the worship of the world.

13:9 He who has an ear, let him hear.

13:10 If anyone is to go into captivity, into captivity he will go. If anyone is to be killed with the sword, with the sword he will be killed.

> *"Those destined for death, to death; those for the sword, to the sword; those for starvation, to starvation; those for captivity, to captivity" (Jeremiah 15:2).*

Whatever is involved in following Christ, the believer in Christ must accept even if it means death.

This calls for patient endurance and faithfulness on the part of the saints.

A similar statement occurs in 13:18, 14:12 and 17:9. Jesus said, *"He who stands firm to the end will be saved" (Matthew 24:13).*

6
The Beast Out of the Earth

13:11 Then I saw another beast, coming out of the earth. He had two horns like a lamb, but he spoke like a dragon.

He speaks as the serpent in Eden spoke, deceitfully and beguilingly. Here marks the universal victory of godless humanism.

Note the warnings of our Lord, and the apostle Paul concerning false teachers whose sole desire is to ravage the flock of God.

> *"Beware of false prophets, who come to you in sheep's clothing, but inwardly are ravenous wolves" (Matthew 7:15).*

> *"I know that after I leave, savage wolves will come in among you and will not spare the flock. Even from your own number men will arise and distort the truth in order to draw away disciples after them. So be on your guard!" (Acts 20:29-31).*

13:12 He exercised all the authority of the first beast on his behalf, and made the earth and its inhabitants worship the first beast, whose fatal wound had been healed.

I believe that this beast is a counterfeit of the third person of the Trinity, the Holy Spirit, who does similar service for the Son. Here, then, we have an Unholy Trinity—The Devil or Anti-Father, the Anti-Christ and the False Prophet or Anti-Holy Spirit.

13:13 And he performed great and miraculous signs, even causing fire to come down from heaven to earth in full view of men.

> *"For false Christs and false prophets will appear and perform great signs and miracles to deceive even the elect—if that were possible"* *(Matthew 24:24).*

> *"The coming of the lawless one will be in accordance with the work of Satan displayed in all kinds of counterfeit miracles, signs and wonders, and in every sort of evil that deceives those who are perishing. They perish because they refused to love the truth and so be saved"* *(2 Thessalonians 2:9-10).*

Many will be deceived and lost because they prefer to believe a lie rather than the truth. Unfortunately, their numbers are legion today.

The Image

13:14 Because of the signs he was given power to do on behalf of the first beast, he deceived the inhabitants of the earth. He ordered them to set up an image in honor of the beast that was wounded by the sword and yet lived.

This could very well be the "abomination" mentioned by Daniel that will be set up at the mid-point of this week of seven years. *"So when you see standing in the holy place 'the abomination that causes desolation,' spoken of through the prophet Daniel—let the reader understand—"* (Matt. 24:15).

Nebuchadnezzar, king of Babylon, did a similar thing requiring his subjects to fall down and worship the golden image or face death in a blazing furnace (Daniel 3:1-6).

According to the *Ascension of Isaiah* (4:11), the Antichrist is to set up his image in every city. Caligula, we are told, tried to do this, but died before he could accomplish it.

13:15 He was given power to give breath to the image of the first beast, so that it could speak and cause all who refused to worship the image to be killed.

257

Speaking statues that performed miracles were not uncommon in ancient literature. Simon Magus is said to have brought statues to life. Part of the False Prophet's pronouncement is a sentence of death on all who refuse to worship it.

Many will comply, and this decision on their part is what Paul terms "the great apostasy" preceding the coming of Christ (2 Thessalonians 2:1-3).

13:16 He also forced everyone, small and great, rich and poor, free and slave, to receive a mark on his right hand or on his forehead,

Note the coupling of opposites. This is a way of stressing totality—no one being exempt.

13:17 so that no one could buy or sell unless he had the mark, which is the name of the beast or the number of his name.

The mark is Antichrist's symbol of possession or ownership rivaling the seal of God on His own. This was a common practice with conquered people. It was a sign of utter possession and subjection. It was degrading and cruel. It signaled unqualified allegiance to the imperial cult. It is the ultimate test of loyalty. To resist meant almost certain death. (Illustration: The three Hebrew children and the fiery furnace)

13:18 This calls for wisdom. If anyone has insight, let him calculate the number of the beast, for it is man's number. His number is 666.

The suggestions for the meaning here are endless. The ancient peoples had no figures for numbers, and the letters of the alphabet did duty for numbers as well. So every word and every proper name could also be a number. Among the Jews, the practice was known as gematria. John writes this in Greek letters: 600, 60, and 6, thus 666. (By the way, Goliath was 6 cubits and a span; his spear 600 shekels. Nebuchadnezzar's image was 60 cubits high and 6 cubits wide. Solomon received 666 talents of gold in one year at the height of his power)

Six is the number of man and beast, both having been created on the sixth day. Man works for six days, and rests on the seventh. It represents man trying to increase his number, attempting to reach beyond himself, as Antichrist here does. It also suggests the number that falls short of perfection—the three sixes representing the evil triumvirate even as three sevens represents Father, Son, and Holy Spirit.

Note that Neron Kesar (Nero Caesar) in the Hebrew gives us 666, and the early Christians may well have made the connection.

CHAPTER 14

7
The Lamb

14:1 Then I looked, and there before me was the Lamb, standing on Mount Zion, and with him 144,000 who had his name and his Father's name written on their foreheads.

Chapter 14 is included here to set the stage for what is about to unfold with the bowls of wrath poured out on an unbelieving world and the seat of Antichrist's power. The sealed remnant have now made it through the Great Tribulation period, and have probably been witnessing to their brethren *"Repent, for the kingdom of God is at hand."* This is not the gospel of salvation to which they witness, but a message of the imminent overthrow of all anti-God forces, and the setting up of God's kingdom on earth. Here they acknowledge their Sovereign Lord, and own Him as the true Messiah of God.

> *"Therefore my people will know my name; therefore in that day they will know that it is I who foretold it. Yes, it is I. How beautiful on the mountains are the feet of those who bring good news, who proclaim peace, who bring good tidings, who proclaim salvation, who say to Zion, "Your God reigns!" (Isaiah 52:6-7).*

They represent a great host in national Israel who will repent and turn to Christ at His coming. The call goes out from the coming Lord of glory in chapter 18 and verse 4, *"Come out of her, my people, so that you will not share in her sins, so that you will not receive any of her plagues . . . "*

Mount Zion is on earth, one of the mountains surrounding Jerusalem on which David built the earthly Jerusalem centuries before. The Old Testament allusions to this event seem to indicate that the scene takes place when Christ returns to Mt. Zion on earth.

II Esdras has an interesting parallel to our text in which Ezra sees upon Mt. Zion a great crowd singing hymns of praise to the Lord. In their midst is a tall young man who places crowns on their heads. Upon inquiry Ezra learns that it is the Son of God whom they acknowledged in mortal life (II Esdras 2:42-47).

It is the Father's name written on their foreheads, not the mark of the beast as above!

Zion
The New Jerusalem

> *"**The ransomed of the LORD** will return. They will enter Zion with singing; everlasting joy will crown their heads. Gladness and joy will overtake them, and sorrow and sighing will flee away"* (Isaiah 51:11).

When the Lord Returns to Zion

> *"Listen! Your watchmen lift up their voices; together they shout for joy. When the LORD returns to Zion, they will see it with their own eyes. Burst into songs of joy together, you ruins of Jerusalem, for the Lord has comforted his people, **he has redeemed Jerusalem.**"*

Notice this will take place when the Lord comes to overthrow the nations.

> *"The Lord will lay bare his holy arm in the sight of all the nations, and all the ends of the earth will see the salvation of our God"* (Isaiah 52:8-10).

> *"And everyone who calls on the name of the Lord will be saved; **for on Mount Zion and in Jerusalem there will be deliverance**, as the Lord has said, among the survivors whom the Lord calls" (Joel 2:32).*

> *"Say **to the Daughter of Zion**, 'See, your Savior comes! See, his reward is with him, and his recompense accompanies him.'" They will be called the Holy People, the Redeemed of the Lord; and you will be called Sought After, the City No Longer Deserted" (Isaiah 62:11-12).*

> *"I will make the lame a remnant, those driven away a strong nation. The Lord will rule over them in Mount Zion from that day and forever" (Micah 4:7).*

The Remnant Pardoned

> *"Who is God like you, who pardons sin and forgives the transgression of the remnant of his inheritance. You do not stay angry forever but delight to show mercy. You will again have compassion on us; you will tread our sins underfoot and hurl all our iniquities into the depths of the sea" (Micah 7:18—19).*

> *"Israel has experienced a hardening in part until the full number of the Gentiles has come in. And so all Israel will be saved, as it is written: 'The deliverer will come from Zion; he will turn godlessness away from Jacob. And this is my covenant with them when I take away their sins' (Rom. 11:25-27).* This is quoted from Isaiah 59:20-21.

14:2 And I heard a sound from heaven like the roar of rushing waters and like a loud peal of thunder. The sound I heard was like that of harpists playing their harps.

The sound from heaven seems to be the sound of the great multitude welcoming the 144,000 as the redeemed of the Lord. See the following:

> *"They held harps given them by God and sang the song of Moses the servant of God and the song of the Lamb" (15:2, 3).*

*"After this I heard what sounded like the roar of a great multitude
in heaven . . . I heard what sounded like a great multitude, like the
roar of rushing waters and like loud peals of thunder, shouting . . . "
(19:1, 6).*

**14:3 And they sang a new song before the throne and before the four
living creatures and the elders. No one could learn the song except
the 144,000 who had been redeemed from the earth.**

The song must be the song of redemption. The "new song" in 5:9 was
also a song of redemption

*"For the Lord will ransom Jacob and redeem them from the hand
of those stronger than they. They will come and shout for joy on the
heights of Zion; they will rejoice in the bounty of the Lord . . . they
will be like a well-watered garden, and they will sorrow no more"
(Jeremiah 31:11, 12).*

The song that the 144,000 sing may well be Psalm 118. It was the
psalm sung by Israel in connection with the Feast of Tabernacles when,
once a year, they traveled to the top of Mount Zion, where the celebration
is held even today. The feast, which occurs exactly five days after the Day
of Atonement, is celebrated only on Mount Zion.

**14:4 These are those who did not defile themselves with women,
for they kept themselves pure. They follow the Lamb wherever
he goes. They were purchased from among men and offered as
firstfruits to God and the Lamb.**

*"Return, **O Virgin Israel**, return to your towns . . . "
(Jeremiah 31:21).*

These are *"the virgin daughter of Zion"* (2 Kings 19:21; Lam. 2:13). They
have kept themselves pure from all defiling relationships with the pagan
world system. The ideal of virginity or celibacy should be understood in
the sense that Paul used it in 2 Corinthians 11:2, *"I am jealous for you with
a godly jealousy. I promised you to one husband, to Christ, so that I might
present you as a pure virgin to him."*

Is the remnant composed only of men? They are spoken of as celibate men. It may be that they are a carefully chosen group by God to call Israel back to absolute loyalty to God, and His kingdom rule.

The latter part of the verse may indicate martyrdom, but not necessarily so. They have received special protection so that they might survive the tribulation period.

Note Jeremiah's reference to Israel's experience of deliverance from Egypt, and God's guiding, protecting hand in the desert wanderings. The language is similar here.

> *"I remember the devotion of your youth, how as a bride you loved me and followed me through the desert, through a land not sown. Israel was holy to the Lord, the **firstfruits** of his harvest."*
> *(Jeremiah 2:2-3).*

"Firstfruits" means that they belong solely to God. The first of anything was a token that not just the part but all belonged to God (the tenth, the first-born etc.) It could also mean that they are the first of a harvest that will follow. Zechariah predicts that a third of Israel will be spared and believe in the last day when the Lord returns.

14:5 No lie was found in their mouths; they are blameless.

> **"The remnant of Israel** *will do no wrong; they will speak no lies, nor will deceit be found in their mouths" (Zephaniah 3:13).*

To pretend to be something you are not is an abhorrent thought throughout the Revelation. (See 2:9; 3:9; 21:8; 22:15) The pagan world, by contrast, *"exchanged the truth about God for a lie" (Rom. 1:25).*

They are also *"without blemish"* which is a term often used in the ritual sense of being sacrificially acceptable. Christ the Paschal Lamb was "blameless." No one could point a finger at them to locate in them sin or fault. They were morally pure.

The significance of the "remnant" that God will spare in the last day is extremely important. Many have tried to spiritualize all these references and make them refer to the Church. But if we do that, language has no meaning.

The Remnant Gathered

*"I myself will gather **the remnant** of my flock out of all the countries where I have driven them and will bring them back to their pasture, where they will be fruitful and increase in number. I will place shepherds over them who will tend them, and they will no longer be afraid or terrified, nor will any be missing," declares the LORD" (Jeremiah 23:3-4).*

The Righteous King

*"The days are coming," declares the LORD, "when I will raise up to David a righteous Branch, a King who will reign wisely and do what is just and right in the land. **In his days Judah will be saved and Israel will live in safety.** This is the name by which he will be called: The LORD Our Righteousness" (Jeremiah 23:5-6).*

The New Covenant With Israel

*"The time is coming", declares the Lord, "when I will **make a new covenant with the house of Israel and with the house of Judah.** It will not be like the covenant I made with their forefathers when I took them by the hand to lead them out of Egypt, because they broke my covenant, though I was a husband to them, "declares the Lord. "This is the covenant I will make with the house of Israel after that time," declares the Lord. "I will put my law in their minds and write it on their hearts. I will be their God, and they will be my People. No longer will a man teach his neighbor, or a man his brother, saying, 'Know the Lord,' because they will all know me, from the least of them to the greatest," declares the Lord. "For I will forgive their wickedness and will remember their sins no more" (Jeremiah 31:31-34).*

*"In those days, at that time," declares the Lord, **"the people of Israel and the people of Judah together will go in tears to***

seek the Lord their God. *They will ask the way to Zion and turn their faces toward it. They will come and bind themselves to the Lord in* **an everlasting covenant** *that will not be forgotten"* *(Jeremiah 50:4-5).*

In the Streets of Jerusalem
The Opposite of Babylon

"Yet in the towns of Judah and the streets of Jerusalem that are deserted, inhabited by neither men nor animals, there will be heard once more the sounds of joy and gladness, the voices of bride and bridegroom, and the voices of those who bring thank offerings to the house of the Lord, saying, "Give thanks to the Lord Almighty, for the Lord is good; his love endures forever." For I will restore the fortunes of the land as they were before,' says the Lord. The days are coming, declares the Lord, when **I will fulfill the gracious promise I made to the house of Israel and to the house of Judah"** *(Jeremiah 33:10-14).*

The Righteous Branch

"In those days and at that time I will make a righteous Branch sprout from David's line; he will do what is just and right in the land. **In those days Judah will be saved and Jerusalem will live in safety**. *This is the name by which it will be called: 'The Lord Our righteousness'" (Jeremiah 33:15-16).*

The Remnant Forgiven

"In those days, at that time," declares the Lord, "search will be made for Israel's guilt, but there will be none, and for the sins of Judah, but none will be found, **for I will forgive the remnant I spare"** *(Jeremiah 50: 20).*

A Remnant Spared

*"In the whole land," declares the LORD, "two-thirds will be struck down and perish; yet one-third will be left in it. This third I will bring into the fire; I will refine them like silver and test them like gold. **They will call on my name and I will answer them;** I will say, `They are my people,' and they will say, `The LORD is our God"* (Zech. 13:8-9).

"A day of the LORD is coming when your plunder will be divided among you. I will gather all the nations to Jerusalem to fight against it; the city will be captured, the houses ransacked, and the women raped. Half of the city will go into exile, but the rest of the people will not be taken from the city. Then the LORD will go out and fight against those nations, as he fights in the day of battle" (Zech. 14:1-3).

On The Mount of Olives

"On that day his feet will stand on the Mount of Olives, east of Jerusalem, and the Mount of Olives will be split in two from east to west, forming a great valley, with half of the mountain moving north and half moving south" (Zech. 14:4).

The Great Earthquake

"You will flee by my mountain valley, for it will extend to Azel. You will flee as you fled from the earthquake in the days of Uzziah king of Judah. Then the LORD my God will come, and all the holy ones with him. On that day there will be no light, no cold or frost. It will be a unique day, without daytime or nighttime—a day known to the LORD. When evening comes, there will be light" (Zech. 14:5-7).

The Seven Administrative Angels in the Final Countdown

What follows now further explains what happens to the two people groups of chapter 7. The 144,000 are seen with the Lord on Mt. Zion, and now we have a glorified Christ coming in the clouds flanked on each side by three angels. Final warnings are issued, the harvest (rapture) of the Church takes place (corresponding to the Marriage Supper of chapter 19), and a second harvest corresponding with the judgment of the nations at Armageddon (also seen in chapter 19 with Christ coming on the white stallion leading his armies into battle. So what follows is a preview of what is explained in fuller detail in subsequent chapters.

1
Angel

Proclaims the Eternal Gospel And Issues Final Warning

14:6 Then I saw another angel flying in midair, and he had the eternal gospel to proclaim to those who live on the earth—to every nation, tribe, language and people.

This is "another" flying angel, signifying that an angel has preceded this one. That angel is probably the "eagle" of Revelation 8:13, *"As I watched, I heard an eagle that was flying in midair call out . . . "*

The "eternal gospel" does not seem to be here the gospel of salvation. It seems to be spelled out in verse 7.

14:7 He said in a loud voice, "Fear God and give him glory, because the hour of his judgment has come. Worship him who made the heavens, the earth, the sea and the springs of water."

It is a final appeal to all men to acknowledge the one true God—Creator of the Universe. Man's moral failure, Paul tells us in Romans 1, began with his failure to glorify God.

It is similar to the proclamation of Paul and Barnabas in Lystra, *"Turn from these vain things to a living God who made the heaven and the earth and the sea and all that is in them" (Acts 14:15).*

It may also correspond to the gospel of the kingdom, *"Repent. The kingdom of God is near."* The coming of the kingdom involves both judgment and salvation.

2
Angel

Announces The Fall of Babylon

14:8 A second angel followed and said, "Fallen! Fallen is Babylon the Great which made all the nations drink the maddening wine of her adulteries (heat of her fornication)."

Here is the second flying angel in a series of three. The language here is definitely borrowed from the prophets. This is the culmination of the great Babylonian system that has been present as the underlying philosophy of nations since ancient Babylon turned away from God in the days of Nimrod. It is uncertain what city is in view here. Rome and Jerusalem have been suggested as well as the actual city of Babylon.

> *"Is not this the great Babylon I have built . . . by my mighty power and my majesty" (Daniel 4:30). "Babylon has fallen, has fallen! All the images of its gods lie shattered on the ground!" (Isaiah 21:9). "Babylon was a gold cup in the Lord's hand; she made the whole earth drunk" (Jeremiah 51:7).*

3
Angel

Final Warning to Those Who Worship the Beast and Receive His Mark

14:9 A third angel followed them and said in a loud voice: "If anyone worships the beast and his image and receives his mark on the forehead or on the hand,

14:10 he, too, will drink of the wine of God's fury, which has been poured full strength into the cup of his wrath. He will be tormented with burning sulfur in the presence of the holy angels and of the Lamb.

Daniel's Seventieth Week is probably now over. This is seen as a warning of the consequences of worshiping the beast and his image, and receiving his mark. The judgment of God on such is undiluted.

Fire and brimstone—like unto the judgment of Sodom and Gomorrah. Note the comparison between *"the maddening wine of her adulteries"* and drinking *"the wine of God's fury."*

> *". . . you who have drunk from the hand of the Lord the cup of his wrath, you who have drained to its dregs the goblet that makes men stagger" (Isaiah 51:17).*

> *"Take from my hand this cup filled with the wine of my wrath and make all the nations to whom I send you drink it. When they drink it, they will stagger and go mad because of the sword I will send among them" (Jeremiah 25:15-16).*

> *"Whoever acknowledges me before men, the Son of Man will also acknowledge him before the angels of God. But he who disowns me before men will be disowned before the angels of God" (Luke 12:809).*

14:11 And the smoke of their torment rises for ever and ever. There is no rest day or night for those who worship the beast and his image, or for anyone who receives the mark of his name."

What we see here is the terrifying reality of divine wrath poured out on those who persist in following and worshiping Antichrist and his image. The language is reminiscent of the judgment of the nations predicted in Isaiah 34:8-10,

> *"For the Lord has a day of vengeance, a year of retribution, to uphold Zion's cause, Edom's streams will be turned into pitch, her dust into burning sulfur; her land will become blazing pitch! It will not be quenched night and day; its smoke will rise forever."*

The Obedient and Faithful Saints

14:12 This calls for patient endurance on the part of the saints who obey God's commandments and remain faithful to Jesus.

This is the same group mentioned at the close of chapter 12 (verse 17), and chapter 13, verse 10.

14:13 Then I heard a voice from heaven say, "Write: Blessed are the dead who die in the Lord from now on."

"Yes," says the Spirit," they will rest from their labor, for their deeds will follow them."

There is a stark contrast here between those who worship the beast and receive his mark, and those who refuse that mark, and are thus put to death. It is unrest as opposed to rest. It is apostasy as opposed to fidelity. God will not forget all his people have endured out of loyalty to Him. Jesus instructed His disciples about this time of great suffering that was to come,

"Do not be afraid of those who kill the body but cannot kill the soul. Rather, be afraid of the One who can destroy both soul and body in hell. Are not two sparrows sold for a penny? Yet not one of them will fall to the ground apart from the will of your Father. And even the very hairs of your head are all numbered. So don't be afraid; you are worth more than many sparrows" (Matthew 10:28-31).

THE HARVEST OF THE EARTH

4
Angel

With the Sickle

14:14 I looked, and there before me was a white cloud, and seated on the cloud was one "like the son of man" with a crown of gold on his head and a sharp sickle in his hand.

This one is not called an angel. Instead, he is identified as one *"seated on the cloud, one 'like the son of man'.* Christ has appeared before as the Angel of the Lord. This person is said to have a gold crown on his head, signifying rule and authority. It could be one of the exalted angels, an archangel, for his description here is unique, and the voice of an archangel will announce the Lord's arrival at His coming (I Thessalonians 4:16).

Even if this is not Christ as the Angel of the Lord, the timing still corresponds with the "cloud-coming" of Christ. The reference to one "like the son of man" reminds us immediately of Daniel's vision and also Revelation 1:13, *"Among the lampstands was someone like a son of man . . . . "*

One reason for taking it to be one of seven angels is that the next angel issues an order for the one sitting on the cloud to reap. In Matthew 24:30f, it is Christ who *"sends His angels with a loud trumpet call to gather His elect from the four winds, from one end of the heavens to the other (v 31).*

*"In my vision at night I looked, and there before me was one like
a son of man, coming with the clouds of heaven. He approached
the Ancient of Days and was led into his presence. He was given
authority, glory and sovereign power; all peoples, nations and men
of every language worshiped him. His dominion is an everlasting
dominion that will not pass away, and his kingdom is one that will
never be destroyed" (Daniel 7:12-14).*

My personal opinion is that this is a preview of Christ's coming.
The same sequence is given in Revelation 19 with the Marriage Supper
of the Lamb consisting of the gathered ones of all ages. Then follows
immediately His Coming with all His angels and saints in the final great
battle. The second harvest in Revelation 14 is certainly a reference to this
battle, Armageddon.

5
Angel

Issues the Order to Reap

**14:15 Then another angel came out of the temple and called in a loud
voice to him who was sitting on the cloud, "Take your sickle and reap,
because the time to reap has come, for the harvest of the earth is ripe."**

**14:16 So he that was seated on the cloud swung his sickle over the
earth, and the earth was harvested.**

Notice, too, how closely it parallels our Lord's description of the
harvest at the end of the age in Matthew 13:

*"Explain to us the parable of the weeds in the field." He answered,
"The one who sowed the good seed is the Son of Man. The field is
the world, and the good seed stands for the sons of the kingdom. The
weeds are the sons of the evil one, and the enemy who sows them is
the devil.* **The harvest is the end of the age, and the harvesters
are angels**. *As the weeds are pulled up and burned in the fire,*

so it will be at the end of the age. The Son of Man will send out his angels, and they will weed out of his kingdom everything that causes sin and all who do evil. They will throw them into the fiery furnace, where there will be weeping and gnashing of teeth. Then the righteous will shine like the sun in the kingdom of their Father. He who has ears, let him hear." (Matthew 13 :36-43).

Now notice the "harvest" language associated with the gathering out of God's people in the rapture.

"At that time the sign of the Son of Man will appear in the sky, and all the nations of the earth will mourn. They will see the Son of Man coming on the clouds of the sky, with power and great glory. And he will send his angels with a loud trumpet call, and they will gather his elect from the four winds, from one end of the heavens to the other" (Matthew 24:3-31).

"According to the Lord's own word, we tell you that we who are still alive, who are left till the coming of the Lord, will certainly not precede those who have fallen asleep. For the Lord himself will come down from heaven, with a loud command with the voice of the archangel, and with the trumpet call of God, and the dead in Christ will rise first. After that, we who are still alive and are left will be caught up together with them in the clouds to meet the Lord in the air. And so we will be with the Lord forever. Therefore encourage each other with these words" (I Thessalonians 4:15-18).

6
Angel

With the Sickle

14:17 Another angel came out of the temple in heaven, and he too had a sharp sickle.

7
Angel

The Fire Angel Issues the Order for The Second Harvest
The Winepress of God's Wrath

14:17 Still another angel, who had charge of the fire, came from the altar and called in a loud voice to him who had the sharp sickle, "Take your sharp sickle and gather the clusters of grapes from the earth's vine, because its grapes are ripe."

14:19 The angel swung his sickle on the earth, gathered its grapes and threw them into the great winepress of God's wrath.

> *"This is what the Lord Almighty, the God of Israel says: 'The Daughter of Babylon is like a threshing floor at the time it is trampled; the time to harvest her will soon come'" (Jeremiah 51:33).*

14:20 They were trampled in the winepress outside the city, and blood flowed out of the press, rising as high as the horse' bridles for a distance of 1,600 stadia (about 180 miles).

There are obviously two harvests in view here—the wheat harvest and the grape harvest. Many believe that both refer to judgment, but in the light of our Lord's teaching regarding the harvest at the end of the age, one harvest refers to deliverance and the other to judgment. The first harvest parallels the harvest of the angels in Matthew 24:31.

Judgment is here pictured in the familiar terms of the harvest and of the winepress. This judgment is to take place outside Jerusalem where, it was held, the Gentiles would be judged. Some say that the judgment here is against Israel as God's Vineyard, but it more fittingly represents His judgment against the nations. In it the risen Christ assigns His angels the task of collecting His own for glory, and the wicked for judgment; and the judgment is so complete that the effect of it covers the whole land.

"The LORD is angry with all nations; his wrath is upon all their armies. He will totally destroy them, he will give them over to slaughter. Their slain will be thrown out, their dead bodies will send up a stench; the mountains will be soaked with their blood. All the stars of the heavens will be dissolved and the sky rolled up like a scroll; all the starry host will fall like withered leaves from the vine, like shriveled figs from the fig tree." (Isaiah 34:2-4).

"I trampled the nations in my anger; in my wrath I made them drunk and poured their blood on the ground." (Isaiah 63:6).

There is unquestionably an allusion here to Joel's graphic description of the nations gathering in the Valley of Jehoshaphat and the Day of the Lord.

"Proclaim this among the nations: Prepare for war! Rouse the warriors! Let all the fighting men draw near and attack. Beat your plowshares into swords and your pruning hooks into spears. Let the weakling say, "I am strong!" Come quickly, all you nations from every side, and assemble there. Bring down your warriors, O Lord! Let the nations be roused; let them advance into the Valley of Jehoshaphat, for there I will sit to judge all the nations on every side. Swing the sickle, for the harvest is ripe. Come, trample the grapes, for the winepress is full and the vats overflow—so great is their wickedness!" Multitudes, multitudes in the valley of decision! For the day of the Lord is near in the valley of decision. The sun and moon will be darkened, and the stars no longer shine. The Lord will roar from Zion and thunder from Jerusalem; the earth and the sky will tremble. But the Lord will be a refuge for his people, a stronghold for the people of Israel" (Joel 3:9-16).

Note that this will probably be the time for the judging of the nations mentioned above and in Matthew 25.

"When the Son of man comes in his glory, and all the angels with him, he will sit on his throne in heavenly glory. All the nations will be gathered before him, and he will separate the people one from another as a shepherd separates the sheep from the goats. he will put the sheep on his right and the goats on his left. Then the

*King will say to those on his right, 'Come, you who are blessed by
my Father; take your inheritance, the kingdom prepared for you
since the creation of the world. For I was hungry and you gave
me something to eat, I was thirsty and you gave me something to
drink, I was a stranger and you invited me in, I needed clothes
and you clothed me, I was sick and you looked after me, I was in
prison and you came to visit me. Then the righteous will answer
him, 'Lord, when did we see you hungry and feed you, or thirsty
and give you something to drink? When did we see you a stranger
and invite you in, or needing clothes and clothe you? When did
we see you sick or in prison and go to visit you?' The King will
reply, 'I tell you the truth, whatever you did for one of the least of
these brothers of mine, you did for me.' Then he will say to those
on his left, 'Depart from me, you who are cursed, into the eternal
fire prepared for the devil and his angels. For I was hungry and
you gave me nothing to eat, I was thirsty and you gave me nothing
to drink, I was a stranger and you did not invite me in, I needed
clothes and you did not clothe me, I was sick and in prison and
you did not look after me.' They also will answer, 'Lord, when did
we see you hungry or thirsty or a stranger of needing clothes or sick
or in prison, and did not help you?' "He will reply, 'I tell you the
truth, whatever you did not do for one of the least of these, you did
not do for me.' Then they will go away to eternal punishment, but
the righteous to eternal life." (Matthew 25:31-46)*

CHAPTER 15

THE REDEEMED IN HEAVEN THE SEVEN BOWL ANGELS

15:1 I saw in heaven another great and marvelous sign: seven angels with the seven last plagues—last, because with them God's wrath is completed.

The wrath of God is said to remain on those who reject the Son.

> *"Whoever believes in the Son has eternal life, but whoever rejects the Son will not see life, for God's wrath remains on him" (John 3:36).*

> It is possible to *"store up wrath against yourself for the day of God's wrath, when his judgment will be revealed" (Rom. 2:5).*

> Those who have been justified by His blood, are *"saved from God's wrath through Him" (Rom. 5:9).*

> Believers are not appointed *"to suffer wrath but to receive salvation through our Lord Jesus Christ" (I Thessalonians 5:9).*

Because they did not respond to the remedial trumpet judgments, God will now complete what he began. The word here for "complete" is the Greek *telos*. It means to realize a goal, to accomplish a predetermined purpose. The time has now arrived for God to accomplish in wrath what he had foretold would occur. We are moving to a climax.

"If after all this you will not listen to me, I will punish you for your sins seven times over" (Lev. 26:18).

The Victorious Saints In Heaven

15:2 And I saw what looked like a sea of glass mixed with fire and, standing beside the sea, those who had been victorious over the beast and his image and over the number of his name. They held harps given them by God.

The Sea of glass, as noted in chapter 4 and verse 6, is probably the heavenly representation of the earthly Brazen Laver. At the conclusion to chapter 14, there was a great Red Sea of blood. Here the saints rejoice in their deliverance as they stand beside the Crystal Sea. It is mixed with fire because soon the fiery wrath of God is to be poured out. In the dedication of Solomon's Temple, the fire came down on the Sea, and the glory of the Lord filled the Temple. (2 Chronicles 6:14-42) Here in verse 8, God's glory fills the Temple, and no one is able to enter until the wrath of God is completed.

It is interesting to note that some kind of vindication of God or of His saints is given before the seals, trumpets and vials.

These could well be the same group the *"great multitude out of the great tribulation"* mentioned in chapter 7:14. They overcame the beast by *"the blood of the Lamb and by the word of their testimony; they did not love their lives so much as to shrink from death" (12:11).*

Later, in chapter 20, John sees *"the souls of those who had been beheaded because of their testimony for Jesus and because of the Word of God. They had not worshiped the beast or his image and had not received his mark on their foreheads or their hands" (20:4).* These who have died partake in the first resurrection at Christ's coming.

15:3 and sang the song of Moses the servant of God and the song of the Lamb:

The Song of Moses in Exodus

"I will sing to the Lord, for he is highly exalted. The horse and its rider he has hurled into the sea. The Lord is my strength and

> *my song; he has become my salvation. He is my God, and I will*
> *praise him, my father's God, and I will exalt him. The Lord is a*
> *warrior; the Lord is his name. Pharaoh's chariots and his army he*
> *has hurled into the sea. The best of Pharaoh's officers are drowned*
> *in the Red Sea. The deep waters have covered them; they sank to*
> *the depths like a stone" (Exodus 15:1-5)*

Here we have the heavenly counterpart of Israel's experience when they stood by the Red Sea and sang the song of deliverance. The theme of victory in Exodus 15 becomes the basis for praise and adoration in the song of the victors. This hymn may have been used in the liturgy of the early church.

"Great and marvelous are your deeds, Lord God Almighty. Just and true are your ways, King of the ages.

15:4 Who will not fear you, O Lord, and bring glory to your name? For you alone are holy. All nations will come and worship before you, for your righteous acts have been revealed.

15:5 After this I looked and in heaven the temple, that is, the tabernacle of Testimony, was opened.

The earthly counterpart is seen in Exodus 38:21. The Ark of the Covenant was the supreme symbol to Israel of God's visible power and presence. It disappeared when the times of the Gentiles began. It will now reappear as the times of the Gentiles ceases, and Israel is restored.

15:6 Out of the temple came the seven angels with the seven plagues. They were dressed in clean, shining linen and wore golden sashes around their chests.

The clean, shining linen garments represent their qualification to perform their awesome task. The golden sashes seem to indicate a special type of angel, perhaps the archangels.

15:7 Then one of the four living creatures gave to the seven angels seven golden bowls filled with the wrath of God, who lives forever and ever.

15:8 And the temple was filled with smoke from the glory of God and from his power, and no one could enter the temple until the seven plagues of the seven angels were completed.

> *"I saw the Lord seated on a throne, high and exalted, and the train of his robe filled the temple . . . . the doorposts and thresholds shook and the temple was filled with smoke" (Isaiah 6:1, 4).*

> *"Then the cloud covered the Tent of Meeting, and the glory of the Lord filled the tabernacle" (Exodus 40:34).*

The judgment issues from the temple and the very throne of God. The temple is filled with His glory and power. None can stay the hand of God. Final judgment has come.

CHAPTER 16

THE SEVEN BOWLS OF WRATH

16:1 Then I heard a loud voice from the temple saying to the seven angels, "Go, pour out the seven bowls of God's wrath on the earth."

> *"Hear that uproar from the city, hear that noise **from the temple**!*
> *It is the sound of the Lord repaying his enemies all they deserve"*
> *(Isaiah 66:6).*

Trumpets warn; bowls are poured out. This is God's own voice that is heard speaking from His throne. The indication is that the bowls are poured out in rapid succession.

The series seems to draw heavily for its symbolism from the ten Egyptian plagues.

THE DAY OF THE LORD

It is my opinion that this describes the beginning of the Day of the Lord. It would be fitting to insert here some of the Old Testament passages that deal with this climactic event.

From The Prophet Joel

> *"What a dreadful day! For the day of the Lord is near; it will come*
> *like a destruction from the Almighty . . . Blow the trumpet in*

Zion; sound the alarm on my holy hill. Let all who live in the land tremble, for the day of the Lord is coming. It is close at hand—a day of darkness and gloom, a day of clouds and blackness. Like dawn spreading across the mountains a large and mighty army comes, such as never was of old nor ever will be in ages to come. . . . Before them the earth shakes, the sky trembles, the sun and moon are darkened, and the stars no longer shine. The Lord thunders at the head of his army; his forces are beyond number, and mighty are those who obey his command . . . I will show wonders in the heavens and on the earth, blood and fire and billows of smoke. The sun will be turned to darkness and the moon to blood before the coming of the great and dreadful day of the Lord" (Joel 1:15; 2:1-2, 10-11, 30-31).

These celestial disturbances are intended to signal one last chance for man to repent. The promise goes out . . ."

"And everyone who calls on the name of the Lord will be saved; for on Mount Zion and in Jerusalem there will be deliverance, as the Lord has said, among the survivors whom the Lord calls" (Joel 2:32)

Does this refer to the remnant of Israel that will be saved when the Lord comes? The 144,000 are seen in chapter 14 with the Lord on Mount Zion. Joel has still more to say:

"In those days and at that time, when I restore the fortunes of Judah and Jerusalem, I will gather all nations and bring them down to the Valley of Jehoshaphat. There I will enter into judgment against them concerning my inheritance, my people Israel . . . Proclaim this among the nations: Prepare for war! Rouse the warriors! Let all the fighting men draw near and attack. Beat your plowshares into swords and your pruning hooks into spears. Let the weakling say, 'I am strong!' Come quickly, all you nations from every side, and assemble there. 'Bring down your warriors, O Lord!" Let the nations be roused; let them advance into the Valley of Jehoshaphat, for there I will sit to judge all the nations on every side. Swing the sickle, for the harvest is ripe. Come, trample the grapes, for the winepress is full and the vats overflow—so great is their wickedness! Multitudes, multitudes in the valley of decision! For the day of

the Lord is near in the valley of decision. The sun and the moon will be darkened, and the stars no longer shine. The Lord will roar from Zion and thunder from Jerusalem; the earth and the sky will tremble. **But the Lord will be a refuge for his people**, *a stronghold for the people of Israel." (Joel 3:1-2; 9-16).*

Here again it is mentioned that a surviving remnant of Israel will be saved.

From the Prophet Amos

Peter's address at the Council of Jerusalem quotes from Amos 9:11, 12, *"After this I will return and rebuild David's fallen tent. Its ruins I will rebuild, and I will restore it, that the remnant of men may seek the Lord, and all the Gentiles who bear my name, says the Lord, who does these things' that have been known for ages. (Acts 15:16-18).*

Amos went on to speak of that terrible day—*"Woe to you who long for the day of the Lord! Why do you long for the day of the Lord? That day will be darkness, not light. It will be as though a man fled from a lion only to meet a bear, as though he entered his house and rested his hand on the wall only to have a snake bite him. Will not the day of the Lord be darkness, not light, pitch-dark, without a ray of brightness?" (Amos 5:18-20).*

From the Prophet Isaiah

"Go into the rocks, hide in the ground from dread of the Lord and the splendor of his majesty! The eyes of the arrogant man will be humbled and the pride of men brought low; the Lord alone will be exalted in that day. The Lord Almighty has a day in store for all the proud and lofty, for all that is exalted (and they will be humbled), for all the cedars of Lebanon, tall and lofty, and all the oaks of Bashan, for all the towering mountains and all the high hills, for every lofty tower and every fortified wall, for every trading ship and every stately vessel. The arrogance of man will be brought

low and the pride of men humbled; the Lord alone will be exalted in that day, and the idols will totally disappear. Men will flee to caves in the rocks and to holes in the ground from dread of the Lord and the splendor of his majesty, when he rises to shake the earth. In that day men will throw away to the rodents and bats their idols of silver and idols of gold, which they made to worship. They will flee to caverns in the rocks and to the overhanging crags from dread of the Lord and the splendor of his majesty when he rises to shake the earth" (Isaiah 2:10-21).

Again in chapter 13, Isaiah picks up the theme of the day of the Lord.

"Listen, a noise on the mountains, like that of a great multitude! Listen, an uproar among the kingdoms, like nations massing together! The Lord Almighty is mustering an army for war. They come from faraway lands, from the ends of the heavens—the Lord and the weapons of his wrath—to destroy the whole country. Wait, for the day of the Lord is near; it will come like destruction from the Almighty. Because of this, all hands will go limp, every man's heart will melt. Terror will seize them, pain and anguish will grip them; they will writhe like a woman in labor. They will look aghast at each other, their faces aflame. See, the day of the Lord is coming—a cruel day, with wrath and fierce anger—to make the land desolate and destroy the sinners within it. The stars of heaven and their constellations will not show their light. The rising sun will be darkened and the moon will not give its light. I will punish the world for its evil, the wicked for their sins. I will put an end to the arrogance of the haughty and will humble the pride of the ruthless. I will make man scarcer than pure gold, more rare than the gold of Ophir. Therefore I will make the heavens tremble; and the earth will shake from its place at the wrath of the Lord Almighty, in the day of his burning anger" (Isaiah 13:4-13).

From the Prophet Ezekiel

Ezekiel warns that there will be a day of reckoning and accountability for His people some day in the future.

"Son of man, prophesy and say: 'This is what the Sovereign Lord says: 'Wail and say, "Alas for that day!" For the day is near, the day of the Lord is near—a day of clouds, a time of doom for the nations." (Ezekiel 30:2-3).

From the Prophet Zephaniah

"The great day of the Lord is near—near and coming quickly. Listen! The cry on the day of the Lord will be bitter, the shouting of the warrior there. That day will be a day of wrath, a day of distress and anguish, a day of trouble and ruin, a day of darkness and gloom, a day of clouds and blackness, a day of trumpet and battle cry against the fortified cities and against the corner towers. I will bring distress on the people and they will walk like blind men, because they have sinned against the Lord. Their blood will be poured out like dust and their entrails like filth. Neither their silver nor their gold will be able to save them on the day of the Lord's wrath. In the fire of his jealousy the whole world will be consumed, for he will make a sudden end of all who live in the earth." Gather together, gather together, O shameful nation, before the appointed time arrives and that day sweeps on like chaff, before the fierce anger of the Lord comes upon you, before the day of the Lord's wrath comes upon you. Seek the Lord, all you humble of the land, you who do what he commands. Seek righteousness, seek humility; perhaps you will be sheltered on the day of the Lord's anger" (Zephaniah 1:14—2:3).

"I have decided to assemble the nations, to gather the kingdoms and to pour out my wrath on them—my fierce anger" (Zephaniah 3:8).

From the Prophet Zechariah

Added to these is Zechariah's testimony concerning Jerusalem:

"A day of the Lord is coming when your plunder will be divided among you. I will gather all the nations to Jerusalem to fight

against it; the city will be captured, the houses ransacked, and the women raped. Half of the city will go into exile, but the rest of the people will be taken from the city. Then the Lord will go out and fight against those nations, as he fights in the day of battle. On that day his feet will stand on the Mount of Olives, east of Jerusalem, and the Mount of Olives will be split in two from east to west, forming a great valley, with half of the mountain moving north and half moving south." (Zechariah 14:1-4)

Israel will use this newly formed valley to flee from the city. It is at this moment that the Lord returns in the clouds—

"Then the Lord my God will come, and all the holy ones with him" (Zechariah 14:5).

He will set up His kingdom—

"On that day living water will flow out form Jerusalem, half to the eastern sea and half to the western sea, in summer and in winter. The Lord will be king over the whole earth. On that day there will be one Lord, and his name the only name" (Zechariah 14:8-9).

1
Bowl

Land

16:2 The first angel went and poured out his bowl on the land, and ugly and painful sores broke out on the people who had the mark of the beast and worshiped his image.

". . . festering boils will break out on men and animals throughout the land" (Exodus 9:9).

The target objects of these painful sores—*"the people who had the mark of the beast."*

2
Bowl

Sea

16:3 The second angel poured out his bowl on the sea, and it turned into blood like that of a dead man, and every living thing in the sea died.

The devastation is complete this time—*"every living thing."* This is reminiscent of the plague in Egypt when the waters of the Nile were turned to blood (Exodus 7:20-21).

3
Bowl

Rivers & Springs of Water

16:4 The third angel poured out his bowl on the rivers and springs of water, and they became blood.

All fresh water sources are affected.

> *"He turned their rivers to blood; they could not drink from their streams" (Psalm 78:44).*

God's Judgments Just

16:5 Then I heard the angel in charge of the waters say:

"You are just in these judgments, you who are and who were, the Holy One, because you have so judged;

God's judgment is not capricious or vengeful, but an expression of his just and holy nature. We are persistently being reminded by the heavenly worship team that God's actions are always just and holy.

16:6 for (because) they have shed the blood of your saints and prophets, and you have given them blood to drink as they deserve.

The "them" here refers to the worshipers of the beast who, having shed innocent blood will now drink blood. God tailors the punishment to fit the crime. *". . . they will be drunk on their own blood, as with wine" (Isaiah 49:26*

16:7 And I heard the altar respond:

"Yes, Lord God Almighty, true and just are your judgments."

These may be the same voices as those of the fifth seal—*"the martyrs under the altar."* They had cried out for vengeance, and here it is rendered (Rev. 6:9-11).

4
Bowl

The Sun

16:8 The fourth angel poured out his bowl on the sun, and the sun was given power to scorch people with fire.

16:9 They were seared by the intense heat and they cursed the name of God, who had control over these plagues, but they refused to repent and glorify him.

Notice that in addition to the searing heat, they had no fresh water to assuage their thirst.

The result is like a refrain—*"they refused to repent and glorify Him."* (see *v 11)* God's unparalleled judgment here fails to call forth repentance.

5
Bowl

Darkness

16:10 The fifth angel poured out his bowl on the throne of the beast, and his kingdom was plunged into darkness.

The symbol of the beast's sovereignty is now targeted.

> *"Then they will look toward the earth and see only distress and darkness and fearful gloom, and they will be thrust into utter darkness" (Isaiah 8:22).*

Note also the plague of darkness in Egypt—Exodus 10:21-29

16:11 Men gnawed their tongues in agony and cursed the God of heaven because of their pains and their sores, but they refused to repent of what they had done.

Associated with the intense darkness is something which causes great suffering signified by the *"biting of their tongues"*. They blaspheme God. Cumulatively, the suffering becomes more intense. They come so quickly that there is no time to recover from the previous one. Again the refrain, *"they refused to repent"*.

6
Bowl

Euphrates

16:12 The sixth angel poured out his bowl on the great river Euphrates, and its water was dried up to prepare the way for the kings from the East.

"Kings of the east" are uncertain. Perhaps an allusion to the Parthian warriors so feared by the Roman rulers, or in our modern context, the vast army that China has put together. God is seen working behind the scenes preparing the way for their ultimate defeat.

> *"He (the Lord) will sweep his hand over the Euphrates River. He will break it up into seven streams so that men can cross over in sandals" (Isaiah 11:15).*

16:13 Then I saw three evil spirits that looked like frogs; they came out of the mouth of the dragon, out of the mouth of the beast and out of the mouth of the false prophet.

The unclean frog-like spirits or demons proceed from the mouths of the unholy triumvirate, and suggest their deceptive propaganda that leads the nations and their rulers to ally themselves with their evil cause.

16:14 They are spirits of demons performing miraculous signs, and they go out to the kings of the whole world, to gather them for the battle on the great day of God Almighty.

> *"The Spirit clearly says that in later times some will abandon the faith and follow deceiving spirits and things taught by demons" (I Timothy 4:1).*

The place is Megiddo, and this is not the first time that God has fought for His people on this plain. Here a still broader coalition of nations is in view, *"the whole world"*.

16:15 "Behold, I come like a thief! Blessed is he who stays awake and keeps his clothes with him, so that he may not go naked and be shamefully exposed."

The message to the church in Sardis was ***"I will come like a thief****, and you will not know at what hour I will come upon you" (3:3)* The letter continues,

> *"Wake up, and strengthen the things that remain, which were about to die; for I have not found your deeds completed in the sight*

of My God . . . . But you have a few people in Sardis who have not soiled their garments; and they will walk with Me in white; for they are worthy. He who overcomes shall thus be clothed in white garments . . . " (3:2; 4-5)

This is reminiscent of what the Lord said in Matthew 24:44, *"so you also must be ready, because the Son of Man will come at an hour you do not expect him."*

Or again in Luke 21:34-36,

*"Be careful, or your hearts will be weighed down with dissipation, drunkenness and the anxieties of life, and that day will close on you unexpectedly like a trap. For it will come upon all those who live on the face of the whole earth. Be always on the watch, and pray that you may be able to escape all that is about to happen, and that you may be able to stand before the Son of Man." "But understand this: If the owner of the house had known at what hour **the thief was coming**, he would not have let his house be broken into. You must be ready, because the Son of Man will come at an hour when you do not expect him" (Luke 12:39-40).*

Paul writes in I Thessalonians 5:4,

*"For you know very well that the day of the Lord will come **like a thief in the night**. While people are saying, "Peace and safety," destruction will come on them suddenly, as labor pains on a pregnant woman, and they will not escape. But you, brothers, are not in darkness so that this day should surprise you like a thief. You are all sons of the light and sons of the day. We do not belong to the night or to the darkness. So then, let us not be like others, who are asleep, but let us be alert and self-controlled."*

This constitutes another reason why I believe the sixth Seal and the sixth Trumpet and the sixth Bowl bring us to Armageddon. The Day of the Lord is the Coming of the Lord in power and great glory! The seventh Seal, seventh Trumpet, and seventh Bowl are climactic and announce His arrival.

ARMAGEDDON!

16:16 Then they gathered the kings together to the place that in Hebrew is called Armageddon.

Har-Magedon means Mountain of Megiddo. It probably refers to the ancient city of Megiddo whose ruins are on the north side of the Carmel ridge and command the strategic pass between the coastal plain and the valley of Jezreel (Jewish) or Esdraelon (Greek) where so many famous battles have taken place. The valley is about 15 miles wide at its widest point.

7
Bowl

FINISHED!

16:17 The seventh angel poured out his bowl into the air, and out of the temple came a loud voice from the throne, saying, "It is done!"

All the events recorded in Revelation 17-19 probably occur while the bowls are being poured out. They are explanatory and give more detail of the Day of the Lord.

Terminus Statement

16:18 Then there came flashes of lightning, rumblings, peals of thunder and a severe earthquake. No earthquake like it has ever occurred since man has been on earth, so tremendous was the quake.

> *"And in my zeal and in My blazing wrath I declare that on that day there will surely be a great earthquake in the land of Israel. And the fish of the sea, the birds of the heavens, the beasts of the field, all the creeping things that creep on the earth, and all the men who are on the face of the earth will shake at My presence; the mountains*

also will be thrown down, the steep pathways will collapse, and every wall will fall to the ground" (Ezekiel 38:19-20).

16:19 The great city split into three parts, and the cities of the nations collapsed.

This is very likely Jerusalem which is in view, and the fulfillment of Zechariah's prophecy that when Christ's feet touch the Mount of Olives it will cleave in its midst forming a great valley (Zech. 14:l-4). This earthquake is unparalleled in its intensity and destructiveness. It reaches well beyond the environs of Jerusalem.

God remembered Babylon the Great and gave her the cup filled with the wine of the fury of his wrath.

16:20 Every island fled away and the mountains could not be found.

This probably means that the islands and the mountains disappear from view into the sea, and thus cease to exist.

The writer to the Hebrews refers to a time of shaking when the Old is replaced by the New.

> *See to it that you do not refuse him who speaks. If they did not escape when they refused him who warned them on earth, how much less will we, if we turn away from him who warns us from heaven? At that time his voice shook the earth, but now he has promised, "Once more I will shake not only the earth but also the heavens." The words once more" indicate the removing of what can be shaken—that is, created things—so that what cannot be shaken may remain. Therefore, since we are receiving a kingdom that cannot be shaken, let us be thankful, and so worship God acceptably with reverence and awe, for our "God is a consuming fire." (Hebrews 12:26-29)*

Huge Hailstones

16:21 From the sky huge hailstones of about a hundred pounds each fell upon men. And they cursed God on account of the plague of hail, because the plague was so terrible.

One can only imagine at the utter devastation such huge hailstones would cause. It would be difficult to find safe refuge from such.

> *"In my wrath I will unleash a violent wind, and in my anger hailstones and torrents of rain will fall with destructive fury"* *(Ezekiel 13:13).*

CHAPTER 17

MYSTERY BABYLON THE GREAT

17:1 One of the seven angels who had the seven bowls came and said to me, "Come, I will show you the punishment of the great prostitute, who sits on many waters.

In verse 15 the "waters" are interpreted as *"peoples, multitudes, nations and languages."* This designation appears frequently in Daniel and here in the Revelation as a description of the people of the earth or the world. It refers to empire authority. There have been seven world empires or kingdoms that have been associated in some way with this ancient Babylonish system first introduced by Nimrod at Babel.

In 21:9, this or another of the bowl angels appears to John and shows him the Bride, the wife of the Lamb. The connection is most certainly not accidental. The great Harlot and the Pure Bride are contrasted.

17:2 With her the kings of the earth committed adultery and the inhabitants of the earth were intoxicated with the wine of her adulteries."

This is religious apostasy at its worst. She represents a world system based on seduction and personal gain.

17:3 Then the angel carried me away in the Spirit into a desert. There I saw a woman sitting on a scarlet beast that was covered with blasphemous names and had seven heads and ten horns.

17:4 The woman was dressed in purple and scarlet, and was glittering with gold, precious stones and pearls. She held a golden cup in her hand, filled with abominable things and the filth of her adulteries.

> *"Babylon was a gold cup in the Lord's hand; she made the whole earth drunk. The nations drank her wine; therefore they have now gone mad" (Jeremiah 51:7).*

17:5 This title was written on her forehead: MYSTERY BABYLON THE GREAT THE MOTHER OF PROSTITUTES AND OF THE ABOMINATIONS OF THE EARTH.

The woman known as "Babylon the Great" is Satan's own ecclesiastical system. All idolatrous systems are her harlot-daughters.

17:6 I saw that the woman was drunk with the blood of the saints, the blood of those who bore testimony to Jesus.

This woman represents the godless anti-Christian system that has consistently opposed God and God's people since the earliest of times beginning with Nimrod who built the first Babylon and erected the Tower of Babel. In John's day, Rome was the Vanity Fair of the world's cities. The description here certainly fits Rome or more specifically The Vatican City. (Research the years of Inquisition, efforts to control politically as well as religiously, accumulation of vast wealth etc.)

When I saw her, I was greatly astonished.

17:7 Then the angel said to me: "Why are you astonished? I will explain to you the mystery of the woman and of the beast she rides, which has the seven heads and ten horns.

17:8 The beast, which you saw, once was, now is not, and will come up out of the Abyss and go to his destruction. The inhabitants of the earth whose names have not been written in the book of life from the creation of the world will be astonished when they see the beast, because he once was, now is not, and yet will come.

Obviously, this is a parody of the Lamb, who was put to death yet came back to life and now is alive forevermore. It is also antithetical to the One *"who is and who was and who is to come."*

17:9 This calls for a mind with wisdom. The seven heads are seven hills on which the woman sits. They are also seven kings.

Some see the seven hills as the seven hills on which Rome was built. In keeping with Daniel's parade of nations, they might be better viewed as seven successive kingdoms or empires. 1. Seven heads—seven mountains (kingdoms) 2. Seven heads—seven kings

17:10 Five have fallen, one is, the other has not yet come; but when he does come, he must remain for a little while.

Since this refers to what will take place in the latter days, its primary reference must be to the successive kingdoms that figured into Israel's history from their slavery in Egypt where they became a nation to the Rome of John's day. Beyond that kingdom there is still another yet to appear.

1. Egypt
2. Assyria
3. Babylon—Daniel's vision onward
4. Persia
5. Greece
6. Rome (the one that is)
7. Ten-Toed or Ten-Horned Confederacy

17:11 The beast who once was, and now is not, is an eighth king. He belongs to the seven and is going to his destruction.

8. Confederated Kingdom of Antichrist

Daniel indicates that the Little Horn will defeat three kings of the 10 who resist his authority—this would make him an eighth king along with the remaining seven. Then all 10 kingdoms submit to his rule and purpose. So he is doubly an "eighth" king.

17:12 The ten horns you saw are ten kings who have not yet received a kingdom, but who for one hour will receive authority as kings along with the beast.

One hour—a brief period of time

> *"The fourth beast is a fourth kingdom that will appear on earth. It will be different from all the other kingdoms and will devour the whole earth, trampling it down and crushing it. The ten horns are ten kings who will come from this kingdom. After them another king will arise, different from the earlier ones; he will subdue three kings. He will speak against the Most High and oppress his saints and try to change the set times and the laws. The saints will be handed over to him for a time, times and half a time" (Daniel 7:23-25).*

Notice this king is an eighth king, but belongs to the seven (v 11 above). The ten kingdoms are the same mentioned in Daniel that correspond to the ten toes (part iron and part clay) of the colossus. They are 10 kings and kingdoms that shall arise in the last day for a short time and support the antichrist in his bid to take over world dominance. They may well be a revived Roman Empire (since the ancient Roman Empire was not completely destroyed) in what is modern Europe. There is a sense in which the nations in Daniel's vision still exist in some form since the colossus composed of four kingdoms plus the end time confederated kingdom will come smashing to the ground and be ground to dust when the rock cut out of the mountain smashes the toes. It must not be overlooked that Israel is presently surrounded by her ancient foes and they are all Islamic nations whose intense hatred for Israel is public record.

17:13 They have one purpose and will give their power and authority to the beast.

The Conquering Lamb!

17:14 They will make war against the Lamb, but the Lamb will overcome them because he is Lord of lords and King of kings—and with him will be his called, chosen and faithful followers."

> *"Then the Lord my God will come, and all the holy ones with him"*
> *(Zechariah 14:5).*

17:15 Then the angel said to me, "The waters you saw, where the prostitute sits, are peoples, multitudes, nations and languages.

17:16 The beast and the ten horns you saw will hate the prostitute. They will bring her to ruin and leave her naked; they will eat her flesh and burn her with fire.

Note Ezekiel's allegory of Unfaithful Jerusalem.

> *"Therefore I am going to gather all your lovers, with whom you found pleasure, those you loved as well as those you hated. I will gather them against you from all around and will strip you in front of them, and they will see all your nakedness . . . Then I will hand you over to your lovers, and they will tear down your mounds and destroy your lofty shrines. They will strip you of your clothes and take your fine jewelry and leave you naked and bare" (Ezekiel 16:37, 39).* See also Ezek. 23:11-35

17:17 For God has put it into their hearts to accomplish his purpose by agreeing to give the beast their power to rule, until God's words are fulfilled.

This is understandable when one considers that the two great beasts set up their own religious system that they fully intend to make universal in its scope and mandatory on all their subjects. Every form of existing worship including this false system will come under its ban. Their existing wealth will be confiscated, their temples, cathedrals, mosques etc. will be rifled, stripped and burned. All who resists will evidently be put to the sword.

17:18 The woman you saw is the great city that rules over the kings of the earth."

Great Babylon in its final revelation is also a local city. It seems more than just an ideal. Rome has been suggested, as has been Jerusalem. But we should not dismiss the idea that the literal city of Babylon could once again be restored and become the seat of the world's religion and commerce. It is true that the ancient predictions seemed to indicate the utter destruction of Babylon, but they have not yet been completely fulfilled (Isaiah 13). Isaiah locates the destruction of Babylon in "the day of the Lord." That day has not yet literally been fulfilled. The Medes and Persians made it one of their royal cities. It was the chosen capital of the Graeco-Macedonian Empire under Alexander. The Syrian kings who succeeded Alexander used it. It still existed in the time of the apostles. As late as A.D. 250, there was a Christian church there. The Babylonian Talmud was issued from their by Jewish academies centered there 500 years after Christ. Sadam Hussein, the former dictator of Iraq fancied himself to be the successor to Nebuchadnezzar, and poured millions of oil revenue dollars into beginning reconstructing the ancient city to its former glory. Zechariah sees the vision of the flying scroll of the curse of God going forth over the face of the whole earth, and he sees the measuring basket and the two women with wings. The prophet wondered what it all meant, and was told that they were taking the basket *"to the country of Babylonia (Shinar) to build a house for it. When it is ready, the basket will be set there in its place."* Inside the basket is the woman of wickedness that may correspond to Mystery Babylon the Great here. (Zechariah 5:1-11). This evil power is the ephah and the talent, symbols of commerce. Leaders in commerce have long recognized that the region of the Euphrates Valley would be an ideal site for a commercial hub among the nations. If the present reconstruction of Iraq is successful in time, it could rise once again to prominence.

CHAPTER 18

THE FALL OF BABYLON

Chapters 17 and 18 describe the same event, the fall of Babylon, both the moral and commercial aspects.

As mentioned above, Zechariah 5:5-11 describes "a woman" and a "house" built in the land of Shinar. The woman seems to move her headquarters from one city to another. The modern name for Shinar is Iraq or Babylon. The whole world will amalgamate in one religious system—a "new age" system.

18:1 After this I saw another angel coming down from heaven. He had great authority, and the earth was illuminated by his splendor.

18:2 With a mighty voice he shouted: "Fallen! Fallen is Babylon the Great! She has become a home for demons and a haunt for every unclean and detestable bird.

> *"But desert creatures will lie there, jackals will fill her houses; there the owls will dwell, and there the wild goats will leap about. Hyenas will howl in her strongholds, jackals in her luxurious palaces. Her time is at hand, and her days will not be prolonged"* (Isaiah 13:21-22).

> *"The desert owl and screech owl will possess it; the great owl and the raven will nest there" (34:11).*

"So desert creatures and hyenas will live there, and there the owl will dwell" (Jeremiah 50:39).

"Babylon will be a heap of ruins, a haunt of jackals, an object of horror and scorn, a place where no one lives" (51:37).

18:3 For all the nations have drunk the maddening wine of her adulteries. The kings of the earth committed adultery with her, and the merchants of the earth grew rich from her excessive luxuries."

18:4 Then I heard another voice from heaven say: "Come out of her, my people, so that you will not share in her sins, so that you will not receive any of her plagues;

This is probably a call to Israel to escape while they can, the rapture having already occurred.

"Leave Babylon, flee from the Babylonians!" (Isaiah 48:20). "Flee out of Babylon; leave the land of the Babylonians . . . " (Jeremiah 50:8).

18:5 for her sins are piled up to heaven, and God has remembered her crimes.

Note Jeremiah's continued warning:

"Flee from Babylon! Run for your lives! Do not be destroyed because of her sins. It is time for the Lord's vengeance; he will pay her what she deserves. Babylon was a gold cup in the Lord's hand; she made the whole earth drunk. The nations drank her wine; therefore they have now gone mad. Babylon will suddenly fall and be broken. Wail over her! Get balm for her pain; perhaps she can be healed. We would have healed Babylon, but she cannot be healed; let us leave her and each go to his own land, for her judgment reaches to the skies, it rises as high as the clouds. Come out of her, my people! Run for your lives! Run from the fierce anger of the Lord." (Jeremiah 51:6-9, 45)

18:6 Give back to her as she has given; pay her back double for what she has done. Mix her a double portion from her own cup.

> *"O Daughter of Babylon, doomed to destruction, happy is he who repays you for what you have done to us—" (Psalm 137:8). "Do to her as she has done to others" Jeremiah 50:15). "Repay her for her deeds; do to her as she has done" (50:29).*

18:7 Give her as much torture and grief as the glory and luxury she gave herself. In her heart she boasts, 'I sit as queen; I am not a widow, and I will never mourn.'

> *"You said, 'I will continue forever—the eternal queen!' But you did not consider these things or reflect on what might happen. Now then, listen, you wanton creature, lounging in your security and saying to yourself, 'I am, and there is none besides me. I will never be a widow or suffer the loss of children.' (Isaiah 47:7-8).*

18:8 Therefore in one day her plagues will overtake her: death, mourning and famine. She will be consumed by fire, for mighty is the Lord God who judges her.

> *"Both of these will overtake you in a moment, on a single day: loss of children and widowhood" (Isaiah 47:9).*

The phrases used emphasize the suddenness and swiftness of the destruction.

18:9 "When the kings of the earth who committed adultery with her and shared her luxury see the smoke of her burning, they will weep and mourn over her.

> *"Babylon will suddenly fall and be broken. Wail over her!" (Jeremiah 51:8).*

18:10 Terrified at her torment, they will stand far off and cry:

Woe, Woe!

"'Woe! Woe, O great city, O Babylon, city of power! In one hour your doom has come!' 18:11 "The merchants of the earth will weep and mourn over her because no one buys their cargoes any more—

Note the similarity in language with The Lament for Tyre in Ezekiel 27.

> *"Your wealth, merchandise and wares, your mariners, seamen and shipwrights, your merchants and all your soldiers, and everyone else on board will sink into the heart of the sea on the day of your shipwreck . . . They will weep over you with anguish of soul and with bitter mourning . . . The merchants among the nations hiss at you; you have come to a horrible end and will be no more" (Ezekiel 27:27, 31, 36).*

Cargo List

18:12 cargoes of gold, silver, precious stones and pearls; fine linen, purple, silk and scarlet cloth; every sort of citron wood, an articles of every kind made of ivory, costly wood, bronze, iron and marble; 18:13 cargoes of cinnamon and spice, of incense, myrrh and frankincense, of wine and olive oil, of fine flour and wheat; cattle and sheep; horses and carriages; and bodies and souls of men.

See the cargo list in Ezekiel 27 of those who traded goods with Tyre.

18:14 "They will say, 'The fruit you longed for is gone from you. All your riches and splendor have vanished, never to be recovered.' 18:15 The merchants who sold these things and gained their wealth from her will stand far off, terrified at her torment. They will weep and mourn

Woe, Woe!

18:16 and cry out: 'Woe! Woe, O great city, dressed in fine linen, purple and scarlet, and glittering with gold, precious stones and

pearls! 18:17 In one hour such great wealth has been brought to ruin!' "Every sea captain, and all who travel by ship, the sailors, and all who earn their living from the sea, will stand far off. 18:18 When they see the smoke of her burning, they will exclaim, 'Was there ever a city like this great city?' 18:19 They will throw dust on their heads, and with weeping and mourning cry out:

Woe, Woe!

'Woe! Woe, O great city, where all who had ships on the sea became rich through her wealth! In one hour she has been brought to ruin!

18:20 Rejoice over her, O heaven! Rejoice, saints and apostles and prophets! God has judged her for the way she treated you.'"

> *"Then heaven and earth and all that is in them will shout for joy over Babylon, for out of the north destroyers will attack her,"* declares the Lord. (Jeremiah 51:48).

18:21 Then a mighty angel picked up a boulder the size of a large millstone and threw it into the sea, and said:

> *"When you finish reading this scroll, tie a stone to it and throw it into the Euphrates. Then say, 'So will Babylon sink to rise no more because of the disaster I will bring upon her. And her people will fall.'"* (Jeremiah 51:63-64).

"With such violence the great city of Babylon will be thrown down, never to be found again. 18:22 The music of harpists and musicians, flute players and trumpeters, will never be heard in you again.

> *"The gaiety of the tambourines is stilled, the noise of revelers has stopped, the joyful harp is silent"* (Isaiah 24:8).

No workman of any trade will ever be found in you again. The sound of a millstone will never be heard in you again. 18:23 The light of a

lamp will never shine in you again. The voice of bridegroom and bride will never be heard in you again.

A similar thing was said regarding those who had turned away from their God in Jerusalem, *"I will bring an end to the sounds of joy and gladness and to the voices of bride and bridegroom . . . " (Jeremiah 7:34)*. But God would eventually reverse this. (Jeremiah 33:10,11). In the case of Babylon there will be no recovery.

Your merchants were the world's great men. By your magic spell all the nations were led astray.

> *"I will banish from them the sounds of joy and gladness, the voices of bride and bridegroom, the sound of millstones and the light of the lamp" (Jeremiah 25:10).*

> *". . . all because of the wanton lust of a harlot, alluring, the mistress of sorceries, who enslaved nations by her prostitution and peoples by her witchcraft" (Nahum 3:4).*

18:24 In her was found the blood of prophets and of the saints, and of all who have been killed on the earth."

> *"Babylon must fall because of Israel's slain, just as the slain in all the earth have fallen because of Babylon" (Jeremiah 51:49).*

CHAPTER 19

THE HALLELUJAH CHORUS

A Great Multitude

19:1 After this I heard what sounded like the roar of a great multitude in heaven shouting: "Hallelujah! Salvation and glory and power belong to our God, 19:2 for true and just are his judgments. He has condemned the great prostitute who corrupted the earth by her adulteries. He has avenged on her the blood of his servants."

These are probably the "great multitude" of chapter 7, verse 9 and following. They are said to have come out of the great tribulation, and washed their robes and made them white in the blood of the Lamb (v 14).

The "great prostitute" is Babylon the Great, the harlot, who has abandoned the truth and prostituted herself for personal gain. This political, economic, and religious system is as old as the ancient Babel established by Nimrod centuries before. The contrast to the harlot is the pure bride of Christ, the Church.

Note: 18:20 commands *"Rejoice over her!"* This is heaven's response.

19:3 And again they shouted: "Hallelujah! The smoke from her goes up for ever and ever."

Note: "Hallelujah" means Praise the Lord!

"It will not be quenched night and day; its smoke will rise forever.
From generation to generation it will lie desolate; no one will ever

pass through it again" (Isaiah 34:10). (God's judgment of the nations, specifically Edom.)

19:4 The twenty-four elders and the four living creatures fell down and worshiped God, who was seated on the throne. And they cried: "Amen, Hallelujah!"

19:5 Then a voice came from the throne, saying: "Praise our God, all you his servants, you who fear him, both small and great!"

> *"Praise the Lord all you servants of the Lord who minister by night in the house of the Lord" (Psalm 134:1). "The Lord . . . will bless those who fear the Lord—small and great" (Psalm 115:13).*

19:6 Then I heard what sounded like a great multitude, like the roar of rushing waters and like loud peals of thunder, shouting: "Hallelujah! For our Lord God Almighty reigns.

Notice the similarity in language to Revelation 14:2,

> *"And I heard a sound from heaven like the roar of rushing waters and like a loud peal of thunder. The sound I heard was like that of harpists playing their harps. And they sang a new song before the throne and before the four living creatures and the elders" (Revelation 14:2).*

Would this indicate that the "great multitude" was already in heaven, and now welcome the 144,000 redeemed ones? Notice, too, that in chapter 15:2, the victorious ones were given harps given to them by God and they sing the song of deliverance, the song of Moses.

Note the progression:

- ➤ Our God saves (7:10; 19:1)
- ➤ Our God judges (19:2)
- ➤ Our God reigns (19:6)

THE WEDDING SUPPER OF THE LAMB

The Rapture & The Resurrection

"I go and prepare a place for you, and if I go and prepare a place for you, I will come back and take you to be with me that you also may be where I am" (John 14:2, 3).

19:7 Let us rejoice and be glad and give him glory! For the wedding of the Lamb has come, and his bride has made herself ready.

"This is a profound mystery—but I am talking about Christ and the church" (Ephesians 5:32).

Jewish weddings in that day were quite unlike weddings in the Western world. First, there was an engagement, usually made by the parents when the prospective bride and groom were quite young. This engagement was binding and could be broken only by a form of divorce. Any unfaithfulness during the engagement was considered adultery (consider Joseph's dilemma). When the public ceremony was to be enacted, the groom would go to the bride's house and claim her for himself. He would take her to his home for the wedding supper, and all the guests would join the happy couple. This feast could last as long as a week.

One of the kingdom parables Jesus told, The Ten Virgins and The Wedding Supper, gives us a good description of what took place.

"At that time the kingdom of heaven will be like ten virgins who took their lamps and went out to meet the bridegroom. Five of them were foolish and five were wise. The foolish ones took their lamps but did not take any oil with them. The wise, however, took oil in jars along with their lamps. The bridegroom was a long time in coming, and they all became drowsy and fell asleep. At midnight the cry rang out: 'Here's the bridegroom! Come out to meet him!' Then all the virgins woke up and trimmed their lamps. The foolish ones said to the wise, 'Give us some of your oil; our lamps are going out.' 'No,' they replied, 'there may not be enough for both us and you. Instead, go to those who sell oil and buy some for yourselves.'

But while they were on their way to buy the oil, the bridegroom arrived. The virgins who were ready went in with him to the wedding banquet. And the door was shut. Later the others also came. 'Sir! Sir!' they said, 'Open the door for us!' But he replied, 'I tell you the truth, I don't know you.' Therefore keep watch, because you do not know the day or the hour." (Matthew 25:1-13).

Her Dress

19:8 Fine linen, bright and clean was given her to wear." (Fine linen stands for the righteous acts of the saints.)

This completes the great multitude mentioned in chapter 7 who were similarly dressed. The rapture of the Church has occurred. *"They were wearing white robes . . . they have washed their robes and made them white in the blood of the Lamb" (v 9, 14).*

> *"I delight greatly in the Lord; my soul rejoices in my God. For he has clothed me with garments of salvation and arrayed me in a robe of righteousness" (Isaiah 61:10).*

> The priestly service in the temple. *"They are to wear linen . . . . "* (Ezekiel 44:18). *"See, I will take away your sin, and I will put rich garments on you" (Zechariah 3:4).*

The Invitation

19:9 Then the angel said to me, "Write: 'Blessed are those who are invited to the wedding supper of the Lamb!' "And he added, "These are the true words of God."

19:10 At this I fell at his feet to worship him. But he said to me, "Do not do it! I am a fellow servant with you and with your brothers who hold to the testimony of Jesus. Worship God! For the testimony of Jesus is the spirit of prophecy."

THE CONQUERING CHRIST

19:11 I saw heaven standing open and there before me was a white horse, whose rider is called Faithful and True. With justice he judges and makes war.

Here we have another sevenfold description:

- ➤ He rides on a white horse.
- ➤ He is faithful and true.
- ➤ In righteousness He judges and makes war.
- ➤ His eyes like blazing fire.
- ➤ On His head many crowns.
- ➤ A name written, that no man knows, but Himself.
- ➤ Clothed in a robe spattered with blood.

> *"Oh, that you would rend the heavens and come down, that the mountains would tremble before you! As when fire sets twigs ablaze and causes water to boil, come down to make your name known to your enemies and cause the nations to quake before you!" (Isaiah 64:1-2).*

> *"They will sing before the Lord, for he comes, he comes to judge the earth. He will judge the world in righteousness and the peoples in his truth" (Psalm 96:13).*

> *"But with righteousness he will judge . . . " (Isaiah 11:4).*

> *"For to us a child is born, to us a son is given, and the government will be on his shoulders. And he will be called Wonderful Counselor, Mighty God, Everlasting Father, Prince of Peace. Of the increase of his government and peace there will be no end. He will reign on David's throne and over his kingdom, establishing and upholding it with justice and righteousness from that time on and forever. The zeal of the LORD Almighty will accomplish this" (Isaiah 9:6-7).*

> *"In love a throne will be established; in faithfulness a man will sit on it—one from the house of David—one who in judging*

seeks justice and speeds the cause of righteousness" (Isaiah 16:5). "The LORD will be king over the whole earth. On that day there will be one LORD, and his name the only name . . . Then the survivors from all the nations that have attacked Jerusalem will go up year after year to worship the King, the LORD Almighty, and to celebrate the Feast of Tabernacles" (Zechariah 14:9, 16).

19:12 His eyes are like blazing fire, and on his head are many crowns. He has a name written on him that no one but he himself knows. 19:13 He is dressed in a robe dipped in blood, and his name is the Word of God.

This is not our Lord's blood, but that of His conquered foes.

"Who is this coming from Edom, from Bozrah, with his garments stained crimson? Who is this, robed in splendor, striding forward in the greatness of his strength? It is I, speaking in righteousness, mighty to save." Why are your garments red, like those of one treading the winepress? I have trodden the winepress alone; from the nations no one was with me. I trampled them in my anger and trod them down in my wrath; their blood spattered my garments, and I stained all my clothing. For the day of vengeance was in my heart, and the year of my redemption has come. (Isaiah 63:1-4).

THE ARMIES OF HEAVEN

19:14 The armies of heaven were following him, riding on white horses and dressed in fine linen, white and clean.

The armies of heaven are probably angels. I Thessalonians 3:13 says,

"To the end he may establish your hearts unblameable in holiness before God, even our Father, at the coming (parousia) of our Lord Jesus Christ with all his saints." Or it could be translated *"with all his holy ones."*

Or again in Zechariah: *". . . and the Lord my God shall come, and all the saints* (the Septuagint reads 'angels') *with thee"* (*Zechariah 14:5*).

Note 2 Thessalonians1:7 *"And to you who are troubled rest with us, when the Lord Jesus shall be revealed from heaven with his mighty angels."*

Or Mark 8:38: *". . . when he comes in the glory of his Father with the holy angels."*

And the parallel passage in Luke 9:26: *". . . when he shall come in his own glory, and in his Father's, and of the holy angels."*

However, we should not dismiss the idea that those who follow him in linen or white robes may also be his followers. For this we refer to Chapter 17 and verse14: *"They will make war against the Lamb, but the Lamb will overcome them because he is Lord of lords and King of kings—and with him will be his called, chosen and faithful followers."*

Note this graphic description of the Day of the Lord in Joel 2, *"The Lord thunders at the head of his army; his forces are beyond number, and mighty are those who obey his command. The day of the Lord is great; it is dreadful. Who can endure it?" (Joel 2:11).* This last question is very similar to that in 6:17 under the sixth seal, *"For the great day of their wrath has come, and who can stand?"* They are parallel passages.

19:15 Out of his mouth comes a sharp sword with which to strike down the nations. "He will rule them with an iron scepter." He treads the winepress of the fury of the wrath of God Almighty.

"They will make war against the Lamb, but the Lamb will overcome them because he is Lord of lords and King of kings—and with him will be his called, chosen and faithful followers" (Rev. 17:14).

"He will strike the earth with the rod of his mouth; with the breath of his lips he will slay the wicked" (Isaiah 11:4).

"You will rule them with an iron scepter; you will dash them to pieces like pottery" (Psalm 2:9).

"Swing the sickle, for the harvest is ripe. Come, trample the grapes, for the winepress is full and the vats overflow—so great is their wickedness!" (Joel 3:13).

19:16 On his robe and on his thigh he has this name written: KING OF KINGS AND LORD OF LORDS.

THE GREAT SUPPER OF GOD

19:17 And I saw an angel standing in the sun, who cried in a loud voice to all the birds flying in midair, "Come, gather together for the great supper of God,

"Has not my inheritance become to me like a speckled bird of prey that other birds of prey surround and attack? Go and gather all the wild beasts; bring them to devour" (Jeremiah 12:9).

19:18 so that you may eat the flesh of kings, generals, and mighty men, of horses and their riders, and the flesh of all people, free and slave, small and great."

"Son of man, this is what the Sovereign Lord says: Call out to every kind of bird and all the wild animals: 'Assemble and come together from all around to the sacrifice I am preparing for you, the great sacrifice on the mountains of Israel. There you will eat flesh and drink blood. You will eat the flesh of mighty men and drink the blood of the princes of the earth as if they were rams and lambs, goats and bulls—all of them fattened animals from Bashan. At the sacrifice I am preparing for you, you will eat fat till you are glutted and drink blood till you are drunk. At my table you will eat your fill of horses and riders, mighty men and soldiers of every kind,' declares the Sovereign Lord" (Ezekiel 39:17-20).

19:19 Then I saw the beast and the kings of the earth and their armies gathered together to make war against the rider on the horse and his army.

> *"A day of the Lord is coming when your plunder will be divided among you. I will gather all the nations to Jerusalem to fight against it; the city will be captured, the houses ransacked, and the women raped. Half of the city will go into exile, but the rest of the people will not be taken from the city. Then the Lord will go out and fight against those nations, as he fights in the day of battle. On that day his feet will stand on the Mount of Olives, east of Jerusalem, and the Mount of Olives will be split in two from east to west, forming a great valley, with half of the mountain moving north and half moving south. You will flee by my mountain valley, for it will extend to Azel. You will flee as you fled from the earthquake in the days of Uzziah king of Judah. Then the Lord my God will come, and all the holy ones with him . . . On that day living water will flow out from Jerusalem, half to the eastern sea and half to the western sea, in summer and in winter. The Lord will be king over the whole earth. On that day there will be one Lord, and his name the only name" (Zechariah 14:1-5, 8-9).*

THE BEAST & FALSE PROPHET CAPTURED AND CONFINED

19:20 But the beast was captured, and with him the false prophet who had performed the miraculous signs on his behalf. With these signs he had deluded those who had received the mark of the beast and worshiped his image. The two of them were thrown alive into the fiery lake of burning sulfur.

Cast into hell—Satan will join them a thousand years later, along with those not recorded in the book of life (20:10, 15).

"Then I continued to watch because of the boastful words the horn was speaking. I kept looking until the beast was slain and its body destroyed and thrown in the blazing fire" (Daniel 7:11).

19:21 The rest of them were killed with the sword that came out of the mouth of the rider on the horse, and all the birds gorged themselves on their flesh.

CHAPTER 20

THE THOUSAND YEARS

Before The 1,000 Years

20:1 And I saw an angel coming down out of heaven, having the key to the Abyss and holding in his hand a great chain.

Note: Abyss—not the same as hell. (9:1-2, 11; 11:7; 17:8). *"(The demons) begged him repeatedly not to order them to go into the Abyss" (Luke 8:31).*

Satan Seized and Imprisoned.

20:2 He seized the dragon, that ancient serpent, who is the devil, or Satan, and bound him for a thousand years.

"In that day the Lord will punish the powers in the heavens above and the kings on the earth below. They will be herded together like prisoners bound in a dungeon; they will be shut up in prison and be punished after many days. The moon will be abashed, the sun ashamed; for the Lord Almighty will reign on Mount Zion and in Jerusalem, and before its elders, gloriously" (Isaiah 24:22-23).

"For if God did not spare angels when they sinned, but sent them to hell, putting them into gloomy dungeons to be held for judgment . . . if this is so, then the Lord knows how to rescue

godly men from trials and to hold the unrighteous for the day of judgment, while continuing their punishment" (2 Peter 2:4, 9).

20:3 He threw him into the Abyss, and locked and sealed it over him, to keep him from deceiving the nations any more until the thousand years were ended. After that, he must be set free a short time.

Judgment Thrones

20:4 I saw thrones on which were seated those who had been given authority to judge.

> *Jesus said to them (his disciples), "I tell you the truth, **at the renewal of all things**, when the Son of Man sits on his glorious throne, you who have followed me will also sit on twelve thrones, judging the twelve tribes of Israel" (Matthew 19:28).*

> *"As I looked, thrones were set in place, and the Ancient of Days took his seat" (Daniel 7:9).*

During The 1,000 Years

The Martyrs

And I saw the souls of those who had been beheaded because of their testimony for Jesus and because of the word of God. They had not worshiped the beast or his image and had not received his mark on their foreheads or their hands. They came to life and reigned with Christ a thousand years.

The First Resurrection

20:5 (The rest of the dead did not come to life until the thousand years were ended.) This is the first resurrection.

". . . you will be repaid at the resurrection of the righteous" (Luke 14:14).

"For the Lord himself will come down from heaven, with a loud command, with the voice of the archangel and with the trumpet call of God, and the dead in Christ will rise first. After that, we who are still alive and are left will be caught up together with them in the clouds to meet the Lord in the air. And so we will be with the Lord forever" (I Thessalonians 4:16-17).

Reigning With Christ

20:6 Blessed and holy are those who have part in the first resurrection. The second death has no power over them, but they will be priests of God and of Christ and will reign with him for a thousand years.

"As you come to him, the living Stone—rejected by men but chosen by God and precious to him—you also, like living stones, are being built into a spiritual house to be a holy priesthood, offering spiritual sacrifices acceptable to God through Jesus Christ" (I Peter 2:4-5).

Isaiah 11 describes conditions when Christ sets up His kingdom:

"And the wolf will dwell with the lamb, and the leopard will lie down with the kid, and the calf and the young lion and the fatling together; and a little boy will lead them. Also the cow and the bear will graze; Their young will lie down together; and the lion will eat straw like the ox. And the nursing child will play by the hole of the cobra, and the weaned child will put his hand on the viper's den. They will not hurt or destroy in all My holy mountain, for the earth will be full of the knowledge of the Lord as the waters cover the sea" (v. 6-9).

The Millennial blessings are partially recited in Isaiah 65:

1. A renovated earth made necessary because of the destruction by fire in the Day of the Lord.

"Behold, I will create new heavens and a new earth. The former things will not be remembered, nor will they come to mind" (65:17).

2.   No sorrow but great joy.

"But be glad and rejoice forever in what I create, for I will create Jerusalem to be a delight and its people a joy. I will rejoice over Jerusalem and take delight in my people; the sound of weeping and crying will be heard in it no more" (65:18-19).

3.   Longevity.

"Never again will there be in it an infant that lives but a few days, or an old man who does not live out his years; he who dies at a hundred will be thought a mere youth; he who fails to reach a hundred will be considered accursed" (65:20).

4.   Permanence and security.

"They will build houses and dwell in them; they will plant vineyards and eat their fruit. No longer will they build houses and others live in them, or plant and others eat. For as the days of a tree, so will be the days of my people; my chosen ones will long enjoy the works of their hands" (65:21-22).

5.   Blessed with successful progeny.

"They will not toil in vain or bear children doomed to misfortune; for they will be a people blessed by the Lord, they and their descendants with them" (65:23).

6.   Speedy answers to prayer.

"Before they call I will answer; while they are still speaking I will hear" (65:24).

7. Restored balance to nature.

"The wolf and the lamb will feed together, and the lion will eat straw like the ox, but dust will be the serpent's food. They will neither harm nor destroy in all my holy mountain" (65:25).

After The 1,000 Years

Satan Is Released For The Final Rebellion

20:7 When the thousand years are over, Satan will be released from his prison

20:8 and will go out to deceive the nations in the four corners of the earth—Gog and Magog—to gather them for battle. In number they are like the sand on the seashore.

"Son of man, set your face against Gog the land of Magog, the chief prince of Meshech and Tubal; prophesy against him and say: This is what the Sovereign Lord says: I am against you, O Gog chief prince of Meshech and Tubal." (Ezekiel 38:2 also 39:1).

20:9 They marched across the breadth of the earth and surrounded the camp of God's people, the city he loves. But fire came down from heaven and devoured them.

"You will come from your place in the far north, you and many nations with you, all of them riding on horses, a great horde, a mighty army. You will advance against my people Israel like a cloud that covers the land. In days to come, O Gog, I will bring you against my land, so that the nations may know me when I show myself holy through you before their eyes" (Ezekiel 38:15-16).

This is probably a reference to the gathering of nations against Jerusalem just before the Lord returns.

Satan's Final Judgment

20:10 And the devil, who deceived them, was thrown into the lake of burning sulfur, where the beast and the false prophet had been thrown. They will be tormented day and night forever and ever.

The Great White Throne

20:11 Then I saw a great white throne and him who was seated on it. Earth and sky fled from his presence, and there was no place for them. 20:12 And I saw the dead, great and small, standing before the throne, and books were opened. Another book was opened, which is the book of life. The dead were judged according to what they had done as recorded in the books.

The Judgment of the Wicked Dead

20:13 The sea gave up the dead that were in it, and death and hades gave up the dead that were in them, and each person was judged according to what he had done.

The Second Death—The Lake of Fire

20:14 Then death and Hades were thrown into the lake of fire. The lake of fire is the second death. 20:15 If anyone's name was not found written in the book of life, he was thrown into the lake of fire.

CHAPTER 21

THE HOLY CITY—NEW JERUSALEM
THE BRIDE OF CHRIST

21:1 Then I saw a new heaven and a new earth, for the first heaven and the first earth had passed away, and there was no longer any sea.

This may not be sequential. After taking his readers to the final judgment, he now goes back, as he frequently does, to pick up the theme of God's people reigning with Christ. See the termination statement in verse 6. He seems to be stating that in the new age, everything will be new or renewed.

Peter seems to place the new heaven and new earth following the destruction of the earth by fire. *"But the day of the Lord will come like a thief. The heavens will disappear with a roar; the elements will melt in the heat. But in keeping with his promise we are looking forward to **a new heaven and a new earth**, the home of righteousness." (2 Peter 3:10-13).*

The Old Testament saints looked for this city. *"For he was looking forward to the city with foundations, whose architect and builder is God" (Hebrews 11:10). ". . . they were longing for a better country—a heavenly one. Therefore God is not ashamed to be called their God, for he has prepared a city for them" (Hebrews 11:16).* Evidently, the author of Hebrews expected the destination of believers to be the heavenly city, the New Jerusalem: *"But you have come to Mount Zion, to the heavenly Jerusalem, the city of the living God. You have come to thousands upon thousands of angels in joyful assembly, to the church of the firstborn, whose names are written in heaven . . . " (Hebrews 12:22-23)/*

The references in Isaiah refer to the kingdom age and not the eternal state.

*"Behold, I will create **new heavens and a new earth**; the former things will not be remembered nor will they come to mind . . . the sound of weeping and of crying will be heard in it no more. Never again will there be in it an infant who lives but a few days, or an old man who does not live out his years; for the youth will die at the age of one hundred and the one who does not reach the age of one hundred shall be thought accursed" (Isaiah 65:17, 19, 20). See also verse 25, "The wolf and the lamb shall graze together, and the lion shall eat straw like the ox; and dust shall be the serpent's food."*

*"As **the new heavens and the new earth** that I make will endure before me," declares the Lord, "so will your name and descendants endure . . . ." (Isaiah 66:11,24).*

21:2 I saw the Holy City, the new Jerusalem, coming down out of heaven from God, prepared as a bride beautifully dressed for her husband.

"Awake, awake, O Zion, clothe yourself with strength. Put on your garments of splendor, O Jerusalem, the holy city. The uncircumcised and defiled will not enter you again. (Isaiah 52:1)

"He has clothed me with garments of salvation, He has wrapped me with a robe of righteousness, as a bridegroom decks himself with a garland, and as a bride adorns herself with her jewels" (Isaiah 61:10).

"But be glad and rejoice forever in what I create, for I will create Jerusalem to be a delight and its people a joy. I will rejoice over Jerusalem and take delight in my people; the sound of weeping and crying will be heard in it no more" (65:18-19).

21:3 And I heard a loud voice from the throne saying, "Now the dwelling of God is with men, and he will live with" them. They will be his people, and God himself will be with them and be their God.

"But will God really dwell on earth with men? The heavens, even the highest heavens, cannot contain you. How much less this temple I have built!" (2 Chronicles 6:18).

"I will make a covenant of peace with them; it will be an everlasting covenant. I will establish them and increase their numbers, and I will put my sanctuary among them forever. My dwelling place will be with them; I will be their God, and they will be my people. Then the nations will know that I the Lord makes Israel holy, when my sanctuary is among them forever."' (Ezekiel 37:26-28) "And the name of the city from that time on will be: The Lord is there." (Ezekiel 48:35).

"Shout and be glad, O Daughter of Zion. For I am coming, and I will live among you," declares the Lord." (Zechariah 2:10).

"For we are the temple of the living God. As God has said: 'I will live with them and walk among them, and I will be their God, and they will be my people'" (2 Corinthians 6:16). Quoted from Leviticus 26:12

21:4 He will wipe every tear from their eyes. There will be no more death or mourning or crying or pain, for the old order of things has passed away."

Tears Wiped Away

"He will swallow up death for all time, and the Lord God will wipe tears away from all faces, and He will remove the reproach of His people from all the earth" (Isaiah 25:8).

". . . the sound of weeping and of crying will be heard in it no more" (Isaiah 65:19).

No More Death

"Then death and Hades were thrown into the lake of fire. The lake of fire is the second death" (Revelation 20:14). "Then the end will come, when he hands over the kingdom to God the Father after he has destroyed all dominion, authority and power. For he

must reign until he has put all his enemies under his feet. The last enemy to be destroyed is death. For he has put everything under his feet." (I Corinthians 15:26,27). ". . . and they can no longer die; for they are like the angels. They are God's children, since they are children of the resurrection" (Luke 20:36).

These things apply to the resurrected ones who will now occupy the eternal city.

Great Gladness and Joy

"And a highway will be there; it will be called the Way of Holiness. The unclean will not journey on it; it will be for those who walk in that Way; wicked fools will not go about on it. No lion will be there, nor will any ferocious beast get up on it; they will not be found there. But only the redeemed will walk there, and the ransomed of the Lord will return. They will enter Zion with singing; everlasting joy will crown their heads. Gladness and joy will overtake them, and sorrow and sighing will flee away" (Isaiah 35:8-10)

21:5 He who was seated on the throne said, "I am making everything new!" Then he said, "Write this down, for these words are trustworthy and true."

Terminus Statement

21:6 He said to me: "It is done. I am the Alpha and Omega, the Beginning and the End. To him who is thirsty I will give to drink without cost from the spring of the water of life.

"It is coming! It will surely take place, declares the Sovereign Lord. This is the day I have spoken of" (Ezekiel 39:8).

"Come, all you who are thirsty, come to the waters . . . " *(Isaiah 55:1.*

21:7 He who overcomes will inherit all this, and I will be his God and he will be my son.

> *"I will be his father, and he will be my son" (2 Samuel 7:14).* (God's promise to David.)

21:8 But the cowardly, the unbelieving, the vile, the murderers, the sexually immoral, those who practice magic arts, the idolaters and all liars—their place will be in the fiery lake of burning sulfur. This is the second death.

The Bride of the Lamb

21:9 One of the seven angels who had the seven bowls full of the seven last plagues came and said to me, "Come, I will show you the bride, the wife of the Lamb."

This occurred in connection with the City of Babylon, and it is obvious that the two cities are contrasted, and gives us a description of what happens to both "brides."

> *"One of the seven angels who had the seven bowls came and said to me, "Come, I will show you the punishment of the great prostitute . . . " (Revelation 17:1). ". . . his bride has made herself ready" (Revelation 19:7).*

21:10 And he carried me away in the Spirit to a mountain great and high, and showed me the Holy City, Jerusalem, coming down out of heaven from God.

> *"In visions of God he took me to the land of Israel and set me on a very high mountain, on whose south side were some buildings that looked like a city" (Ezekiel 40:2).*

21:11 It shone with the glory of God, and its brilliance was like that of a very precious jewel, like a jasper, clear as crystal.

"Arise, shine, for your light has come, and the glory of the Lord rises upon you. See, darkness covers the earth and thick darkness is over the peoples, but the Lord rises upon you and his glory appears over you. Nations will come to your light, and kings to the brightness of your dawn" (Isaiah 60:1-3). "And I saw the glory of the God of Israel coming from the east. His voice was like the roar of rushing waters, and the land was radiant with his glory" (Ezekiel 43:2).

21:12 It had a great, high wall with twelve gates, and with twelve angels at the gates. On the gates were written the names of the twelve tribes of Israel.

"These will be the exits of the city: Beginning on the north side, which is 4,500 cubits long, the gates of the city will be named after the tribes of Israel. The three gates on the north side will be the gate of Reuben, the gate of Judah and the gate of Levi. On the east side, which is 4,500 cubits long, will be three gates: the gate of Joseph, the gate of Benjamin and the gate of Dan. On the south side, which measures 4,500 cubits, will be three gates: the gate of Simeon, the gate of Issachar and the gate of Zebulun. On the west side, which is 4,500 cubits long, will be three gates: the gate of Gad, the gate of Asher and the gate of Naphtali" (Ezekiel 48:31).

21:13 There were three gates on the east, three on the north, three on the south and three on the west. 21:14 The wall of the city had twelve foundations, and on them were the names of the twelve apostles of the Lamb.

". . . fellow citizens with God's people and members of God's household, built on the foundation of the apostles and prophets, with Christ Jesus himself the chief cornerstone" (Ephesians 2:20).

21:15 The angel who talked with me had a measuring rod of gold to measure the city, its gates and its wall.

"He took be there, and saw a man whose appearance was like bronze; he was standing in the gateway with a linen cord and a measuring rod in his hand" (Ezekiel 40:3).

21:16 The city was laid out like a square, as long as it was wide. He measured the city with the rod and found it to be 12,000 stadia in length, and as wide and high as it is long.

If we take this literally, it would be approximately 1,400 miles and would exceed the whole land area of Palestine. The vast dimensions here, a number twelve times one thousand, is probably suggesting not exact size, but vastness. Twelve is the perfect cube—"the city lies foursquare."

21:17 He measured its wall and it was 144 cubits thick (200 ft.), by man's measurement, which the angel was using.

Numbers have symbolic meaning. Here is still another multiple of 12—12 x 12. In connection with the 144,000 in chapters 7 and 14, it is 12 x 1,000 x 12. Again, it is not suggesting an exact number, but indicating a vast number.

Notice the other number 12's in the context:

1. 12 gates
2. 12 angels
3. 12 names of tribes
4. 12 foundations—12 stones
5. 12 pearls—gates
6. 12 names of apostles
7. 12 crops, tree of life

21:18 The wall was made of jasper, and the city of pure gold, as pure as glass.

21:19 The foundations of the city walls were decorated with every kind of precious stone. The first foundation was jasper, the second sapphire, the third chalcedony, the fourth emerald,

> "O afflicted city, lashed by storms and not comforted, I will build you with stones of turquoise, your foundations with sapphires. I will make your battlements of rubies, your gates of sparkling jewels, and all your walls of precious stones" (Isaiah 54:11-12)

21:20 the fifth sardonyx, the sixth carnelian, the seventh chrysolite, the eighth beryl, the ninth topaz, the tenth crysophrase, the eleventh jacinth, and the twelfth amethyst.

21:21 The twelve gates were twelve pearls, each gate made of a single pearl. The street of the city was of pure gold, like transparent glass.

21:22 I did not see a temple in the city, because the Lord God Almighty and the Lamb are its temple.

If this section describes the New Jerusalem as the capital city of the New Age—the Millennial Age, then what place would Ezekiel's vision of the rebuilt temple have? It is worth mentioning that Ezekiel's temple is not in Jerusalem per se (Ezekiel 48:8-22) and thus could be set up with the accompanying sacrifices as memorial sacrifices. But wouldn't this contradict the New Testament teaching of Christ's death as a finished and complete work? We must remember that the Old Testament sacrifices never were efficacious. The individual in Old Testament times was saved by faith in the finished work of Messiah, which was to be accomplished in the future, but portrayed in the sacrifices. The Old Testament believer looked forward in faith; the New Testament saint looks back in faith. But the object of faith is the same—the work of Christ. The millennial sacrificial system is mentioned also in Isaiah 56:5-7; 60:7, 13; 66:20-23, Jeremiah 33:15-22 and Zechariah 14:16-21. It is possible that God meant for Israel to "get it right,", and thus reintroduces the temple and sacrifices for Israel, much as the Lord's Supper serves the Church by way of remembrance. God has always dealt with His people, Israel, differently than He has with His Church.

Would it be possible that we have during the millennial age both a visible, material kingdom and temple in view in which God's glory shines as of old, and an invisible, spiritual kingdom with the temple being the presence and glory of God that fills all. Israel, in the Old Testament lived with that reality, the visible tabernacle and temple being earthly representations of the heavenly reality. And Paul stresses that the believer in Christ is simultaneously a creature of two worlds, the material and the spiritual. The material world we access by our senses, and the spiritual world we access by our spirit. He suggests that we can be seated here in a room on a chair, and seated with Christ *in the heavenlies* at one and the same time. He underscores the truth that the quality of our life here in the material world is directly related to our appropriation by faith of the vast inheritance of grace that is ours in Christ. In Hebrews, the author seems to speak of this reality of living in two worlds, the shakeable and the unshakeable. Speaking in the presence tense, he says, *"You have come to Mount Zion, to the heavenly Jerusalem, the city of the living God. You have come to thousands upon thousands of angels in joyful assembly, to the church of the firstborn, whose names are written in heaven. You have come to God, the judge of all men, to the spirits of righteous men made perfect, to Jesus the mediator of a new covenant, and to the sprinkled blood that speaks a better world than the blood of Abel"* (Hebrews 12:22-24). He says that the Old Testament saints were not looking for a material country or city, but a heavenly one, and God has prepared for them this city. He is the architect and builder of this city with foundations (Hebrews 11:10, 15).

Or still another suggestion might be that the The Holy City New Jerusalem is visible, but of another dimension, and the resurrected believer possessed of a resurrection body could move back and forth between the two worlds much as Jesus did following His resurrection and before His ascension.

If, on the other hand, this section indeed describes the eternal state, then the Millennium is the antechamber of and the preparation for the eternal state. Its glories are less than those of eternity, but they are of the same nature. God's time of blessing is eternal. It starts at the beginning of the Millennium and continues into the eternal state, interrupted only briefly by Gog's fall, the great white throne. Such a view, however, does not deal adequately with the thought expressed in Rev. 21:4, *"They came to life and reigned with Christ a thousand years."* From where? Obviously, they reign in and from the New Jerusalem.

21:23 The city does not need the sun or the moon to shine on it, for the glory of God gives it light, and the Lamb is its lamp.

The moon will be abashed, the sun ashamed; for the Lord Almighty will reign on Mount Zion and in Jerusalem, and before its elders, gloriously" (Isaiah 24:23). *"The sun will no more be your light by day, nor will the brightness of the moon shine on you, for the Lord will be your everlasting light, and your God will be your glory. Your sun will never set again, and your moon will wane no more;*

the Lord will be your everlasting light, and your days of sorrow will end. (Isaiah 60:19-20)

21:24 The nations will walk by its light, and the kings of the earth will bring their splendor into it.

"Nations will come to your light, and kings to the brightness of your dawn. . . . Then you will look and be radiant, your heart will throb and swell with joy; the wealth on the seas will be brought to you, to you the riches of the nations will come" (Isaiah 60:3, 5).

"In the last days the mountain of the Lord's temple will be established as chief among the mountains; it will be raised above the hills, and all nations will stream to it. Many people will come and say, 'Come, let us go up to the mountain of the Lord, to the house of the God of Jacob. He will teach us his ways, so that we may walk in his paths.' The law will go out from Zion, the word of the Lord from Jerusalem. He will judge between the nations and will settle disputes for many peoples. They will beat their swords into plowshares and their spears into pruning hooks. Nation will not take up sword against nation, nor will they train for war anymore. Come, O house of Jacob, let us walk in the light of the Lord" (Isaiah 2:2-5).

21:25 On no day will its gates ever be shut, for there will be no night there.

In that day this song will be sung in the land of Judah: We have a strong city; God makes salvation its walls and ramparts" (Isaiah 26:1). "Open the gates that the righteous nation may enter, the nation that keeps faith (Isaiah 26:2).

Arise, shine, for your light has come, and the glory of the LORD rises upon you. See, darkness covers the earth and thick darkness is over the peoples, but the LORD rises upon you and his glory appears over you. Nations will come to your light, and kings to the brightness of your dawn (Isaiah 60:1-3).

"Your gates will always stand open, they will never be shut, day or night, so that men may bring you the wealth of the nations—their kings led in triumphal procession (Isaiah 60:11).

21:26 The glory and honor of the nations will be brought into it.

Pass through, pass through the gates! Prepare the way for the people. Build up, build up the highway! Remove the stones. Raise a banner for the nations (Isaiah 62:10).

21:27 Nothing impure will ever enter it, nor will anyone who does what is shameful or deceitful, but only those whose names are written in the Lamb's book of life.

Awake, awake, O Zion, clothe yourself with strength. Put on your garments of splendor, O Jerusalem, the holy city. The uncircumcised and defiled will not enter you again (Isaiah 52:1).

Then you will know that I, the Lord your God, dwell in Zion, my holy hill. Jerusalem will be holy; never again will foreigners invade her (Joel 3:17).

CHAPTER 22

THE RIVER OF LIFE

22:1 Then the angel showed me the river of the water of life, as clear as crystal, flowing from the throne of God and of the Lamb

> *"You give them drink from your river of delights, for with you is the fountain of life . . . (Psalm 36:8-9). There is a river whose streams make glad the city of God, the holy place where the Most High dwells" (Psalm 46:4).*

> *On that day living water will flow out from Jerusalem, half to the eastern sea and half to the western sea, in summer and in winter. The Lord will be king over the whole earth. On that day there will be one Lord, and his name the only name (Zechariah 14:8-9).*

> *In that day the mountains will drip new wine, and the hills will flow with milk; all the ravines of Judah will run with water. A fountain will flow out of the Lord's house and will water the valley of acacias (Joel 3:18).*

22:2 down the middle of the great street of the city. On each side of the river stood the tree of life, bearing twelve crops of fruit, yielding its fruit every month. And the leaves of the tree are for the healing of the nations.

> *"The man brought be back to the entrance of the temple, and I saw water coming out from under the threshold of the temple toward the east (for the temple faced east). The water was coming down from under the south side of the temple, south of the altar. He then brought me out through the north gate and led me around the outside to the outer gate facing east, and the water was flowing from the south side . . . Then he led me back to the bank of the river. When I arrived there, I saw a great number of trees on each side of the river . . . fruit trees of all kinds will grow on both banks of the river. Their leaves will not wither, nor will their fruit fail. Every month they will bear, because the water from the sanctuary flows to them. Their fruit will serve for food and their leaves for healing" (Ezekiel 47:1-2, 6-7, 12).*

22:3 No longer will there be any curse. The throne of God and of the Lamb will be in the city, and his servants will serve him.

> *"It will be inhabited; never again will it be destroyed. Jerusalem will be secure" (Zechariah 14:11).*
> *"Therefore, they are before the throne of God and serve him day and night in his temple . . . " (Rev. 7:15).*

22:4 They will see his face, and his name will be on their foreheads.

> *". . . a seal on the foreheads of the servants of our God" (Rev. 7:3).*

22:5 There will be no more night. They will not need the light of a lamp or the light of the sun, for the Lord God will give them light. And they will reign forever and ever.

> *"It will be a unique day, without daytime or nighttime—a day known to the Lord. When evening comes, there will be light" (Zechariah 14:7).*

"No longer will violence be heard in your land, nor ruin or destruction within your borders, but you will call your walls Salvation and your gates Praise.

The Everlasting Light

"The sun will no more be your light by day, nor will the brightness of the moon shine on you, for the LORD will be your everlasting light, and your God will be your glory. Your sun will never set again, and your moon will wane no more; the LORD will be your everlasting light, and your days of sorrow will end. Then will all your people be righteous and they will possess the land forever. They are the shoot I have planted, the work of my hands, for the display of my splendor" (Isaiah 60:18-21).

"For Zion's sake I will not keep silent, for Jerusalem's sake I will not remain quiet, till her righteousness shines out like the dawn, her salvation like a blazing torch" (Isaiah. 62:1).

The New Name

"The nations will see your righteousness, and all kings your glory; you will be called by a new name that the mouth of the Lord will bestow. You will be a crown of splendor in the Lord's hand, a royal diadem in the hand of your God. No longer will they call you Deserted, or name your land Desolate. But you will be called Hephzibah, and your land Beulah; for the Lord will take delight in you, and your land will be married."

The Figure of the Bride & Bridegroom

". . . *as a bridegroom rejoices over his bride, so will your God rejoice over you" (Isaiah 62:2-5).*

Pass Through the Gates

"Pass through, pass through the gates! Prepare the way for the people. Build up, build up the highway! Remove the stones. Raise a banner for the nations" (Isaiah 62:10).

"Then the sovereignty, power and greatness of the kingdoms under the whole heaven will be handed over to the saints, the people of the Most High. His kingdom will be an everlasting kingdom, and all ruler will worship and obey him" (Daniel 7:27).

THE EPILOGUE

Note a number of similarities with the Prologue

Genuine prophecy
    1:3; 22:6, 9-10, 18-19
A duly commissioned prophet
    1:1, 9-10; 22:8-10
To be read in the churches
    1:3, 11; 22:18
For the encouragement of the faithful
    1:3; 22:7, 12, 14

22:6 The angel said to me, "These words are trustworthy and true. The Lord, the God of the spirits of the prophets, sent his angel to show his servants the things that must soon take place.

All true prophecy originates with God and comes through men moved by the Holy Spirit (2 Peter 1:21).

Echoes verse 1 of chapter 1

> *"Write this down, for these words are trustworthy and true"* *(Revelation 21:5).*

> *"The spirit of the prophets is subject to the control of the prophets"* *(I Corinthians 14:32).*

1
I Am Coming Soon!

22:7 "Behold, I am coming soon! Blessed is he who keeps the words of the prophecy in this book."

See 1:3; 22:17, 20 "quickly" What about a postponed consummation? An infallible timetable would do away with the attitude of expectancy that has characterized the church through the ages. This word comes with renewed force for every generation until God's redemptive purpose is completed.

> *"For the Son of Man is going to come in his Father's glory with his angels, and then he will reward each person according to what he has done" (Matthew 16:27).*

22:8 I, John, am the one who heard and saw these things. And when I had heard and seen them, I fell down to worship at the feet of the angel who had been showing them to me.

This must have been one impressive angel! This is the second time John attempts to direct worship to an angel (19:10). See Hebrews 1:14.

22:9 But he said to me, "Do not do it! I am a fellow servant with you and with your brothers the prophets and of all who keep the words of this book. Worship God!"
22:10 Then he told me, "Do not seal up the words of the prophecy of this book, because the time is near.

> *"The vision of the evenings and mornings that has been given you is true, but seal up the vision, for it concerns the distant future."* *(Daniel 8:27; 12:9, 13).*

22:11 Let him who does wrong continue to do wrong; let him who is vile continue to be vile; let him who does right continue to do right; and let him who is holy continue to be holy."

The perspective is considered to be so close that there is no longer time to alter the character and habits of men. Men are certain to reap the consequences of the kinds of lives they have lived when our Lord returns. Man's deliberate choice has fixed his fate.

> *"Many will be purified, made spotless and refined, but the wicked will continue to be wicked. None of the wicked will understand, but those who are wise will understand" (Daniel 12:10).*

2
I Am Coming Soon!

22:12 "Behold, I am coming soon! My reward is with me, and I will give to everyone according to what he has done.

Coming without delay—quickly. The distribution of rewards on the basis of works is taught throughout Scripture.

> *"I the Lord search the heart and examine the mind, to reward a man according to his conduct, according to what his deeds deserve" (Jeremiah 17:10).*

> *"God will render to every man according to his works" (Romans 2:6).*

> *"See, the Sovereign Lord comes with power, and his arm rules for him. See, his reward is with him, and his recompense accompanies him. He tends his flock like a shepherd: He gathers the lambs in his arms and carries them close to his heart; he gently leads those that have young" (Isaiah 40:10-11).*

> *"Say to the Daughter of Zion, 'See, your Savior comes! See, his reward is with him, and his recompense accompanies him. They will be called the Holy People, the Redeemed of the Lord; and you will be called Sought After, the City No Longer Deserted" (Isaiah 62:11-12).*

The quality of a man's life and works provide the ultimate indication of what he really believes and who he really is.

22:13 I am the Alpha and the Omega, the First and the Last, the Beginning and the End.

Unlimited in any temporal sense. Nothing precedes Him, nothing comes after Him. See 1:8; 1:17; 21:6

22:14 "Blessed are those who wash their robes, that they may have the right to the tree of life and may go through the gates into the city.

> *"These are they who have come out of the great tribulation; they have washed their robes and made them white in the blood of the Lamb." (7:14).*

Eternal life is the reward of faithfulness in the face of tribulation. Eternal blessedness. The tree of life—a symbol of immortality.

22:15 Outside are the dogs, those who practice magic arts, the sexually immoral, the murderers, the idolaters and everyone who loves and practices falsehood.

1. magic arts
2. sexually immoral
3. murderers
4. idolaters
5. loves falsehood
6. practices falsehood (See 21:8)

Describes the future with the imagery of the present.

For The Churches

22:16 "I, Jesus, have sent my angel to give you (plural) this testimony for the churches.

Our Lord's letters to the 7 churches is just as much for us today as Paul's letters to the seven churches to which he wrote are relevant for us today. They were specific churches then, but the message is universal. **I am the Root and the Offspring of David, and the bright Morning Star."**

> *". . . until the day dawns and the morning star rises in your hearts . . . " (2 Peter 1:19).*

Balaam's prophecy: *"I see him, but not now; I behold him, but not near. A star will come out of Jacob; a scepter will rise out of Israel" (Numbers 24:17).*

> *The* long night of tribulation is all but over, and the new day dawns.

The Four Invitations

22:17 The Spirit and the bride say, "Come!" And let him who hears say, "Come!" Whoever is thirsty, let him come; and whoever wishes, let him take the free gift of the water of life.

The second half interprets the first half of the verse.

The Warning

22:18 I warn everyone who hears the words of the prophecy of this book: if anyone adds anything to them, God will add to him the plagues described in this book.

> *"Do not add to what I command you and do not subtract from it, but keep the commands of the Lord your God that I give you" (Deuteronomy 4:2). Also 12:32*

22:19 And if anyone takes words away from this book of prophecy, God will take away from him his share in the tree of life and in the holy city, which are described in this book.

"Every word of God is flawless; he is a shield to those who take refuge in him. Do not add to his words, or he will rebuke you and prove you a liar" (Proverbs 30:5-6).

3
I Am Coming Soon!

Maranatha!

22:20 He who testifies to these things says, "Yes, I am coming soon."

Amen. Come, Lord Jesus.

22:21 The grace of the Lord Jesus be with God's people. Amen.

> Watch for Me
> Wait for Me
> Work for Me

CONCLUSION

WAITING FOR HIS SON FROM HEAVEN

The Epilogue of Revelation ends with statements that seem to indicate that Christ's coming was not to a time in the distant future, but to a time that is imminent. "I am coming quickly" (22:6-7), "the time is at hand" (22:10), "Behold, I am coming quickly" (22:12), "surely I am coming quickly" (22:20).

Full Preterists believe these and other time-frame references should be taken literally, and the events in Matthew 24 were all fulfilled in the destruction of Jerusalem in 70 A.D. Jesus' reference to "this generation" would refer to the generation living then. They believe that these references of our Lord to his "quick" return were actually fulfilled in the parousia of our Lord in connection with the destruction of Jerusalem. Partial preterists believe that most of the events in the Olivet Discourse refer to A.D. 70, but the coming of Christ in the clouds was *a* parousia, but not *the* parousia which is still future. The full preterist view would virtually eliminate a future hope for the church. Radical preterism sees the entire New Testament eschatology as having been realized already including the rapture and the resurrection (viewed as spiritual not bodily). Its fatal flaw, I think, is in its treatment of the final rapture and resurrection, more specifically the timing of it. There is absolutely no record that the rapture of the living and the resurrection of the dead occurred in the first century. There can be only one Resurrection of believers, and this Resurrection, which coincides with the Rapture, will take place on the Last Day. Partial preterists make a sharp distinction between the judgment-coming of Christ to the Jews at the end of the Jewish age and his parousia and final coming to the world at the end of history. For the former the great resurrection and the rapture occurred in the past. For the latter, they remain in the future.

Here we are two thousand years later, and the imminent nature of Christ's words still underscore for us today the need for readiness. I think that it is exactly why our Lord used these time-frame references. To hold on to the promise of the Second Coming, therefore, is a test of faith's endurance. His coming will be dramatic and glorious, and all of us await that climactic moment in time when our Lord returns. There is a sense of urgency about the message of the Gospel writers. *"Repent, for the kingdom of heaven is at hand." "The kingdom of heaven is near."* What do we do with the urgency inherent in the Advent message? How are we to live joyfully and expectantly in the face of apparent delay? Two thousand years have gone by since that note of urgency and immediacy was sounded.

1
The Certainty of His Coming

Be Sure!

The Scriptures leave no room for doubt that our Lord is coming back again. Matthew 25:31 reads, *"When the Son of man comes . . . "* Not "if" but "when."

When I was pastor of a church in Laramie, Wyoming a number of years ago, we had a sizable group of students who attended from the University of Wyoming, which was just a block away. I still remember the strange mixture of pride and joy and excitement I felt when I heard a group of them, while putting on a musical evening for the congregation, sing Almeda Pearce's great hymn,

> When He shall come, resplendent in His glory,
> To take His own from out this vale of night,
> O may I know the joy at His appearing—
> Only at morn to walk with Him in white!
>
> When I shall stand within the court of heaven
> Where white-robed pilgrims pass before my sight—
> Earth's martyred saints and blood-washed overcomers—
> These then are they who walk with Him in white!

When He shall call, from earth's remotest corners,
All who have stood triumphant in His might,
O to be worthy then to stand beside the,
And in that morn to walk with Him in white!

It sounds the unquestionable note of certainty—Jesus is coming back for His own!

His Visible Coming

The Scriptures say that His coming will be *visible*. There will be nothing hidden or secret about it. *"Behold, He is coming with clouds, and **every eye will see Him . . . **" (Revelation 1:7).* Matthew 25:31 says, *"**They will see** the Son of Man coming . . . "* Our Lord's words in Mark's Gospel underscore his visible return, *"**You will see the son of Man** sitting at the right hand of the Mighty One (the Power), and coming with the clouds of heaven" (Mark 14:62).*

This One is the First and the Last, the One who lives, and was dead, and is alive forevermore, the One who has the keys of Hades and of Death! (Revelation 1:17-18). Every eye will see Him!

His Bodily Coming

At the ascension, Jesus is taken up from his adoring followers into the clouds, and while they looked steadfastly toward heaven as He went up, two men stood by them in white apparel, and said to them, *"Men of Galilee, why do you stand gazing up into heaven? This same Jesus, who was taken up from you into heaven, **will so come in like manner** as you saw Him go into heaven" (Acts 1:11).*

After the resurrection, Jesus appeared to his disciples several times, first appearing and then disappearing, trying, I suppose, to get them used to His not being present with them, at least in bodily form. He left no doubt in their minds that the resurrection body, though different, was still one that could be touched. It was a body that still bore the marks of nail and spear. It was, in short, a very real, recognizable body. And it is in that same body, He will return!

Now, we have never seen Him as the disciples did. How then will we recognize him? There will be no doubt. His coming will be *glorious!*

His Glorious Coming

There will be those false Christs who come claiming to be Him. Jesus says that we should not be taken in my their lies and trickery. His coming will be unmistakable. It will be *"in the Father's glory."* He will be sitting on His *"throne of heavenly glory"* (Matthew 25:31). He will be *"sitting at the right hand of the Mighty One"* (Mark 14:62). Furthermore, he will come *"on the clouds of the sky,"* and *"with His angels,"* and *"with power and great glory"* (Matthew 24:30). And Paul adds the sound effects in I Thessalonians 4:16, *"For the Lord Himself will descend from heaven with a shout, with the voice of the archangel, and with the trumpet of God . . . "* No one will be left in doubt about whom it is who suddenly arrives from heaven to ring down the curtain on things as we now know them. Charles Wesley sang about it.

> Lo, He comes with clouds descending,
> Once for favored sinners slain;
> Thousands thousand saints attending,
> Swell the triumph of His train:
> Alleluia! Alleluia! God appears on earth to reign.
>
> Every eye shall now behold Him,
> Robed in dreadful majesty;
> Those who set at naught and sold Him,
> Pierced and nailed Him to the tree,
> Deeply wailing, deeply wailing,
> Shall the true Messiah see.

2
The Uncertainty in His Coming

Be Cautious!

The second coming prophecy as found in the synoptic gospels presents a paradox for the believer. There is both certainty **and** uncertainty. Jesus promises a sure return, but its time is undisclosed. *"The Son of Man **will** *come . . . "* That strikes the note of assurance. *"At an hour **when you do not expect Him."*** There is uncertainty. We can be certain of the "what," but we cannot be certain about the "when." Now I am confident that that this paradox is by God's design. He desires to create a certain kind of response in His servants, first that of assurance regarding His return—He **is** coming back, and also that of patient expectancy—for we do not know **when** He will come back. This tension has been present in every generation of believers—and God intended it to be so.

So He tells the parable of the fig tree, which underscores the certainty. When the branches of the tree become soft with sap and begin to bud, summer is fast approaching. This natural order recognized by all who were familiar with the tree is confirmation that something will come soon. As surely as summer follows the signals observed in the fig tree, the second coming of Jesus follows the signs He identifies in Matthew 24. This gives us a clue as to the approximate time of His coming, but not the exact day. So He sounds the note of certainty, *"As soon as its twigs get tender and its leaves come out, **you know** that summer is near. Even so, when you see all these things, **you know** that it is near, right at the door" (Matthew 24:32, 33).*

But there is that opposing reality, ***"No one knows** about that day or hour, not even the angels in heaven, nor the Son, but only the Father"*

3
We Must Wait With a Sense of Expectancy

Be Ready!

Jesus stresses that the believer must live in a state of expectancy, anticipating an event that must come at some time, and may arrive at any time. The tension between the knowing and not knowing, the certainty and the uncertainty, keeps us at our spiritual peak. It is to a life of faith that we are called. We must be constantly in a sense of readiness, living a dynamic life, not static. Coming at an unexpected hour means that His followers must be ready and watchful in every hour.

This reminds me of a story that comes out of the classroom. A teacher, seeking to get her students to keep their desks clean and in order, announced that she would give at a certain time in the future a nice reward for the students who kept their desks neat and clean. The students asked the teacher when the reward would be given out, and she said she would not tell them; it would be a surprise. One of the pupils got the point immediately and said, "I guess we will have to keep our desks clean all the time, so that we will be ready the day the reward is announced."

And that is exactly why this note of uncertainty has been present down through the ages. Believers in every age have lived with the certainty of His coming and the reward presented on that day for all who have loved his appearing.

Peter, of course, caught the meaning of His Lord's words when he wrote in his second letter, *"Since everything will be destroyed in this way (that is, at the coming of the Lord), what kind of people ought you to be? You ought to live holy and godly lives as you look forward to the day of God and speed its coming" (2 Peter 3:11, 12).* Or John stresses the same thought in his first epistle, *"We know that when he appears, we shall be like him, for we shall see him as he is. Everyone who has this hope in him purifies himself, just as he is pure" (I John 3:2, 3).*

The only way to be ready is to abide in Him moment by moment, day in and day out. The only way to know what God is going to do next is to be walking with Him in the now so that when He speaks we will hear Him and when He moves we will know it and move with Him.

This note of expectancy is sounded again and again. No one knows the day or the hour except the Father—no, not even the angels in heaven or the Son. He will come *"on a day when he does not expect him and at an hour he is not aware of." "So you also must be ready, because the Son of Man will come at an hour when you do not expect him" (Matthew 24:44).*

A student gets ready for the final exam. A business gets ready for a year-end audit. An athlete gets ready for the Olympic challenge. And we must ready ourselves for that moment when we stand before our Lord. Paul warns that *"we must all appear before the judgment seat of Christ, that each one may receive what is due him for the things done while in the body, whether good or bad" (2 Corinthians 5:10).* And he precedes that with these words, *"So we make it our goal to please Him . . . "*

4
We Must Watch With A Sense of Immediacy

Be Alert!

Jesus talks about being awake and alert so that thieves will not break in unexpectedly, and steal our goods away. Believers will not be surprised because they believe His word and are living in the light of his truth; unbelievers will be surprised—because they live in darkness and have grown careless. Such is the warning Paul gives the Thessalonian believers.

> *"The day of the Lord will come like a thief in the night. While people are saying, "Peace and safety," destruction will come on them suddenly, as labor pains on a pregnant woman, and they will not escape. But you, brothers, are not in darkness so that this day should surprise you like a thief. You are all sons of the light and sons of the day" (I Thessalonians 5:2-5).*

The thief-like coming of our Lord is mentioned almost uniformly in connection with the Day of the Lord or the Day of God. Peter writes, *"But the day of the Lord will come like a thief" (2 Peter 3:10).* He mentions scoffers who say, *"Where is His coming" as he promised? Ever since our fathers died, everything goes on as it has since the beginning of creation" (2 Pet. 3:3, 4).* And he reminds them that they *"deliberately forget . . . "* They chose to forget that people at the time of the flood went blithely on their daily way doing the things they always had done, even though Noah had faithfully warned them of impending doom. They laughed at him; they scorned his words; they refused to repent, and then judgment came suddenly and swept them all away. They were not watching and they were not waiting. And Peter says, that same sort of scenario will take place in the End. *"By the same word the present heavens and earth are reserved for fire, being kept for the Day of Judgment and destruction of ungodly men" (2 Pet. 3:7).*

We as believers need to know what's happening in our world without becoming unduly alarmed at all the "sign seekers." We should not allow the world to "pour us into its mold." We must not be conformed to its attitudes, its spirit, and its life-style. We should not become too complacent

351

or comfortable since our stay here is only temporary. We are looking for, waiting for another world, a renewed, renovated world, where Christ reigns and righteousness prevails.

Immediacy does not necessary mean that nothing need come between now and His coming in the clouds as if His coming were likely to happen "any moment" without further delay. It only underscores the necessity to be always in a state of watchful waiting. Nor does it mean we can never go to sleep, for sleep is a necessary requirement for health and functionality. The command to stay awake strikes a note of alertness. Every waking moment must be lived in the light of His soon return. Imminent means it could happen without delay. It was not understood by the early church to mean a signless coming—that no prophecy need be fulfilled before his coming. Jesus clearly indicates that certain things will take place immediately preceding his return—a period of persecution and suffering, a great turning away as the hearts of people grow cold, and great celestial disturbances.

It may well be that the many references in Matthew 24 about being ready, and watching should be understood in the light of the immediate context. The readiness and the watchfulness would then begin when certain signs begin to appear such as the celestial disturbances He mentions that occur just before His coming in the clouds. Luke adds weight to this view by saying, *"When these things (the heavenly bodies shaken) take place, stand up and lift up your heads, because your redemption is drawing near" (21:28).*

5
We Must Wait With A Sense of Urgency

Be Active!

There is not only a sense of expectancy and immediacy that must be engendered in our hearts as we look for His appearing, but also a sense of urgency. And unfortunately, this sense of urgency is often missing from our evangelical churches today.

Peter reminds us that there is a very good reason why God delays to bring about the dissolution of all things and the judgment of the wicked at the second coming of His Son in glory.

> *"Do not forget this one thing, dear friends: With the Lord a day is*
> *like a thousand years, and a thousand years are like a day. The Lord*
> *is not slow in keeping his promise, as some understand slowness.*
> *(And here's the reason)* **He is patient with you,** *not wanting*
> *anyone to perish, but everyone to come to repentance" (2 Pet. 3:9).*

There is urgency to our message that is not determined by our clocks or calendars. We cannot judge the infinite God by the dictates of finite time—*"With the Lord a day is like a thousand years, and a thousand years are like a day."* In other words, if we see time from God's view point, only a couple of days have gone by since our Lord was crucified, arose and ascended to the Father's right hand. The third day has now dawned. Will He now arise with healing in His wings, and return to earth for His own?

But I would ask my readers to consider one further important and related thought in regard to His coming.

6
The Finality of His Coming

Be Decisive!

Jesus underlines, as we have seen, that no one knows the day or the hour when He will return—except the Father. It will be sudden and it will be marked by **finality.** And this note of finality stresses the climactic nature of His coming.

Where did we ever get the idea that when our Lord returns, there will be a second chance? In that climactic moment when He returns, all opportunity is over.

All of us live with the certainty of Jesus Return—His Coming again in the clouds of glory.

As we said in our introduction, we also live with the uncertainty of when that will be. And it is that very uncertainty which our Lord uses to keep us **ready**, with a sense of expectancy; **alert,** with a sense of immediacy; **steadfast**, with a sense of urgency.

While we watch, we wait, and while we wait, we work. This is no time for a casual or careless walk, but a life committed to His purposes in the world.

Let us hear Paul's challenge as he throws it out in Ephesians chapter 5,

> *Wake up, O sleeper*
> *Rise from the dead,*
> *And Christ will shine on you.*
>
> *Be careful, then, how you live—not as unwise but as wise,*
> *making the most of every opportunity, because the days are evil.*
> *Therefore do not be foolish, but understand what the Lord's will*
> *is." (Eph. 5:14-17)*

That is a summary of what it means to live with the certainty of His coming, but the uncertainty of when that will be.